The Complete Guide to

PLUMBING

Updated 8th Edition

Completely Updated to Current Codes

COOL
SPRINGS
PRESS

Quarto.com

© 2023 Quarto Publishing Group USA Inc.
Text © 2015, 2019, 2023 Quarto Publishing Group USA Inc.

First Published in 2015 by Cool Springs Press, an imprint of
The Quarto Group, 100 Cummings Center, Suite 265-D, Beverly, MA 01915, USA.
T (978) 282-9590 F (978) 283-2742

Cool Springs Press titles are also available at discount for retail, wholesale, promotional,
and bulk purchase. For details, contact the Special Sales Manager by email at
specialsales@quarto.com or by mail at The Quarto Group, Attn: Special Sales Manager,
100 Cummings Center, Suite 265-D, Beverly, MA 01915, USA.

27 26 25 24   3 4 5

ISBN: 978-0-7603-8114-4

Digital edition published in 2023
eISBN: 978-0-7603-8115-1

Library of Congress Cataloging-in-Publication Data available

Page Layout: *tabula rasa* graphic design

Illustrations by Ada Keesler on pages 18, 19, 20, 21, 40, 41, 47, 48, 49, 64, 65, 86, 87, 88,
89, 95, 96, 97, 126, 127, 215, 216, 217, 219, 220, 221, 272, 273

Printed in China

BLACK+DECKER The Complete Guide to Plumbing, 8th Edition
Created by: The Editors of Cool Springs Press, in cooperation with BLACK+DECKER. BLACK+DECKER and the BLACK+DECKER logo are
trademarks of The Black + Decker Corporation and are used under license. All rights reserved.

NOTICE TO READERS

For safety, use caution, care, and good judgment when following the procedures described in this book. The publisher and
BLACK+DECKER cannot assume responsibility for any damage to property or injury to persons as a result of misuse of the
information provided.

The techniques shown in this book are general techniques for various applications. In some instances, additional
techniques not shown in this book may be required. Always follow manufacturers' instructions included with products,
since deviating from the directions may void warranties. The projects in this book vary widely as to skill levels required:
some may not be appropriate for all do-it-yourselfers, and some may require professional help.

Consult your local building department for information on building permits, codes, and other laws as they apply to
your project.

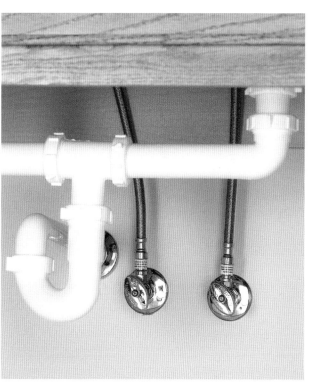

Partial-house shutoffs are often found in medium- to large-size homes. They control water flow to large areas of the house. They are found in pairs, one for hot and one for cold water. Turning off a pair of these may shut off water to a floor or to an entire bathroom or kitchen.

Fixture shutoff valves, also called stop valves, control water to a specific faucet, toilet, or fixture. They are also usually found in pairs, one for hot and one for cold. However, toilets, icemakers, and other cold-water-only fixtures will have only one stop valve. If you live in an older home that lacks stop valves, it's a good idea to install them.

 ## SMART LEAK DETECTORS AND VALVE CONTROLLERS

Leak detectors are placed in high-risk spots, such as the lowest area of a basement floor, where leak water is likely to show up first. The detector transmits an alert to your smart phone or to a smart valve controller that will automatically shut off the water supply. Less-expensive smart valve controllers are battery operated with simple mechanisms that physically close the valve. These can be installed in less than an hour by anyone with basic tools. Pricier systems are plumbed right into a supply line and act as an internal valve. They usually require a direct power source, and often come with proprietary apps for your smart phone. They should be installed by a professional.

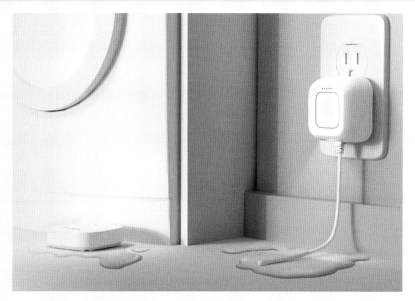

The problem with shut-off valves? They can stop the flow to a leak only after the leak has likely done some (and often a lot of) damage. Smart leak detectors and valve controllers are the latest innovation that promises to get the jump on leaks—even if you're not around to detect them.

Gray Water Systems

Water is increasingly precious. Drought conditions in several areas of the country have led to increasing water prices, private wells that run dry or no longer reliably produce, and difficulty maintaining even drought-tolerant landscapes.

The answer? Use your water more than once.

A gray water system reuses water from bathing, laundering clothes, and washing dishes to irrigate nonedible plants or, in some cases, to flush toilets. This type of piped system can be as simple as plumbing a fixture to an exterior outlet that directly waters plants, or as complicated as a self-contained turnkey system that reuses water from multiple fixtures.

The cost of a gray water system varies widely. A single-appliance, direct irrigation line is a doable DIY project that could be installed in a weekend for less than a $100. You could, however, purchase a whole-house filtration system collecting from multiple fixtures and distributing to both irrigation and toilets, for several thousand dollars.

Those costs will be offset by the fact that recycled water is going to save on your water bill. Depending on where you live, those savings can be significant. In fact, the U.S. Environmental Protection Agency (EPA) estimates that one-third of residential water usage is directed to landscaping irrigation.

This large gray water reservoir is connected to multiple appliances through the back wall of the home, creating a simple method for irrigating the yard during the dry months.

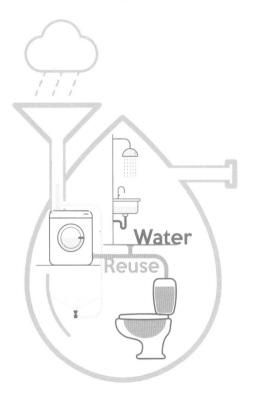

Plumb It Yourself

The most basic gray water option is to use PVC pipe and fixtures to tap into your clothes washing machine waste outlet, and direct the waste water out through a hole in the wall to gravity-feed lines connected to off-the-shelf drip-irrigation. You can also plumb multiple fixtures this way.

The water is usually only enough for one area of your yard. The plumbing must include a three-way diverter valve at each appliance on the system. This allows you to redirect the flow to the waste line in cases where the water contains bleach or other contaminants (such as when you're cleaning paint brushes in a sink), or in situations where the ground outside is already saturated from precipitation.

Homeowners who install gray water systems usually change to biodegradable personal hygiene products (if the shower drain feeds into the system), soaps, and detergents. The by-products of many ecologically friendly soaps and cleansers may actually feed certain plants.

Filtering for Convenience

The problem with any direct-feed DIY gray water system is that chemicals and other contaminants from the appliance can potentially still make their way to your landscaping, even when you're being careful. Not only can this endanger plants, it can also harm wild and domesticated animals, and possibly even children who play in the yard.

That's where the next step up comes in—a filter plumbed into the line. There are several on the market, and all are meant to remove both particulates and some pollutants. These are rarely if ever used for drinking water; the filter protects plant life and any animals that might come in contact with the irrigation.

A big step up from a simple in-line filter, whole-house recycling systems collect, filter, and distribute water efficiently ensuring that very little is ever wasted. Generally, the more complex the reclamation system is, the more maintenance it will require. Upkeep can entail changing filters on a schedule, or even swapping out UV bulbs in the most sophisticated systems.

Reclaiming Outside Water

It rains even where there is an ongoing drought. The problem is, that rain often runs off before it can do any good, and it's not there when you need it most, such as during hot, dry summer months. That's why several manufacturers make rainwater recycling systems that are designed to capture whatever precipitation falls, no matter when it rains.

Making your own is an achievable DIY option. PVC pipe attached to gutter drop outlets on one end and a plastic barrel or barrels on the other, can trap a significant amount of rainwater and is as simple as it is useful.

Gray Water Guidelines

1. Always start by checking local building and health departments to determine the codes that dictate gray water use in your locality, and what permits you'll need for the work. One advantage of hiring a licensed plumber is that a professional will know exactly what rules and regulations govern gray water systems in your area.

2. Be careful to match the water produced by the system's fixtures to the needs of your plants, if you're using an outside irrigation system. Consult a gardener if you have any doubt about your yard or garden needs.

3. Never irrigate edible plants with gray water. This includes fruit trees and bushes, as well as vegetable gardens.

4. Don't store gray water for more than a day, and don't direct it to any area where it will pool or run off.

5. Use only biodegradable products in the water routed to the gray water system (divert it to sewer or septic, as necessary). Be careful not to allow any harsh chemicals to go into the system. Avoid any that contain salts, boron, or chlorine bleach.

6. Never route water that has come in contact with feces—from toilets or diaper washing—into a gray water system.

Even if a full-scale gray water is out of the question, you can use a recapture system to collect rainwater and use it for irrigating dry areas of the yard.

BLACK WATER

Any water that comes from a toilet or chemical fixture like a water softener is called "black water" and is not suitable for recycling or reuse. Toilet water could potentially cause disease outbreak and other health problems. Although bathroom showers, sinks, and bathtubs can all be drained into a gray water system, toilets should never be connected to anything but the sewer or septic system.

Plumbing Tools, Materials + Skills

Although most plumbing projects use common tools found in most every homeowner's toolbox, you'll also need a few that are particular to the pipes and fixtures that populate home plumbing systems. As with all other tools, plumbing essentials can be broken down into two basic categories: hand tools and power tools. Most importantly of all, though, is the safety equipment that will reduce your risk of injury. Those include a sturdy pair of heavy-duty work gloves (and another pair with rubber finger and palm pads for when things get slippery), safety eyewear meant for construction work, and—occasionally—a mask to avoid inhaling dust and airborne contaminants.

As far as the materials you'll use, PEX pipe continues to grow in popularity. There are few places plumbers today won't use this adaptable type of pipe, including to replace or cut into copper or PVC pipe. With that in mind, this edition of *The Complete Guide to Plumbing* includes an expanded section on PEX, and discusses a device that makes good use of PEX's unique, easy-to-fabricate nature—the manifold. It allows for simple and quick whole-house and single-area water supply.

Of course, any home plumber will inevitably have to work with existing pipes that may be PVC, copper, or cast iron (replace any galvanized pipes in your home). All of those have their uses, and all require different tools and skills to modify or fabricate. Fortunately, you'll discover everything you need to know about those materials and how to work with them, in the pages that follow.

In this chapter:
- Plumbing Tools
- Plumbing Materials
- Copper
- PEX Pipe
- PVC
- Cast Iron
- Outdoor Flexible Pipe
- Fittings
- Valves + Hose Bibs

Plumbing Tools

Depending on the project, home plumbing tasks may require little more than the tools you already own, or they may call for specialized gear that can be used for no other tasks. However, in plumbing even more than in other areas of home repair, the right tool can be the difference between a successful job and one that you come to regret.

The tools shown here are the most commonly used for plumbing projects small and large. Unless you plan on doing a lot of plumbing work, it's wise to rent larger, more specialized tools and power tools. In any case, always make sure you have the correct tool for the plumbing job at hand. You'll thank yourself when it's done.

Safety First

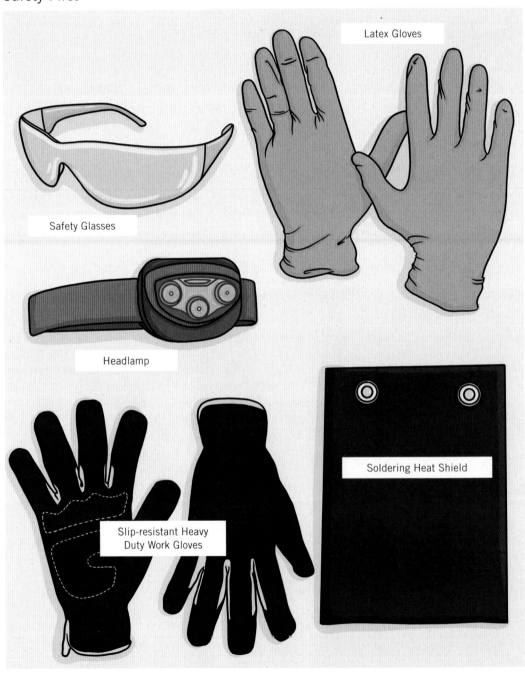

Latex Gloves

Safety Glasses

Headlamp

Soldering Heat Shield

Slip-resistant Heavy Duty Work Gloves

Plumbing Tools: Cutting + Prepping

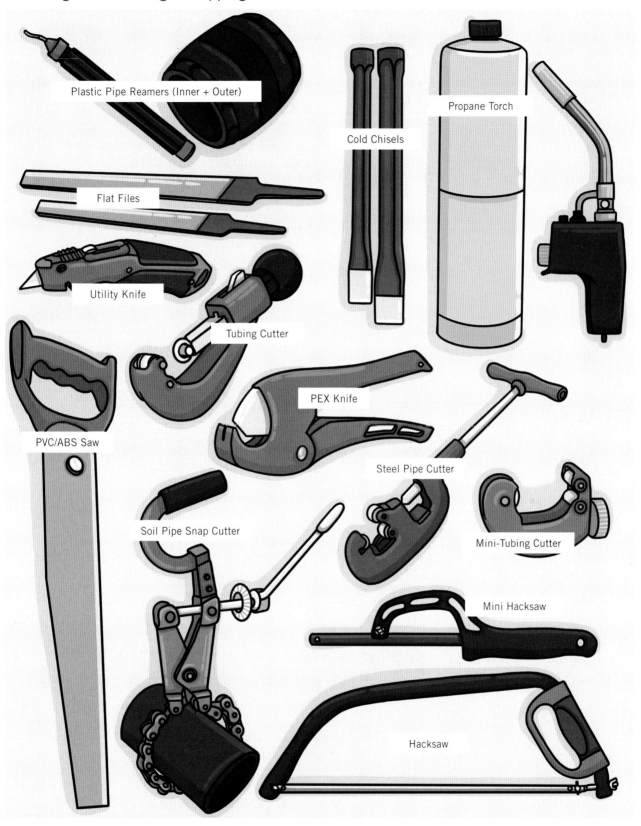

Plastic Pipe Reamers (Inner + Outer)

Cold Chisels

Propane Torch

Flat Files

Utility Knife

Tubing Cutter

PEX Knife

PVC/ABS Saw

Steel Pipe Cutter

Mini-Tubing Cutter

Soil Pipe Snap Cutter

Mini Hacksaw

Hacksaw

(continued)

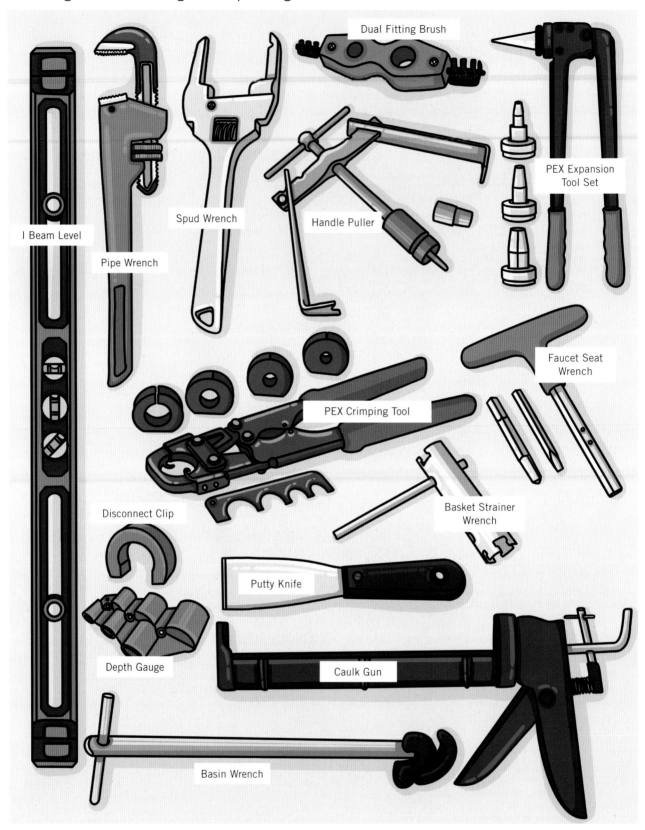

Dual Fitting Brush

PEX Expansion Tool Set

Spud Wrench

Handle Puller

I Beam Level

Pipe Wrench

Faucet Seat Wrench

PEX Crimping Tool

Disconnect Clip

Basket Strainer Wrench

Putty Knife

Depth Gauge

Caulk Gun

Basin Wrench

Plumbing Tools: Repairing

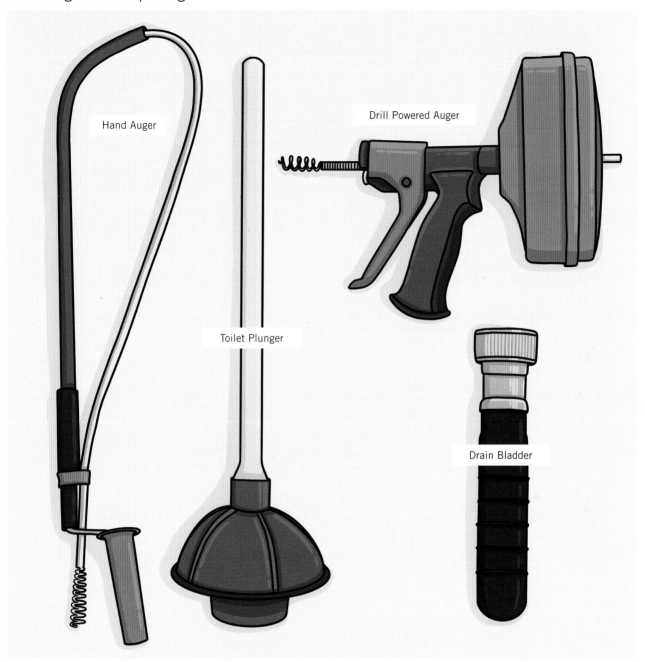

Hand Auger

Toilet Plunger

Drill Powered Auger

Drain Bladder

Plumbing Materials

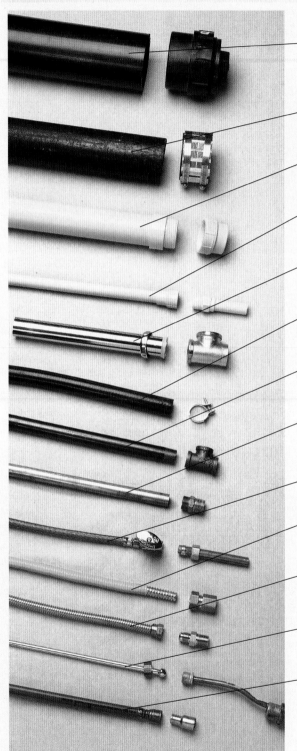

BENEFITS + CHARACTERISTICS

Acrylonitrile butadiene styrene (ABS) is an approved DWV pipe (although it has its detractors) and is commonly used in many markets, especially in the western U.S.

Cast iron is strong but hard to work with. Repairs should be made with plastic pipe.

Polyvinyl chloride (PVC) is rigid plastic that resists heat and chemicals. Schedule 40 is the minimum wall thickness, although Schedule 80 pipe minimizes water noi

Chlorinated polyvinyl chloride (CPVC) rigid plastic is inexpensive and withstands high temperature and pressure.

Chromed brass has an attractive shiny surface and is used for drain traps where appearance is important.

Polyethylene (PE) plastic is a black or bluish flexible pipe sometimes used for main w service lines as well as irrigation systems.

Black pipe (iron pipe) generally is threaded at the ends to accept female-threaded fittings. Usually used for gas lines; it is not for potable water.

Rigid copper is used for water supply pipes. It resists corrosion and has smooth surfa for good water flow.

Braided metal is used for water supply tubes that connect shutoff valves to fixtures.

Flexible stainless-steel (protective coated) connectors are used to attach gas applian to supply stopcocks.

Flexible stainless-steel (uncoated) connectors are used to attach gas appliances to supply stopcocks.

Chromed copper supply tube is used in areas where appearance is important. It is ea bend and fit.

Cross-linked polyethylene (PEX) is flexible and is approved by major building codes fo water supply.

Flexible copper tubing (not shown) bends easily and requires fewer couplings than rigid copper.

COMMON USES	LENGTHS	DIAMETERS	FITTING METHODS	TOOLS USED FOR CUTTING
DWV pipes, sewer pipes, drain traps	10'	1¼, 1½, 2, 3, 4"	Solvent cement, threaded fittings, or mechanical couplings	Tubing cutter, miter box, or hacksaw
DWV pipes, sewer pipes	5', 10'	1½, 2, 3, 4"	Oakum + lead, banded neoprene couplings	Snap cutter or hacksaw
DWV pipes, sewer pipes, drain traps	10', 20'; or sold by linear feet	1¼", 1½", 2", 3", 4"	Solvent cement, threaded fittings, or mechanical couplings	Tubing cutter, miter box, or hacksaw
Hot + cold water supply pipes	10'	⅜", ½", ¾", 1"	Solvent cement + plastic fittings, or with compression fittings	Tubing cutter, miter box, or hacksaw
Valves + shutoffs; drain traps, supply risers	Lengths vary	1¼", ½", ¾", 1¼", 1½"	Compression fittings or with metal solder	Tubing cutter, hacksaw, or reciprocating saw
Outdoor cold water supply pipes	Sold in coils of 25 to hundreds of feet	¼" to 1"	Rigid PVC fittings + stainless steel hose clamps	Ratchet-style plastic pipe cutter or miter saw
Gas supply pipe	Sold in lengths up to 10'	⅜, 1, 1¼, 1½"	Threaded connectors	Hacksaw, power cutoff saw, or reciprocating saw with bi-metal blade
Hot + cold water supply pipes	10', 20'; or sold by linear feet	⅜", ½", ¾", 1"	Metal solder, compression fittings, threaded fittings, press connect fittings, push connect fittings, flared fittings	Tubing cutter, hacksaw, or jigsaw
Supply tubes	12", 20", 30"	⅜, ½, ¾"	Attached threaded fittings	Do not cut
Gas ranges, dryers, water heaters	12" to 60"	⅝", ½" (OD)	Attached threaded fittings	Do not cut
Gas ranges, dryers, water heaters	12" to 60"	⅝", ½" (OD)	Attached threaded fittings	Do not cut
Supply tubing	12", 20", 30"	⅜"	Brass compression fittings	Tubing cutter or hacksaw
Hot + cold water supply; PEX-AL-PEX (usually orange) is used in radiant floors	Sold in coils of 25 feet to hundreds of feet	¼" to 1"	Crimp fittings, push fittings, or compression fittings	PEX cutter
Gas supply; hot + cold water supply	30', 60' coils; or by linear feet	¼", ⅜", ½", ¾", 1"	Brass flare fittings, solder, compression fittings	Tubing cutter or hacksaw

Copper

Copper is nearly ideal for water supply pipes. A purely natural (and consequently environmentally friendly) material, it resists corrosion and has a smooth surface that allows efficient water flow. The pipes are available in several diameters, but most home plumbing is done with ½- or ¾-inch pipe. The pipe comes in both rigid and flexible forms, although any copper pipe is going to be somewhat rigid.

The drawbacks to copper pipe are its susceptibility to leaks if it comes in contact with highly acidic well water, as well as its expense—also, traditional soldering or "sweating" of copper fittings is a skill that takes some practice to get right. PEX is an increasingly popular alternative because it is cheaper and the semiflexible tubes can be quickly and easily routed through framing without concern for kinks or the need for meticulous bending.

Rigid copper, sometimes called hard copper, is approved for home water supply systems by all local codes. It comes in three wall-thickness grades: Types M, L, and K. Type M is the thinnest, the least expensive, and a good choice for do-it-yourself home plumbing.

Rigid Type L usually is required by code for commercial plumbing systems. Because it is strong and solders easily, Type L may be preferred by some professional plumbers and do-it-yourselfers for home use. Type K has the heaviest wall thickness and is used most often for underground water service lines.

Flexible copper, also called soft copper, comes in two wall-thickness grades: Types L and K. Both are approved for most home water supply systems, although flexible Type L copper is used primarily for gas service lines. Because it is bendable and will resist a mild frost, Type

Soldering is a traditional way to join copper pipe and fittings, but it takes some practice to master (lead-free solders, now a requirement, can be a little more finicky). But push-fit fittings and other connection and material options are largely replacing soldered fittings and pipe.

L may be installed as part of a water supply system in unheated indoor areas, such as crawl spaces. Type K is used for underground water service lines.

Copper pipes are connected with soldered, compression, flare, or push-fit fittings (see chart below). Always consult your local code for the correct types of pipes and fittings allowed in your area.

COPPER PIPE + FITTING CHART

FITTING METHOD	RIGID COPPER			FLEXIBLE COPPER		GENERAL COMMENTS
	TYPE M	TYPE L	TYPE K	TYPE L	TYPE K	
Soldered	yes	yes	yes	yes	yes	Inexpensive, strong, and trouble-free fitting method. Requires some skill.
Compression	yes	not applicable		no	no	Makes repairs and replacement easy. More expensive than solder. Best used on flexible copper.
Flare	no	no	no	yes	yes	Use only with flexible copper pipes. Usually used as a gas-line fitting. Requires some skill.
Push-fit fittings	no	yes	yes	no	no	Easy to use. Flexible and inexpensive.

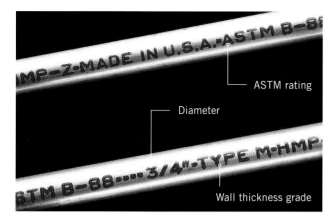

Grade stamp information includes the pipe diameter, the wall-thickness grade, and a stamp of approval from the ASTM (American Society for Testing and Materials). Type M pipe is identified by red lettering, Type L by blue lettering.

Bend flexible copper pipe with a coil-spring tubing bender to avoid kinks. Select a bender that matches the outside diameter of the pipe. Slip the bender over the pipe using a twisting motion. Bend pipe slowly until it reaches the correct angle, but not more than 90º.

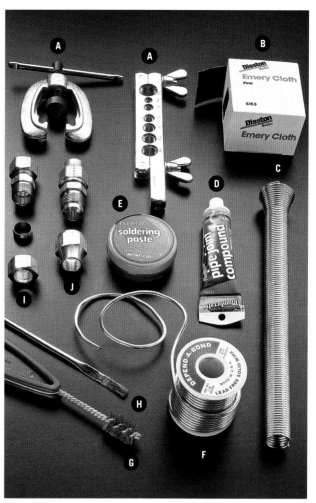

Specialty tools and materials for working with copper include: flaring tools (A), emery cloth (B), coil-spring tubing bender (C), pipe joint compound (D), soldering paste (flux) (E), lead-free solder (F), wire brush (G), flux brush (H), compression fitting (I), flare fitting (J).

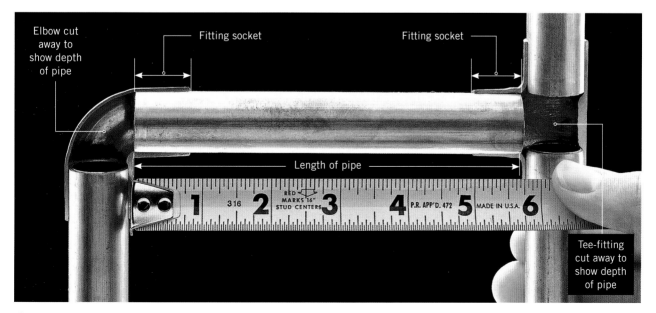

Find the length of copper pipe needed by measuring between the bottom of the copper fitting sockets (fittings shown in cutaway). Mark the length on the pipe with a felt-tipped pen.

Cutting + Soldering Copper

The best way to cut rigid and flexible copper pipe is with a tubing cutter. A tubing cutter makes a smooth, straight cut, an important first step toward making a watertight joint. Remove any metal burrs on the cut edges with a reaming tool or round file.

Copper can be cut with a hacksaw. A hacksaw is useful in tight areas where a tubing cutter will not fit. Take care to make a smooth, straight cut when cutting with a hacksaw.

A soldered pipe joint, also called a sweated joint, is made by heating a copper or brass fitting with a propane torch until the fitting is just hot enough to melt the solder. The heat draws the solder into the gap between the fitting and pipe to form a watertight seal. A fitting that is overheated or unevenly heated will not draw in solder. Copper pipes and fittings must be clean and dry to form a watertight seal.

SOLDERING TIPS

Use caution when soldering copper. Pipes and fittings become very hot and must be allowed to cool before handling.

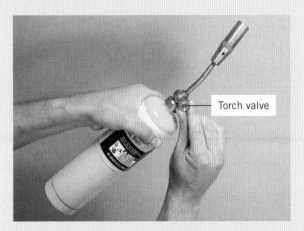

Torch valve

Prevent accidents by shutting off the torch immediately after use. Make sure the valve is closed completely.

TOOLS + MATERIALS

Tubing cutter with reaming tip (or hacksaw + round file)	Channel pliers
	Copper pipe
	Copper fittings
Wire brush	Emery cloth
Flux brush	Soldering paste (flux)
Propane torch	Soldering sheild
Spark lighter (or matches)	Lead-free solder
Round file	Rag
Cloth	Eye protection
Adjustable wrench	Work gloves

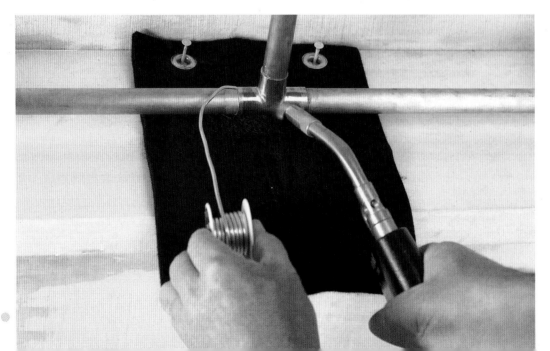

Protect wood from the heat of the torch flame while soldering. Use an old cookie sheet, two sheets of 26-gauge metal, or a fiber shield, as shown.

How to Cut Rigid + Flexible Copper Pipe

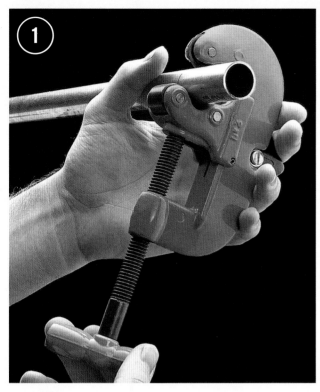

Place the tubing cutter over the pipe and tighten the handle so that the pipe rests on both rollers and the cutting wheel is on the marked line.

Slowly and carefully turn the tubing cutter one rotation so that the cutting wheel scores a continuous straight line around the pipe.

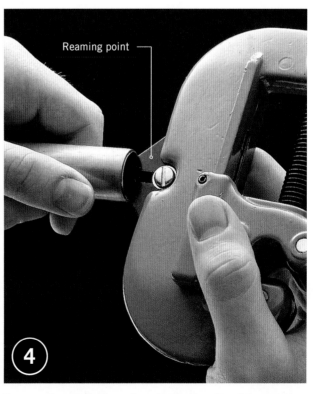

Rotate the cutter in the opposite direction, tightening the handle slightly after every two rotations, until the cut is complete.

Remove sharp metal burrs from the inside edge of the cut pipe using the reaming point on the tubing cutter.

How to Solder Copper Pipes + Fittings

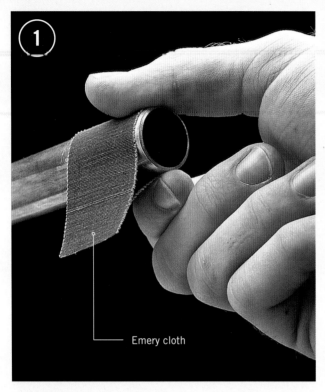

Emery cloth

Clean the end of each pipe by sanding with an emery cloth. Ends must be free of dirt and grease to ensure that the solder forms a good seal.

Clean the inside of each fitting by scouring with a wire brush or emery cloth.

Flux brush

Plumbcraft® soldering paste

NON CORROSIVE • CLEANS AS IT FLUXES

CAUTION: EYE IRRITANT. HARMFUL IF SWALLOWED. READ PRECAUTIONARY MEASURE ON BACK OF CAN.

NET WT. 2 OZ.

Apply a thin layer of soldering paste (flux) to the end of each pipe using a flux brush. Soldering paste should cover about 1" of the pipe end. Don't use too much flux. Apply a thin layer of flux to the inside of the fitting.

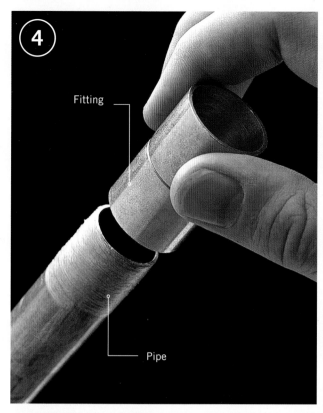

Fitting

Pipe

Assemble each joint by inserting the pipe into the fitting so it is tight against the internal shoulder. Twist each fitting slightly to spread the soldering paste.

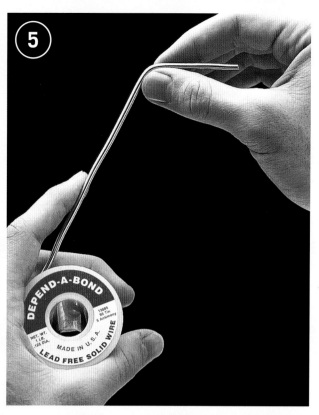

Use a clean dry cloth to remove excess flux before soldering the assembled fitting. Prepare the wire solder by unwinding 8" to 10" of wire from the spool. Bend the first 2" of the wire to a 90° angle.

Open the gas valve and trigger the spark lighter to ignite the torch. Adjust the torch valve until the inner portion of the flame is 1" to 2" long.

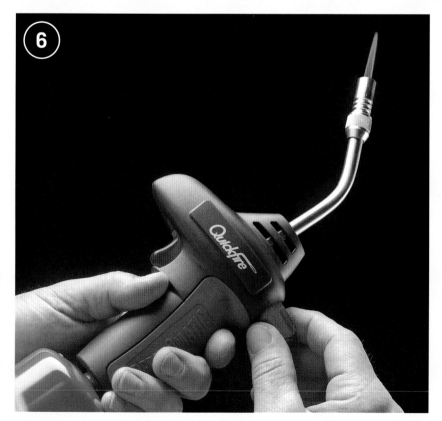

(continued)

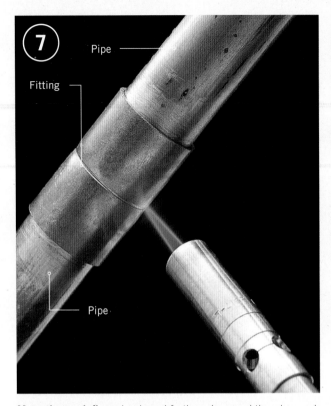

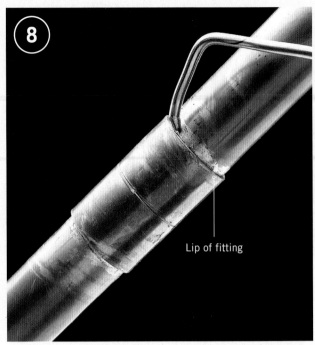

Move the torch flame back and forth and around the pipe and the fitting to heat the area evenly. Heat the other side of the copper fitting to ensure that heat is distributed evenly. Touch the solder to the pipe. The solder will melt when the pipe is at the right temperature.

When the solder melts, remove the torch and quickly push ½" to ¾" of solder into each joint. Capillary action fills the joint with liquid solder. A correctly soldered joint should show a thin, even bead of solder around the lips of the fitting. Allow the joint to cool briefly, then wipe away excess solder with a dry rag.

CAUTION: Pipes will be hot. If joints leak after water is turned on, disassemble and resolder.

 How to Take Apart Soldered Joints

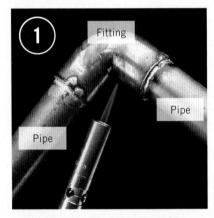

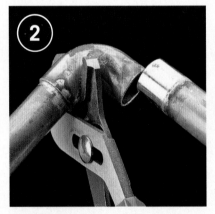

Turn off the water and drain the pipes by opening the highest and lowest faucets in the house. Light your torch. Hold the flame tip to the fitting until the solder becomes shiny and begins to melt.

Use channel pliers to separate the pipes from the fitting.

Remove old solder by heating the ends of the pipe with your torch. Use a dry rag to wipe away melted solder quickly. Use emery cloth to polish the ends of the pipe down to bare metal. Never reuse fittings.

CAUTION: Pipes will be hot.

PEX Pipe

PEX (cross-linked polyethylene) pipe is flexible plastic tubing invented in Germany in 1968. It quickly became the home water-supply plumbing of choice across Europe. In America, because of concerns about durability and potential pipe failures, PEX use was limited to radiant heating tubing from the 1980s onward. However, the use of PEX pipes in American home water supply systems has exploded over the last two decades.

The growing popularity of PEX is due to the fact that early concerns about reliability were misplaced, and the fact that PEX is much cheaper than copper, with many advantages over that traditional material. It is about the same price per linear foot as CPVC, but easier to use because there is no glue involved in the connections. Although PEX use was limited to professionals in the early years, tools, materials, and especially connection methods have advanced to the point that PEX is a completely realistic option for the home DIYer.

This type of pipe is flexible, making it possible to install it in very long, uninterrupted runs. The pipe can also be routed wherever it needs to go with fewer fittings, such as elbows. This can translate to a more stable water pressure and decrease possibility of leaks. PEX's flexibility can completely eliminate water hammer and pipe noise. The plastic also has a degree of elasticity, which means it is less likely than copper to rupture or split if frozen.

PEX comes in three colors: white, red, and blue. There is no physical difference between the three, but plumbing cold lines with blue and red lines for hot water allows you to tell at a glance what type of service any line is carrying.

There are three common types of PEX: A, B, and C. PEX-C is not used for home plumbing (it's limited to radiant heat or other hot-water, non-potable applications). You also may come across "oxygen barrier" PEX and PEX-AL-PEX, two types that are not normally used for home water supply; they are meant for closed-loop hydronic systems, such as radiant floor heating and ice-dam melting setups.

PEX-A is the highest quality PEX pipe and the most flexible. It is most often used with expansion fittings. PEX-B is the best value, because it is cheaper than copper or PEX-A. It is most often used with crimp-style connecters. Both A and B are extremely durable and should last as long as copper piping if not damaged or exposed to excessive UV light or chlorine. A sign of the longevity of the material is that PEX manufacturers regularly warranty their products for fifteen years or longer.

PEX can be used in conjunction with other materials, including CPVC and copper. The tubing is sold in most home improvement centers in coils or lengths (sometimes called "sticks") in diameters that include ½, ¾, and 1 inch. You'll also find a wide selection of fittings and connection tools and materials.

NOTE: Don't combine PEX-A with PEX-B in a single project. Use pipe, fittings, and connectors from the same manufacturer, because competing products are often not compatible.

TOOLS + MATERIALS

Tape measure

Non-permanent marker

Connection tool

Tubing cutter

PEX pipe

Manifolds

Safety plates (as needed)

PEX fittings

Utility knife

Plastic manifold hangers

PEX Materials

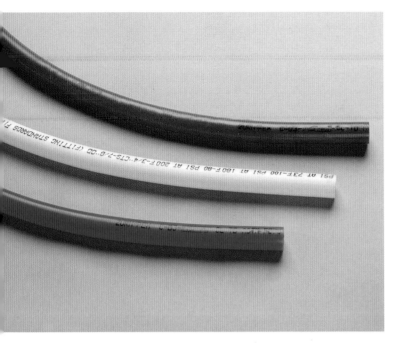

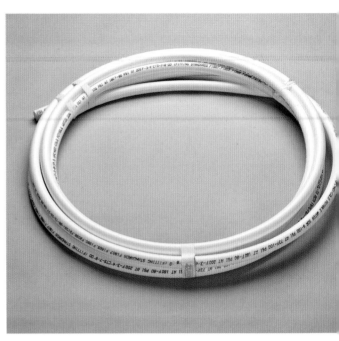

PEX pipe is manufactured in red, white, and blue. The intention is to use red for hot water lines and blue for cold water. However, the color does not affect price, and you may decide to use one color for the entire project.

PEX combines the flexibility of plastic tubing with the durability of rigid supply pipe. It is sold in coils of common supply-pipe diameters.

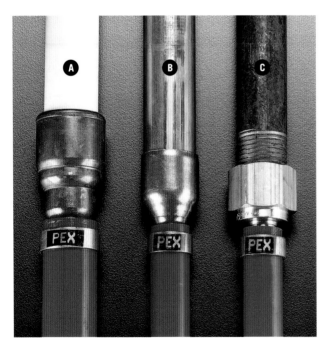

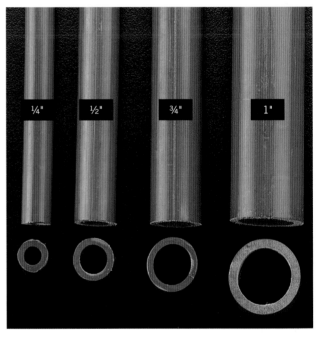

PEX is connected to other water supply materials with transition fittings, including CPVC-to-PEX (A), copper-to-PEX (B), and iron-to-PEX (C).

Generally, you should use the same diameter PEX as is specified for rigid supply tubing.

System Designs

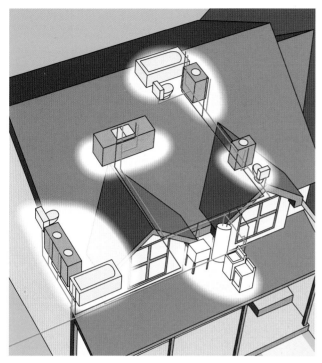

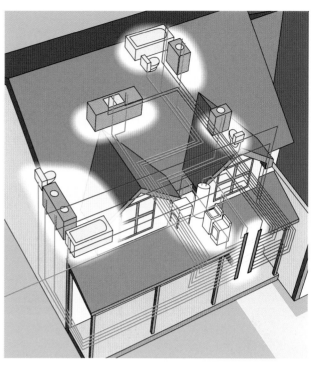

Trunk-and-branch systems are configured in much the same way as traditional rigid copper or PVC supply systems. A main supply line (the trunk line) carries water to all of the outlets via smaller branch lines that tie into the trunk and serve a few outlets in a common location.

Home run systems rely on one or two central manifolds to distribute the hot and cold water very efficiently. Eliminating the branch fittings allows you to use thinner supply pipe in some situations.

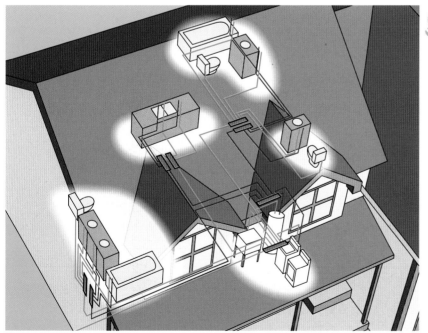

Remote manifold systems are a hybrid between traditional trunk-and-branch systems and home run systems. Instead of relying on just one or two manifolds, they employ several smaller manifolds downline from a larger manifold. Each smaller manifold services a group of fixtures, as in a bathroom or kitchen.

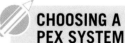

CHOOSING A PEX SYSTEM

- For maximum single-fixture water pressure: Trunk-and-branch

- For economy of materials: Trunk-and-branch or remote manifold

- For minimal wait times for hot water (single fixture): Home run

- For minimal wait times for hot water (multiple fixtures used at same approximate time): Trunk-and-branch or remote manifold

- For ease of shutoff control: Home run

- For lowest number of fittings and joints: Home run

PEX Installation

Most codes now allow for the use of PEX pipe and manifolds in residential plumbing, although you should always check with your local building department. Local codes may limit the use of PEX in some locations.

- Do not install PEX in aboveground exterior applications, because it degrades quickly from UV exposure.

- Do not use PEX for gas lines.

- Do not use plastic solvents or petroleum-based products with PEX (they can dissolve the plastic).

- Keep PEX at least 12" away from recessed light fixtures and other potential sources of high heat.

- Do not attach PEX directly to a water heater. Make connections at the heater with metallic tubing (either flexible water-heater connector tubing or rigid copper) at least 18" long; then join it to PEX with a transition fitting.

- Do not install PEX in areas where there is a possibility of mechanical damage or puncture. Always fasten protective plates to wall studs that house PEX pass-throughs.

- Always leave some slack in installed PEX lines to allow for contraction and in case you need to cut off a bad crimp. Add a loop in any run of 30' or more.

- Use the same minimum branch and distribution supply-pipe dimensions for PEX that you'd use for copper or CPVC, according to your local plumbing codes.

- You can use push fittings to join PEX to itself or to CPVC or copper. See page 56. Some professionals avoid using push fittings inside enclosed walls.

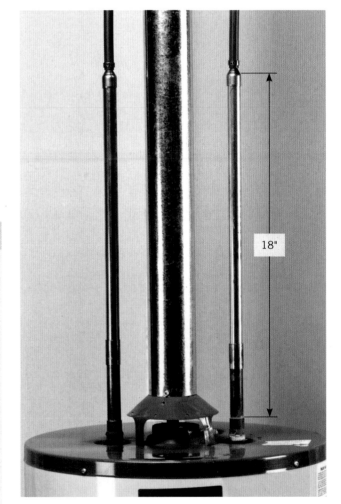

Do not connect PEX directly to a water heater. Use metal connector tubes. Solder the connector tubes to the water heater before attaching PEX. Never solder metal tubing that is already connected to PEX lines.

GENERAL CODES FOR PEX

PEX has been endorsed for residential use by all major building codes, although some municipal codes may be more restrictive. The specific design standards may also vary, but here are some general rules:

- For PEX, maximum horizontal support spacing is 32" and maximum vertical support spacing is 10'.

- PEX is designed to withstand 210°F water for up to 48 hours. For ongoing use, most PEX is rated for 180°F water up to 100 pounds per square inch of pressure.

- Directional changes of 90 degrees or more require a guide fitting.

- A mid-story guide is required for most PEX installations in walls. The guide should prevent movement perpendicular to the pipe direction.

Connectors for PEX systems are not interchangeable and all require specific crimping or connecting tools. The most common types you'll find in building centers today are: (A) clamping tool with jaws that snag a tab on a stainless-steel ring, drawing the ring tight when the tool is squeezed; (B) stainless-steel sleeve crimping tool that is similar to the full-circle crimping tool (below) but uses stainless-steel sleeves with flared ends; (C) expansion connectors with conical tips that fit into the PEX and a nylon union ring, temporarily expand it as a barbed fitting is inserted, then squeeze tight as the memory in the PEX causes it to shrink back to a nonexpanded state.

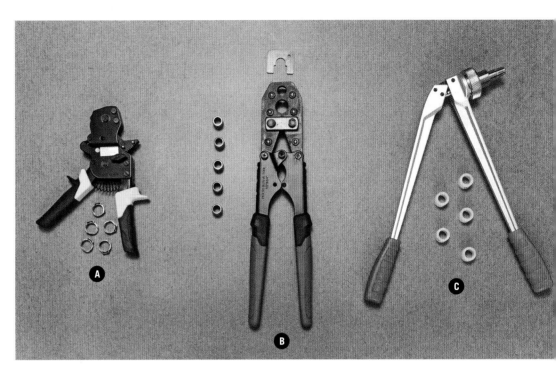

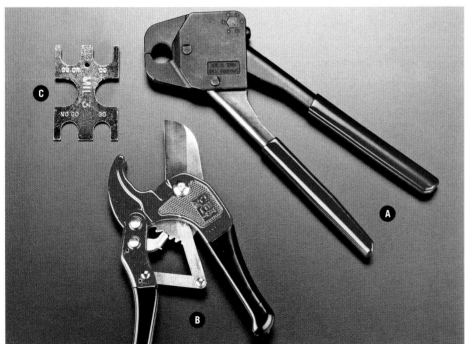

A full-circle crimping tool (A) compresses a crimping ring (usually copper) onto the PEX union to seal the joint. It was the original system used by most professionals before the PEX options expanded into more DIY-friendly systems. Crimping tools and rings are still used widely and are very reliable. With any PEX system you'll need a PEX cutter (B) for clean, square cuts, and a go/no-go gauge (C) to test connectors to make sure they fit properly after installation.

Choosing PEX Pipe and Connectors

Deciding on a connection method for your PEX pipes can seem confusing as first, given that some connectors can only work with certain types of PEX. There are four possible connection types: push-to-connect fittings will work with any PEX pipe, compression fittings work only with PEX-AL-PEX, expansion connectors work only with PEX-A, and crimp fittings will work with any PEX pipe. The types most commonly used in home plumbing are crimp fittings and expansion fittings. Both are extremely reliable, but expansion fittings take a bit more practice and expertise. They are also marginally more expensive, but the fittings themselves feature a larger internal diameter, which translates to improved water flow.

How to Make PEX Crimp Connections

Cut the pipe to length, making sure to leave enough extra material so the line will have a small amount of slack once the connections are made. A straight, clean cut is very important. For best results, use a PEX cutter.

Inspect the cut end to make sure it is clean and smooth. If necessary, deburr the end of the pipe with a sharp utility knife. Slip a crimp ring over the end.

Insert the barbed end of the fitting into the pipe until it is snug against the cut edges. Position the crimp ring so it is ⅛" to ¼" from the end of the pipe, covering the barbed end of the fitting. Pinch the fitting to hold it in place.

Fit the crimping tool with the appropriate head for the size pipe and fitting you're crimping. Align the jaws of the tool over the crimp ring (the ring should be exactly perpendicular to the pipe) and squeeze the handles to apply strong, even pressure to the ring until you hear a click.

Test the connection to make sure it is mechanically acceptable using a go/no-go gauge. If the ring does not fit into the gauge properly, cut the pipe near the connection and try again.

How to Make PEX Clamp Connections

Press the release button on the clamp tool handle to unlock the tool, and test to make sure the ratcheting action occurs when you squeeze the handles together.

Slip a ring over the cut end of the PEX. Grasp the tab "knuckle" on the ring in the ends of the tool jaws. Partially tighten the ring to keep it from sliding, but do not fully tighten.

Insert the fitting or union into the PEX opening so it is fully seated. Adjust the ring so it is parallel to the cut end of the PEX and ⅛" back from the tube end. With the ring knuckle in the tool jaws, squeeze several times to further tighten the ring—four to six squeezes total is typical. On some tool models, an on-board alert light will glow when you have achieved the right amount of torque. Release the ring from the tool.

OPTION: If you are not satisfied with the connection or need to undo it for any reason, slip the ring knuckle into the slot in the end of the ring removal tool. Hold the PEX joint securely and twist the removal tool back and forth until the ring snaps and can be removed easily.

How to Make PEX Expansion Connections

Fit the expansion connector tool with the head that corresponds to the diameter of the fitting and PEX pipe. Lightly grease the head.

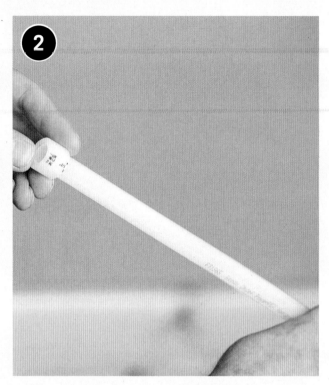

Slide the expansion ring onto the end of the PEX pipe (PEX-A only) until you reach the stop at the end of the ring. The ring should be flush against the cut end of the tubing.

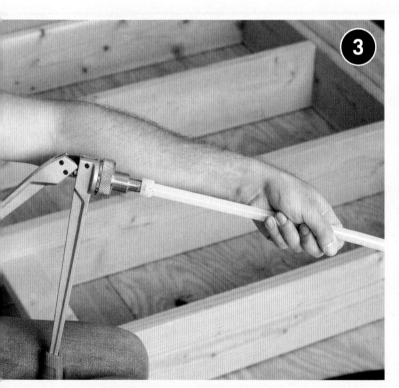

Insert the expansion tool head into the end of the PEX pipe and begin opening and closing the expansions jaws. Push the PEX pipe onto the head as it widens until the edge of the PEX pipe is flush against the base of the expansion head.

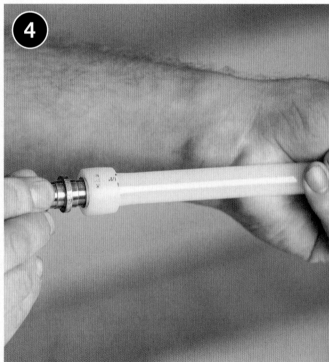

When the pipe and expansion sleeve are fully expanded, quickly remove the expansion tool head and slip the fitting into the end of the pipe. Allow the pipe to return to its original shape, firmly grabbing the fitting's barbed end, before using.

Routing PEX

In general, routing PEX supply lines is easier than routing rigid copper or PVC. That's one of the benefits of using this innovative material. However, it's important to follow best standards and practices when routing PEX lines to avoid leaks or other issues. Here are basic rules to follow, but you should always consult your local codes for more specific guidance.

- **Planning is key.** Know exactly the route your PEX lines will follow, and how you're going to make any bends and loops in the runs. It's always wise to plan for extra length to account for any cutting or fitting errors. Look for construction features that will allow you to route the PEX pipe with a minimum of fittings, which will save time, money, and effort.

- **Provide adequate support.** Horizontal PEX runs should be supported every 24 to 32 inches; vertical runs should be supported at least every 10 feet, but every 6 feet is better if possible. Keep in mind that some slack should be maintained in any PEX run.

- **Loop it.** On any PEX run of 30 feet or more, loop the line to allow for expansion and contraction. If you can afford the extra PEX pipe, it's not a bad idea to loop any run over 20 feet.

- **Protect underground runs.** Where unavoidable, such as in an uninsulated belowground basement or crawlspace, insulate hot water supply lines to avoid heat loss.

- **Follow recommendations.** Use fasteners only specified by the specific manufacturer of the PEX pipe you buy.

- **Support manifolds.** Whether they're home-run manifolds or smaller branch manifolds, any PEX manifold should be fully supported and mounted on a wall surface or sufficient blocking for the entire body of the manifold. Ideally, manifolds should not be enclosed in a wall. They can be mounted horizontally or vertically when properly supported.

- **Avoid heat.** Keep PEX pipe at least 12 inches away from any heat source. This includes less-obvious sources such as recessed lighting fixtures, gas vents, or heating fixtures such as baseboard units and radiators.

- **Protect pass-throughs.** Use nailing plates on stud edges for any stud through which PEX pipe passes.

- **Avoid stress.** Place support clamps at every fitting in a way that relieves any stress on the connection or on any bend in the PEX pipe.

PEX should be secured along runs to joists or wall studs with the correct size pipe strap or hangers specifically approved for use with PEX. It's essential that any support not kink or crush the pipe. Keep cold and hot water lines at least 2 inches apart on runs, to avoid any heat transfer

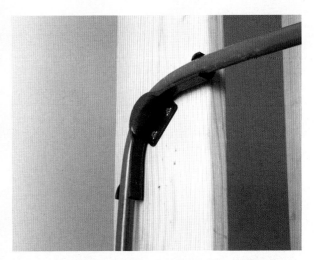

Make 90° bends in any PEX line using either a plastic snap-in guide, as shown here, or a barbed 90° elbow cut into the line. Installing guides is, however, easier and quicker where appropriate.

- **Bundle carefully.** Don't tape bundled runs of PEX pipe, and don't bundle hot and cold supply lines together. You can use plastic ties to hold bundles together, but make sure there is enough slack to allow for expansion and contraction of any pipe in the bundle.

PEX Manifolds

Although a whole-house home-run PEX system requires a large central manifold, most home DIYers are more likely to tackle installing a local or "branch" manifold (also called "remote manifold systems"), which distributes water to one room or a small area of the home. These are useful for plumbing additions or retrofitting a bathroom. Branch manifolds are simpler and easier to install than a home-run manifold. Here are considerations for choosing the right manifold.

• **Material.** PEX manifolds come in brass, copper, and plastic. Metal versions are more expensive and susceptible to corrosion, and often contain integral shut-off valves. Those won't matter as much if you are enclosing the manifold in a wall or ceiling. Plastic manifolds are usually mated to a specific type of PEX.

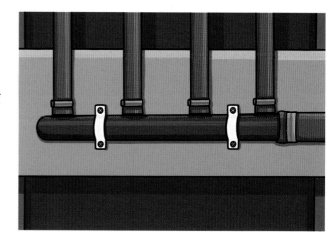

If you have already purchased the pipe for project, that may limit available choices.

• **Size.** Manifold size is defined by number of "branches" and inlet diameter. The most common is a ¾ inch inlet with ½ inch outlets. However, outlet size may be ⅜" in some circumstances (which will conserve energy and improve efficiency) or may need to be ¾"—depending on the length of the branch PEX lines. Consult the manufacturer's recommendations and local codes for appropriate size.

• **Connection method.** Plain barbed inlet and outlet connections are the least expensive. However, manifolds also come with compression and push-fit connections. Push-fit, in particular, can make installation easier and quicker, but are more expensive.

MANIFOLD OPTIONS

Different PEX manifolds serve different purposes. The home run manifold (A) is meant to serve all or most of a home; simple plastic remote "branch" manifolds (B) can work in with a home run manifold or alone, and are best to serve fixtures with their own shutoff valves; brass or copper branch manifolds (C) often come with integral shutoff valves.

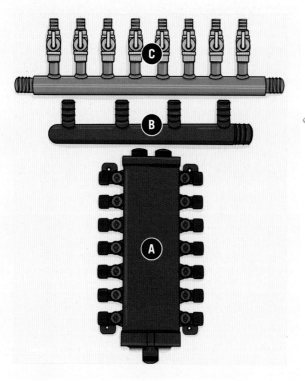

TOOLS + MATERIALS

Level	PEX pipe
Carpenter's pencil	PEX crimps or clamps
Drill + bits	PEX crimping or clamping
Screwdriver	tools
PEX manifold	Plastic pipe straps
Mounting straps or brackets	

How to Install a PEX Branch Manifold

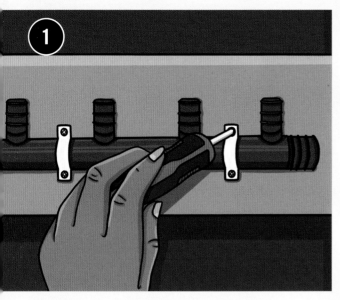

Check for level and mark the location of the manifold. Securely fasten the manifold to a wall, brace between studs, or along a joist (depending on location). Fasten the manifold with pipe straps, manifold brackets, or the manufacturer's supplied brackets.

Note: Some manufacturers recommend attaching the PEX pipe to the manifold prior to securing the manifold in place, but this is normally a less convenient method of installation.

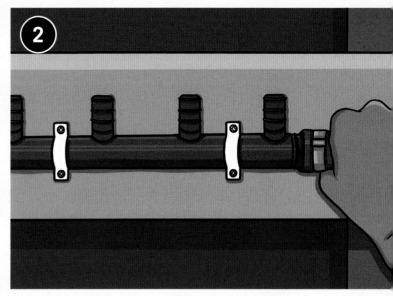

Connect the ¾" water supply to the manifold's open-end inlet. In this case, the manifold is connected to a PEX line from the main home run manifold.

Note: If this were a home-run manifold manifold, the connections would usually be made between the manifold and copper water supply line.

Connect the ½" individual fixture PEX supply lines to the manifold. Secure each one with a crimp ring.

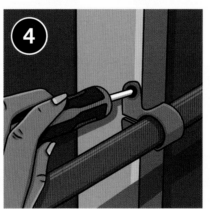

Route each line to its fixture, securing it with plastic pipe straps along the way. Plastic hangers are normally better than metal ones because they are more forgiving of PEX expansion and contraction.

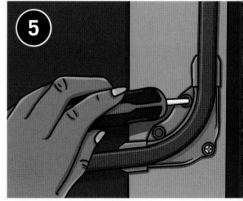

Avoid kinks in the PEX along the route to the fixture hookup. Install a 90° support channel for severe changes in direction. For long runs of more than 30 feet, loop the PEX at least once between clamps or straps to allow for some movement.

Rigid Plastic Pipe

Cut rigid ABS, PVC, or CPVC plastic pipes with a tubing cutter, power saw, or hacksaw. Cuts must be straight to ensure watertight joints.

Rigid plastics are joined with plastic fittings and solvent cement. Use a solvent cement that is made for the type of plastic pipe you are installing. For example, do not use ABS solvent on PVC pipe. Some solvent cements, called "all-purpose" or "universal" solvents, may not comply with local plumbing codes.

Solvent cement hardens in about 30 seconds, so test-fit all plastic pipes and fittings before cementing the first joint. For best results, the surfaces of plastic pipes and fittings should be dulled with emery cloth and liquid primer before they are joined. However, there are several new self-priming cements on the market that eliminate the need for a separate primer. These save time, effort, and expense.

Liquid solvent cements and primers are toxic and flammable. Provide adequate ventilation when fitting plastics, and store the products away from any source of heat.

Solvent welding is a chemical bonding process used to permanently join PVC pipes and fittings. The primer is always purple but may not be needed if you use a self-priming cement.

TOOLS + MATERIALS

Tape measure	Utility knife	Fittings	Rag
Marker	Channel pliers	Emery cloth	Petroleum jelly
Tubing cutter (or miter box or hacksaw)	Gloves	PVC primer and cement	Eye protection
	Plastic pipe		Latex gloves

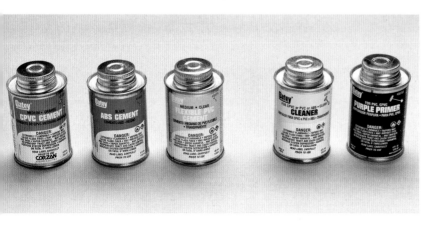

Primer and solvent cement are specific to the plumbing material being used. Avoid using all-purpose or multi-purpose products. Light to medium body cements are appropriate for DIYers as they allow the longest working time and are easiest to use. When working with large pipe, 3 or 4" in diameter, buy a large can of cement, which has a larger dauber. If you use the small dauber (which comes with the small can), you may need to apply twice, which will slow you down and make connections difficult. (The smaller can of primer is fine for any other size pipe, since there's no rush in applying primer.) Cement (though not primer) goes bad in the can within a month or two after opening, so you may need to buy a new can for a new project.

How to Cut Rigid Plastic Pipe

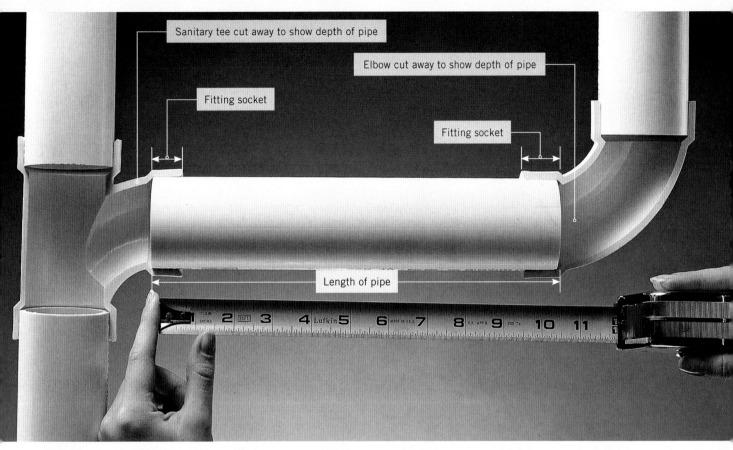

Sanitary tee cut away to show depth of pipe

Elbow cut away to show depth of pipe

Fitting socket

Fitting socket

Length of pipe

Find the length of plastic pipe needed by measuring between the bottoms of the fitting sockets (fittings shown in cutaway). Mark the length on the pipe with a felt-tipped pen.

Plastic tubing cutters do a fast, neat job of cutting. They are not interchangeable with metal tubing cutters and don't work on larger-diameter pipe.

The best cutting tool for PVC and some other plastic pipe is a power miter saw with a fine-tooth woodworking blade.

A ratcheting plastic-pipe cutter can cut smaller diameter PVC and CPVC pipe in a hurry.

How to Cement PVC Pipe

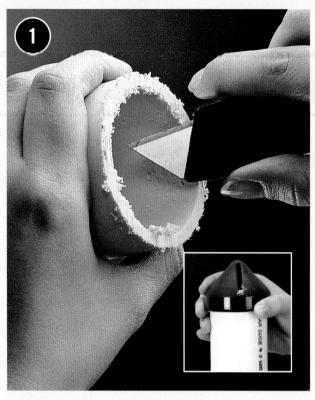

Remove rough burrs on cut ends of plastic pipe using a utility knife or deburring tool (inset).

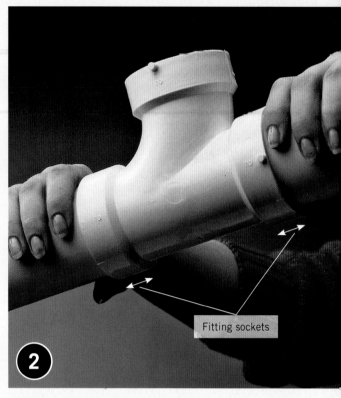

Fitting sockets

Test-fit all pipes and fittings. Pipes should fit tightly against the internal shoulders of the fittings.

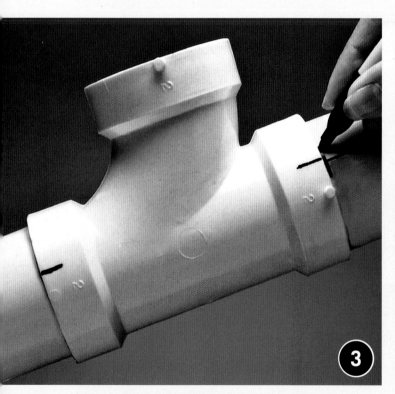

Mark the depth of the fitting sockets on the pipes. Make key marks where needed to maintain positioning of pipe and fittings when disassembled.

Apply a light coat of primer to the ends of the pipes and to the insides of the fitting sockets. Primer dulls glossy surfaces and ensures a good seal. (Skip this step if using a self-priming cement.)

Cement each joint by applying a thick coat of solvent cement to the end of the pipe. Apply a thin coat of solvent cement to the inside surface of the fitting socket. Work quickly: solvent cement hardens in about 30 seconds.

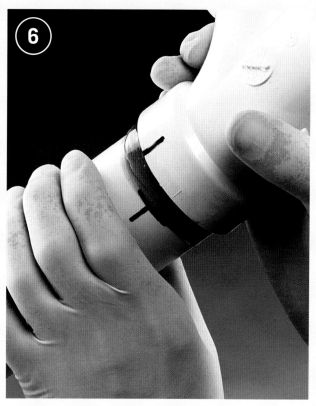

Quickly position the pipe and fitting so that the key marks are offset by about 2". Force the pipe into the fitting until the end fits flush against the internal shoulder.

Spread solvent by twisting the pipe until the marks are aligned. Hold the pipe in place for about 20 seconds to prevent the joint from slipping.

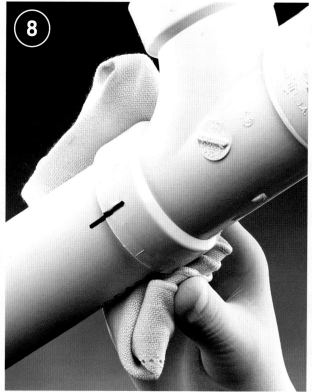

Wipe away excess solvent cement with a rag. Do not disturb the joint for 30 minutes after gluing.

Working with Cast-Iron Pipe

Cast iron was once the preferred material for waste lines in homes across the country. If your house was built before the mid 1970s, it's likely that you have cast-iron soil pipes. After that point, residential builders adopted PVC as the material of choice for waste lines, and much of the plumbing in the home.

There were three reasons for that transition: expense, durability, and ease or fabrication. Properly installed PVC will last as long, if not longer, than cast iron. It is lighter, easier to cut and join, and is less prone to corrosion, rust, or build-up inside the pipe— the principle negatives of cast-iron pipes. All that is why homeowners and the vast majority of builders use PVC. Even so, it's easier to remove or repair individual fixtures with cast-iron replacements, and the material is still required for soil stacks by local codes in a few municipalities.

Given that the best-case anticipated lifespan of cast-iron pipes is fifty to sixty years, you will probably be facing a repair or replacement of any cast-iron plumbing in your home, sooner rather than later. The techniques described here will help you accurately cut the pipe, and make leak-free, stable connections to new sections or fixtures.

Unique Connections

Cast-iron plumbing is not cemented like PVC, nor is it physically welded as with a soldered copper pipe joint. There are no push-fit or compression fittings for cast-iron pipe. Instead, these pipes are connected one of two ways: hub-and-spigot, or banded coupling. (The third option offered below is specifically for splicing a fixture into an existing cast-iron pipe.)

• **Hub-and-spigot.** The "hub" is a preformed cup flare on the end of a cast-iron pipe—cast-iron pipe is sold in standard lengths with hubs at both ends, one end, or neither. The spigot is simply an unflared, plain pipe end. The spigot is secured in the hub in one of two ways. The longstanding method that is rarely used these days, except in some commercial applications, is lead-and-oakum packing. Oakum is loose fiber caulking. The "lead" is lead wool. The joint is formed by first fully seating the spigot into the joint, and then using a blunt chisel or similar tool to tamp oakum down into the joint all the way around. The joint is finished by topping the layer of oakum with a layer of lead wool, tamped into in the joint in the same way.

GALVANIZED STEEL

Galvanized steel is no longer used for home plumbing pipes. The material was prone to corrosion, rust, and other issues and should be replaced as time and opportunity allows. Although these pipes are threaded, be aware that it is easier to simply cut out galvanized pipes because the threads on older galvanized-steel pipes are usually resolutely rusted in place.

Many cast-iron pipes installed in homes have come to the end of their useful lives.

How to Cut Cast-Iron Pipe

Use a white grease pencil or similar to mark the cut line all around the pipe's circumference. Align the tool on the pipe with the cutting wheels contacting the marked cut line. Make sure the cutting wheels are square to the pipe end, so that the cut will be square and clean.

Compress the handle just enough to score the surface. Rotate the tool, and repeat. Finally, apply steady, firm pressure to the snap cutter handle until the pipe breaks along the scored line.

• **Banded coupling.** This is the preferred option for its simplicity and adaptability. The two pipe ends are mated with a neoprene gasket. A stainless steel band is then slide over the gasket and tightened down, holding the pipes in place. A banded coupling is only used on plain-end pipes, but it is a way to join PVC pipe to cast iron, as well as cast iron to cast iron. The union is durable and quick to install.

• **Cast-iron threaded fitting to PVC.** Where you've cut a cast-iron Y or T fitting into an existing waste line, you can use a threaded arm and fit it with a threaded PVC adapter. A new PVC extension can be cemented into the adapter's inlet to create an incredibly stable connection.

Making the Cut

Cutting cast iron is not as easy as cutting PVC or even copper. Although you can cut a cast-iron pipe with a hacksaw, you'll save quite a bit of effort and time by using a snap cutter. This is a specially designed tool, with a chain that tightens around the pipe, and cutting wheels that bite into the surface. Alignment is key no matter what tool you use, but one of the most important factors in using a snap cutter.

For tight spaces, or if you don't have access to a snap cutter or hacksaw, you can also cut a cast-iron pipe with a hammer and cold chisel. This is labor intensive and requires marking the circumference of the pipe accurately, and then carefully chiseling out along the marked line.

TOOLS + MATERIALS

Heavy-duty work gloves	60 inch-pound torque wrench
Safety glasses	
Thick latex gloves	Rubber mallet
File	Hammer
Snap cutter	Pipe puller (optional)
Grease pencil or white marker	Hubless banded coupling
	Adhesive pipe lubricant
⁵⁄₁₆" nut driver	Scrap 2 × 4

Additional Considerations

The most obvious trait that distinguishes cast iron from PVC or even copper is its formidable weight. Given that it is significantly heavier than any other option, cast-iron pipes—especially larger diameters—must be properly supported. Whether you're just inspecting your existing plumbing or actively repairing older cast-iron waste pipe, it's wise to check existing supports—which are themselves often subject to corrosion—for structural integrity.

It may seem overkill, but it's well worth the minimal time and effort to install sturdy stack clamps on any vertical cast-iron pipe. A little extra attention and effort can head off a rather disgusting situation in which a vertical waste stack leaks, or experiences a pipe break. Adequate support is even more vital if you are making a cut in a cast-iron vertical stack that runs up to a second story. Always check that that the pipe is well supported on the floor above.

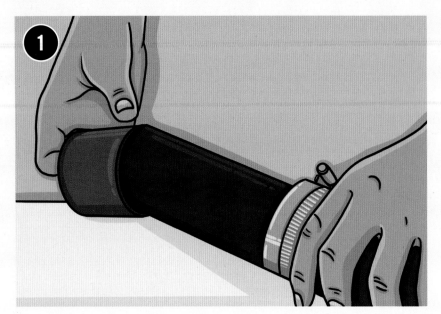

Make sure the ends of both pipes are smooth and clean. Use a coupling that conforms to local codes. Slide the coupling collar onto one pipe end. Insert the pipe end into the coupling gasket until it is securely seated and contacting any inner shoulder.

Slide the other pipe end into the opposite end of the gasket, seating it securely. Slide the collar over the gasket, so that it is perfectly aligned with the gasket edges on both ends, all around the pipe. Initially tighten the clamp with a $\frac{5}{16}$" nut driver. Tighten a little on each side, alternating as you work. Finish tightening the clamp with a 60 inch-pound torque wrench, or whatever torque is required by code.

How to Join Cast-Iron Pipe: Hub-and-Spigot

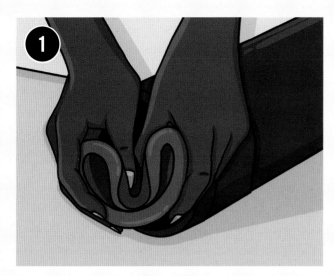

Use a file to remove any sharp edges from the hub and spigot pipe ends. Squeeze and fold the gasket, and slip it into the hub's mouth.

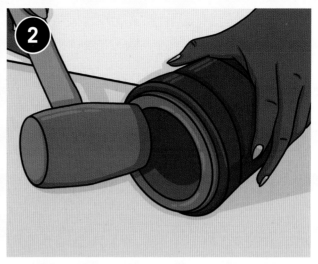

Manipulate the gasket so the lip is even all the way around the edge of hub. Use a rubber mallet to tap the gasket lip and ensure it is securely seated in the hub.

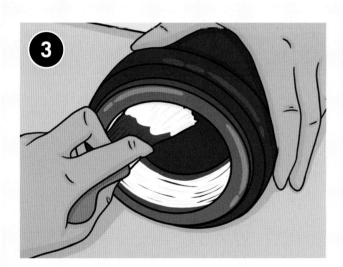

Lubricate the inside of the compression gasket with pipe lubricant (any pipe larger than 5" in diameter should be lubricated with adhesive lubricant). Spread lubricant on the end of the spigot pipe.

Note: Pipe lubricant contains toxic chemicals; use only in a well-ventilated space with rubber or latex gloves. Avoid any contact with your skin or eyes.

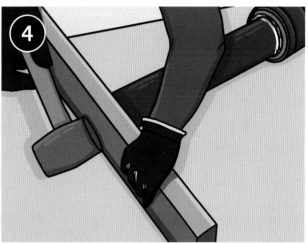

Align the spigot pipe end with the gasket opening, and push the spigot end in. Use a pipe puller to securely seat the spigot pipe in the hub. You can also use a scrap 2 × 4 or 2 × 6 on the opposite end of the spigot, hitting it with a hard mallet or hammer until the pipe fully seats.

Working with Outdoor Flexible Plastic Pipe

Flexible PE (polyethylene) pipe is used for underground cold water lines. Very inexpensive, PE pipe is commonly used for automatic lawn sprinkler systems and for extending cold water supply to utility sinks in detached garages and sheds.

Unlike other plastics, PE is not solvent-cemented but is joined using "barbed" rigid PVC fittings and stainless-steel hose clamps. In cold climates, outdoor plumbing lines should be shut off and drained for winter.

TOOLS + MATERIALS

Tape measure	Flexible pipe
Tubing cutter	Fittings
Screwdriver or wrench	Hose clamps
Pipe joint compound	Utility knife

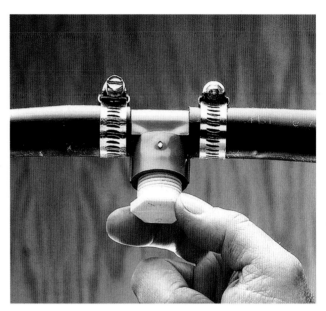

Connect lengths of PE pipe with a barbed PVC fitting. Secure the connection with stainless steel hose clamps.

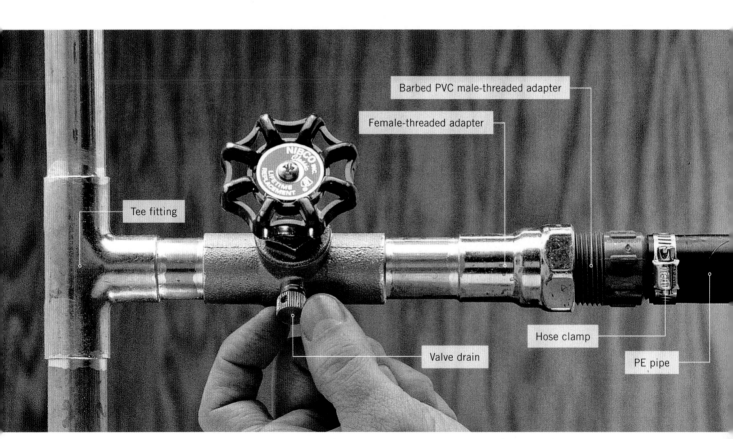

Barbed PVC male-threaded adapter

Female-threaded adapter

Tee fitting

Valve drain

Hose clamp

PE pipe

Connect PE pipe to an existing cold water supply pipe by splicing in a tee fitting to the copper pipe and attaching a drain-and-waste shutoff valve and a female-threaded adapter. Screw a barbed PVC male-threaded adapter into the copper fitting, then attach the PE pipe. The drain-and-waste valve allows you to blow the PE line free of water when winterizing the system.

How to Cut + Join Outdoor Flexible Plastic Pipe

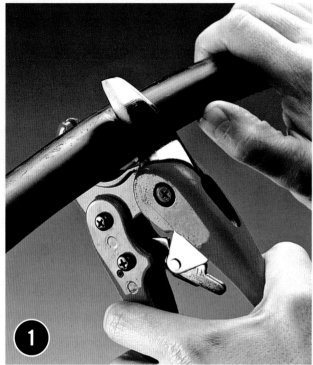

(1) Cut flexible PE pipe with a plastic tubing cutter, or use a miter box or sharp knife. Remove any rough burrs with a utility knife.

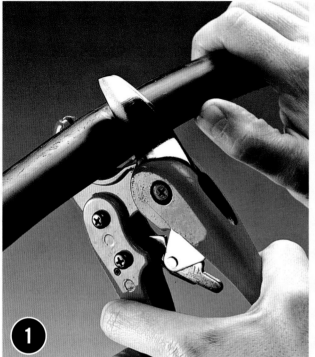

OPTION: To ensure a tighter fit, dab some pipe joint compound onto the barbs so they are easier to slide into the flexible plastic pipe. Apply pipe joint compound to the barbed ends of the tee fitting. Work each end of PE pipe over the barbed portions of the fitting and into position.

Fit stainless-steel hose clamps over the ends of the flexible pipes being joined.

(2)

Slide the hose clamps over the joint ends. Hand tighten each clamp with a screwdriver or wrench.

(3)

Pipe Fittings

Use the photos on these pages to identify the plumbing fittings specified in the project how-to directions found in this book. Each fitting shown is available in a variety of sizes to match your needs.

Pipe fittings come in a variety of shapes to serve different functions within the plumbing system. DWV fittings include:

Vents: In general, the fittings used to connect vent pipes have very sharp bends with no sweep. Vent fittings include the vent tee and vent 90-degree elbow. Standard drain pipe fittings can also be used to join vent pipes.

Horizontal-to-vertical drains: To change directions in a drain pipe from the horizontal to the vertical, use fittings with a noticeable sweep. Standard fittings for this use include waste tee fittings and 90-degree elbows. Wye fittings and 45-degree and 22½-degree elbows can also be used for this purpose.

Vertical-to-horizontal drains: To change direction from the vertical to the horizontal, use fittings with a very pronounced, gradual sweep. Common fittings for this purpose include the long-radius wye tee fitting and some wye fittings with 45-degree elbows.

Horizontal offsets in drains: Wye fittings, 45-degree elbows, 22½-degree elbows, and long sweep 90-degree elbows are used when changing directions in horizontal pipe runs. Whenever possible, horizontal drain pipes should use gradual, sweeping bends rather than sharp turns.

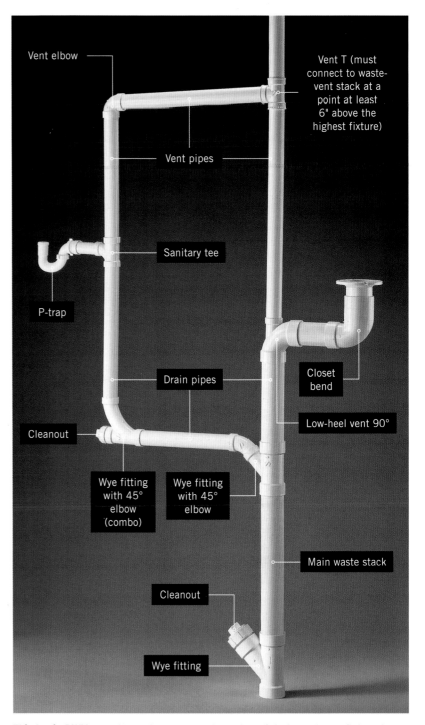

This basic DWV tree shows the correct orientation of drain and vent fittings in a plumbing system. Bends in the vent pipes can be very sharp, but drain pipes should use fittings with a noticeable sweep. Fittings used to direct falling waste water from a vertical to a horizontal pipe should have bends that are even more sweeping. Your local plumbing code may require that you install cleanout fittings where vertical drain pipes meet horizontal runs.

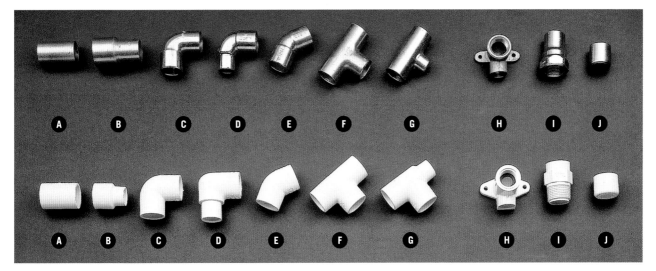

Water supply fittings are available for copper (top), CPVC plastic (center), and PEX (bottom). Fittings for CPVC and copper are available in many shapes, including: unions (A), reducers (B), 90° elbows (C), reducing elbows (D), 45° elbows (E), tee fittings (F), reducing tee fittings (G), drop-ear elbows (H), threaded adapters (I), and caps (J). Common PEX fittings (bottom) include unions (K), PEX-to-copper unions (L), 90° elbows (M), tee fittings (N), plugs (O), drop-ear elbows (P), and threaded adapters (Q). Easy-to-install push fittings are also available.

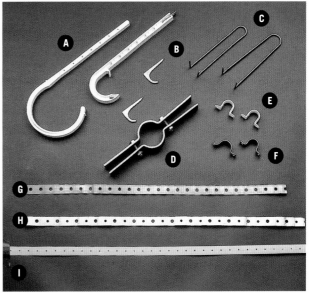

Water supply valves are available in brass or plastic and in a variety of styles, including: drain-and-waste valves (A), gate valve (B), full-bore ball valves (C), fixture shutoff valve (D), vacuum breaker (E), and hose bib (F).

Support materials for pipes include: plastic pipe hangers (A), copper J-hooks (B), copper wire hangers (C), riser clamp (D), plastic pipe straps (E), copper pipe straps (F), flexible copper, steel, and plastic pipe strapping (G, H, I). Do not mix metal types when supporting metal pipes; use copper support materials for copper pipe and steel for steel and cast-iron pipes.

Tee Fittings

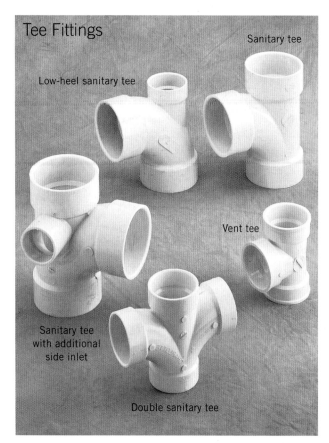

Low-heel sanitary tee

Sanitary tee

Vent tee

Sanitary tee with additional side inlet

Double sanitary tee

Elbows

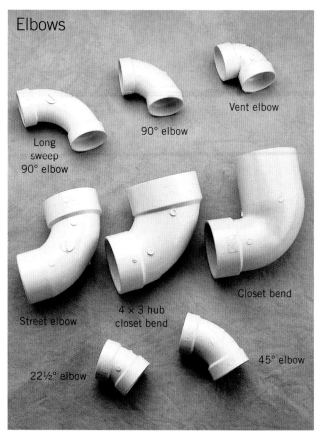

Long sweep 90° elbow

90° elbow

Vent elbow

Street elbow

4 × 3 hub closet bend

Closet bend

22½° elbow

45° elbow

Wye Fittings

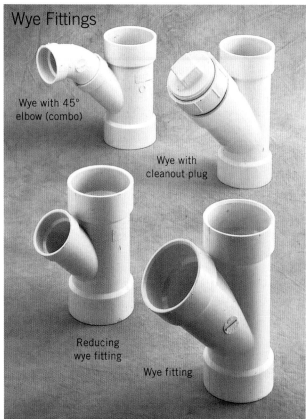

Wye with 45° elbow (combo)

Wye with cleanout plug

Reducing wye fitting

Wye fitting

Specialty Fittings

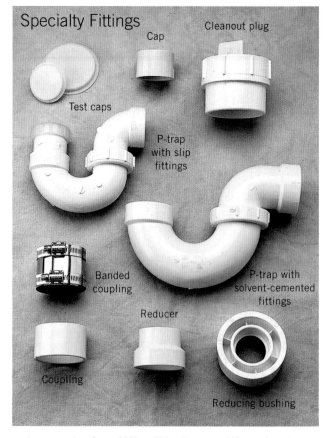

Cap

Cleanout plug

Test caps

P-trap with slip fittings

Banded coupling

P-trap with solvent-cemented fittings

Reducer

Coupling

Reducing bushing

Fittings for DWV pipes are available in many configurations, with openings ranging from 1¼" to 4" in diameter. When planning your project, buy plentiful numbers of DWV and water supply fittings from a reputable retailer with a good return policy. It is much more efficient to return leftover materials after you complete your project than it is to interrupt your work each time you need to shop for a missing fitting.

How to Use Transition Fittings

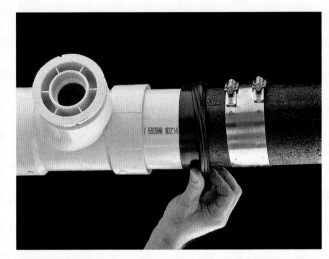

Connect plastic to cast iron with banded couplings. Rubber sleeves cover ends of pipes and ensure a watertight joint.

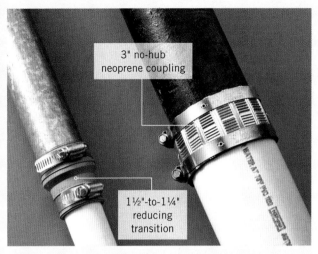

3" no-hub neoprene coupling

1½"-to-1¼" reducing transition

Make transitions in DWV pipes with rubber couplings. The two products shown here can be used to connect pipes of different materials.

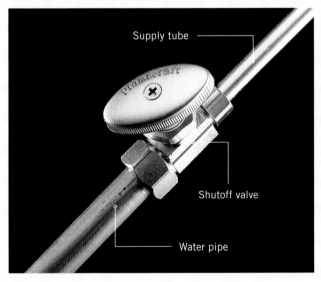

Supply tube

Shutoff valve

Water pipe

Connect a water pipe to any fixture supply tube using a shutoff valve.

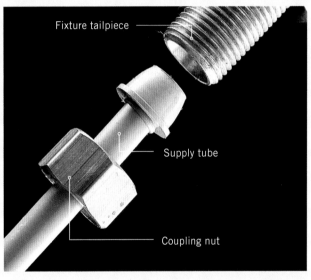

Fixture tailpiece

Supply tube

Coupling nut

Connect any supply tube to a fixture tailpiece with a coupling nut. The coupling nut compresses the bell-shaped end of the supply tube against the fixture tailpiece.

Specialty supply fittings can be used to supply portable water fixtures, such as icemakers and hot water dispensers.

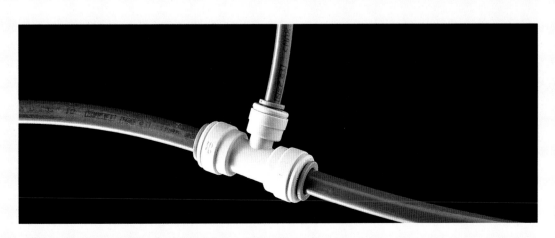

Push-Fit Fittings

Also known as "push-to-connect," push-fit fittings have been around roughly since the turn of the latest century. They were originally developed for naval use, which is an indicator of how reliable they are—when installed correctly and under the right circumstances. These are the height of ease-of-use in plumbing connections, requiring no soldering, chemicals such as glue or solvent, or even tools.

The fittings are manufactured with a ring of stainless-steel teeth pointed to allow the fitting to slide over the end of a pipe and secure it in place. An EPDM rubber O-ring makes a watertight connection around the outside of the pipe, and the O-ring is pre-lubricated to ensure it seals on the surface of the pipe and remains supple.

Push-fit fittings can be used on copper, CPVC, and PEX-A and -B pipes. When used with PEX pipe, a plastic sleeve is fitted inside the pipe and stiffens the PEX to allow the fitting to hold tight. This plastic sleeve must be removed from the push-fit fittings when they are used with copper and CPVC. In every case, the fittings themselves are generally rated at about 200 psi and 200°F.

Still, cost may ultimately affect whether you choose push-fit fittings; the fittings are far more expensive than their more traditional counterparts. That's why most homeowners and professionals tend to use the fittings for small projects and repairs.

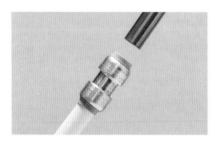

Push-fit fittings may be used on several types of supply pipes and can even join dissimilar pipes in the same run. The fittings freely spin on a pipe end, making their application more versatile. Given that you don't need any tools to install them, these are great options for tight spaces that would not allow for a soldering iron, torch, or other tools.

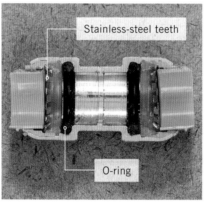

Stainless-steel teeth

O-ring

Plastic sleeve (PEX only)

Shown cutaway

Push-fit fittings make a watertight seal with a EPDM rubber O-ring. A row of stainless-steel teeth grab and hold the pipe in place. Plastic insert sleeves (right) are employed only when the fitting is used with PEX and should be removed for copper or CPVC joints.

DOS FOR USING PUSH-FIT FITTINGS

- Start with a clean cut. The fitting's seal relies on solidly sitting on the end of the pipe. Use a copper pipe cutter—not a saw—when cutting copper pipe for push-fit fittings, and cut PEX with a PEX cutter.

- Limit reuse. Although manufacturers regularly specify that these fittings can be reused four or five times in some cases, most professionals tend to limit reuse to two or three times. There is concern that the lubricant that helps the O-ring maintain a seal could wear away and leak after too many reuses.

- Ream carefully. Clean up the end of any pipe that will be used with these fittings. Even a small burr can damage push-fit rubber O-rings.

DON'TS FOR USING PUSH-FIT FITTINGS

- Never use a push-fit fitting in a system weatherized with glycol, such as in a plumbed recreational vehicle. The glycol may react with the O-ring lubricant and damage the seal.

- Do not use push-fit fittings with any lubricants, glues, solvents, Teflon tape, or other compounds.

- Don't sand the end of copper pipe prior to installing a push-fit fitting.

- Never use push-fit fittings with PEX-AL-PEX (PEX-A and PEX-B are fine).

- Don't use the fittings for exterior applications where they'll be consistently exposed to sunlight.

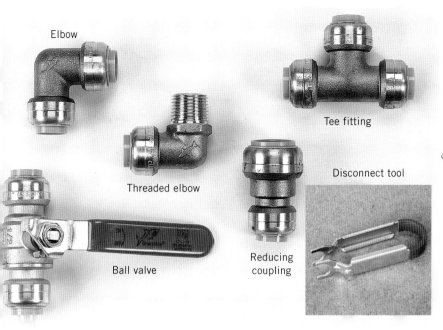

Elbow

Threaded elbow

Tee fitting

Ball valve

Reducing coupling

Disconnect tool

Push-fit fittings for copper pipe are available as couplings, elbows, tees, and even shutoff valves. A special tool (some have handles and some don't) can be purchased to make it easier to disassemble push-fit joints (inset).

TOOLS + MATERIALS

Pipe cutter
Push-fit fitting
Deburr tool or utility knife
Depth gauge or ruler
Marker
Disconnect tool (optional)

 ## How to Install Push-Fit Fittings

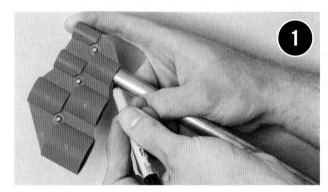

Cleanly cut the end of the pipe with a cutter meant for use on the pipe's material. Clean up the cut end and deburr with the manufacturer's tool. Use the manufacturer's depth gauge or a ruler to mark the pipe with the proper fitting depth.

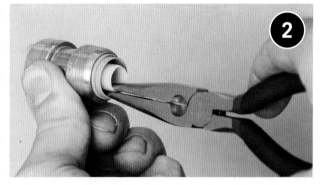

Remove the fitting's plastic sleeve if you're working with any pipe other than PEX. Slide the fitting onto the end of the pipe all the way until you reach the depth gauge mark. Pull on the fitting to ensure it is securely fixed to the pipe.

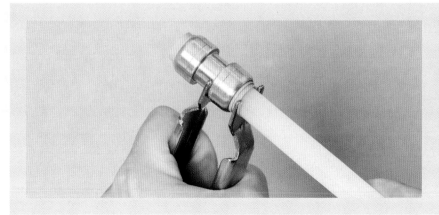

OPTION: If you need to remove the fitting for any reason, slip the removal tool over the pipe, snug it to the bottom of the fitting, and slowly pull the tool and the fitting off the pipe, twisting both as you pull.

Shutoff Valves

Worn-out shutoff valves or supply tubes can cause water to leak underneath a sink or other fixture. First, try tightening the fittings with an adjustable wrench. If this does not fix the leak, replace the shutoff valves and supply tubes.

Shutoff valves are available in several fitting types. For copper pipes, valves with compression-type fittings are easiest to install. For plastic pipes, use compression valves.

Older plumbing systems often were installed without fixture shutoff valves. When repairing or replacing plumbing fixtures, you may want to install shutoff valves if they are not already present.

TOOLS + MATERIALS

Hacksaw	Marker
Tubing cutter	Shutoff valves
Adjustable wrench	Supply tubes
Tubing bender	Pipe joint compound

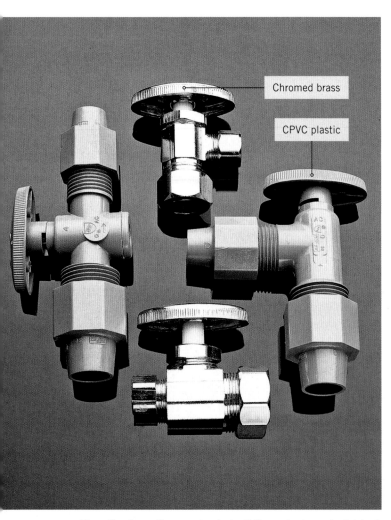

Chromed brass

CPVC plastic

Shutoff valves allow you to shut off the water to an individual fixture so it can be repaired. They can be made from durable chromed brass or lightweight plastic. Shutoff valves come in ½" and ¾" diameters to match common water pipe sizes.

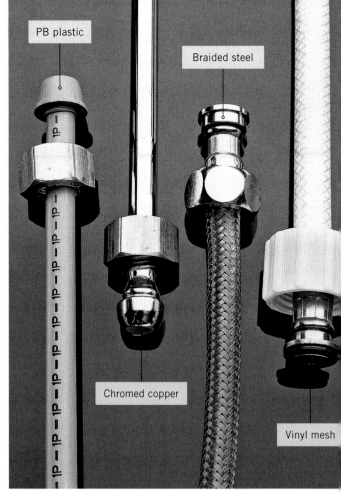

PB plastic

Braided steel

Chromed copper

Vinyl mesh

Supply tubes are used to connect water pipes to faucets, toilets, and other fixtures. They come in 12", 20", and 30" lengths. PB plastic and chromed copper tubes are inexpensive. Braided steel and vinyl mesh supply tubes are easy to install.

How to Install Shutoff Valves + Supply Tubes

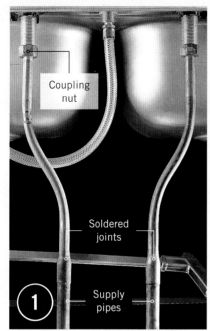

Turn off water at the main shutoff valve. Remove old supply pipes. If pipes are soldered copper, cut them off just below the soldered joint using a hacksaw or tubing cutter. Make sure the cuts are straight and deburred. Unscrew the coupling nuts and discard the old pipes.

Slide a compression nut and a compression ring over the copper water pipe. Threads of the nut should face the end of the pipe.

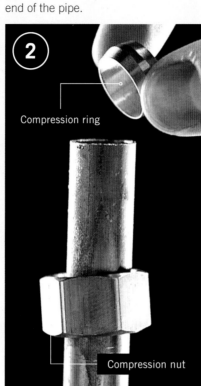

Apply pipe joint compound to the threads of the shutoff valve or compression nut. Screw the compression nut onto the shutoff valve and tighten with an adjustable wrench.

Bend the chromed copper supply tube to reach from the tailpiece of the fixture to the shutoff valve using a tubing bender. Bend the tube slowly to avoid kinking the metal.

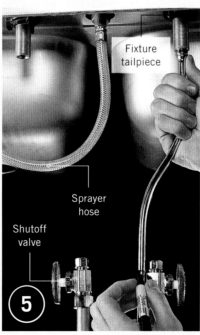

Position the supply tube between the fixture tailpiece and the shutoff valve, and mark the tube to length. Cut the supply tube with a tubing cutter.

Attach the bell-shaped end of the supply tube to the fixture tailpiece with a coupling nut, then attach the other end to the shutoff valve with a compression ring and nut. Tighten all fittings with an adjustable wrench.

Valves + Hose Bibs

Valves make it possible to shut off water at any point in the supply system. If a pipe breaks or a plumbing fixture begins to leak, you can shut off water to the damaged area so that it can be repaired. A hose bib is a faucet with a threaded spout, often used to connect rubber utility or appliance hoses.

Valves and hose bibs leak when washers or seals wear out. Replacement parts can be found in the same universal washer kits used to repair compression faucets. Coat replacement washers with faucet grease to keep them soft and prevent cracking.

If you have the opportunity to replace a shutoff valve, install a ball valve, which has proven to be the most reliable type. Remember to turn off the water before beginning work.

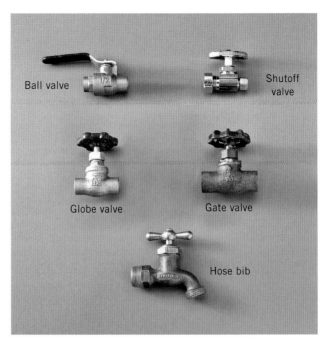

With the exception of chromed shutoff valves that are installed at individual fixtures, valves and hose bibs are heavy-duty fittings, usually with brass bodies. They are installed in-line to regulate water flow. Gate valves and globe valves are similar and are operated with a wheel-type handle that spins. Ball valves are operated with a handle much like a gas pipe stopcock and are considered by pros to be the most reliable. Hose bibs are spigots with a threaded end designed to accept a female hose coupling.

TOOLS + MATERIALS

Screwdriver	Universal washer kit
Adjustable wrench	Faucet grease

How to Fix a Leaky Hose Bib

Remove the handle screw and lift off the handle. Unscrew the packing nut with an adjustable wrench.

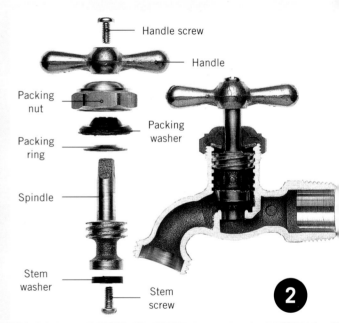

Unscrew the spindle from the valve body. Remove the stem screw, and replace the stem washer. Replace the packing washer, and reassemble the valve.

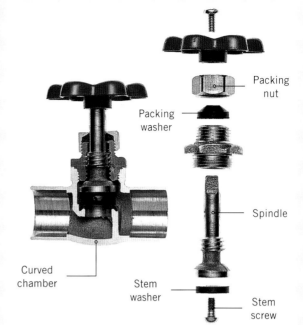

Gate valves have a movable brass wedge, or "gate," that screws up and down to control water flow. Gate valves may develop leaks around the handle. Repair leaks by replacing the packing washer or packing string found underneath the packing nut.

Globe valves have a curved chamber. Repair leaks around the handle by replacing the packing washer. If a valve does not fully stop water flow when closed, replace the stem washer.

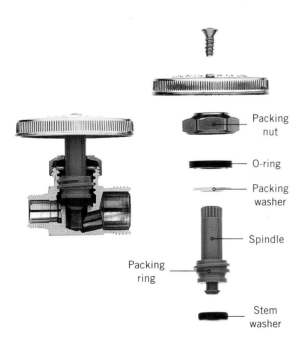

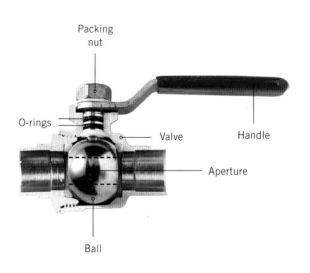

Shutoff valves control water supply to one or more fixtures. A shutoff valve has a plastic spindle with a packing washer and a snap-on stem washer. Repair leaks around the handle by replacing the packing washer. If a valve does not fully stop water flow when closed, replace the stem washer. Shutoff valves with multiple outlets are available to supply several fixtures from a single supply.

Ball valves contain a metal ball with an aperture (or hole) in the center. The ball is controlled by a handle. When the handle is turned, the hole is positioned parallel to the valve (open) or perpendicular (closed).

Compression Fittings

Compression fittings are used to make connections that may need to be taken apart. Compression fittings are easy to disconnect and are often used to install supply tubes and fixture shutoff valves. Use compression fittings in places where it is unsafe or difficult to solder, such as in crawl spaces.

Compression fittings are used most often with flexible copper pipe. Flexible copper is soft enough to allow the compression ring to seat snugly, creating a watertight seal. Compression fittings also may be used to make connections with Type M rigid copper pipe.

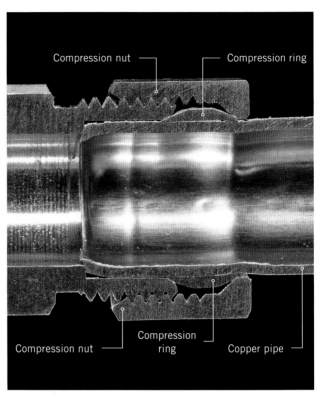

This compression fitting (shown in cutaway) shows how a threaded compression nut forms a seal by forcing the compression ring against the copper pipe. The compression ring is covered with pipe joint compound before assembly to ensure a perfect seal.

TOOLS + MATERIALS

Marker
Tubing cutter or hacksaw
Adjustable wrenches

Brass compression fittings
Pipe joint compound or Teflon tape

How to Attach Supply Tubes to Fixture Shutoff Valves with Compression Fittings

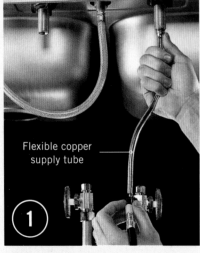

1

Bend flexible copper supply tube and mark to length. Include ½" for the portion that will fit inside valve. Cut the tube.

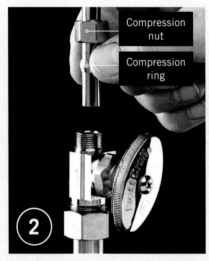

2

Slide the compression nut and then the compression ring over the end of the pipe. The threads of the nut should face the valve.

3

Apply a small amount of pipe joint compound to the threads to lubricate them.

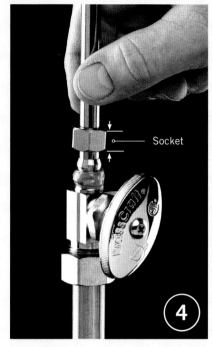

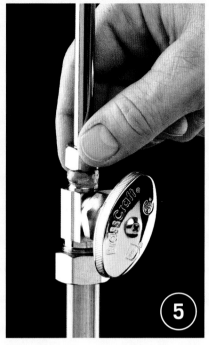

Insert the end of the pipe into the fitting so it fits flush against the bottom of the fitting socket.

Slide the compression ring and nut against the threads of the valve. Hand tighten the nut onto the valve.

Tighten the compression nut with adjustable wrenches. Do not overtighten. Turn on the water and watch for leaks. If the fitting leaks, tighten the nut gently.

 ## How to Join Two Copper Pipes with a Compression Union Fitting

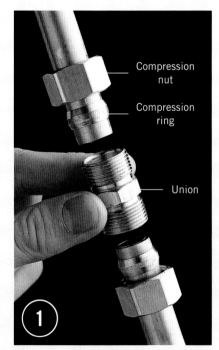

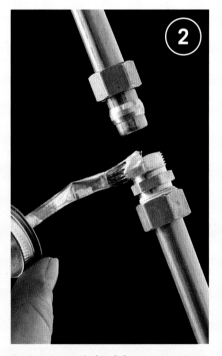

Slide compression nuts and rings over the ends of pipes. Place a threaded union between the pipes.

Apply a layer of pipe joint compound or Teflon tape to the union's threads, then screw compression nuts onto the union.

Hold the center of the union fitting with an adjustable wrench and use another wrench to tighten each compression nut one complete turn. Turn on the water. If the fitting leaks, tighten the nuts gently.

Creating Flared Fittings

Although you likely won't often need to often make a flared connection, it's useful to know how they are made. Fortunately, these connections are incredibly simple and require only attention to detail and a flaring tool. Flared connections are used only for high-pressure water lines or gas lines. In either case, the flare creates an incredibly secure seal to head off catastrophic leaks. Only copper tubing is flared.

TOOLS + MATERIALS

Tubing cutting and deburring tool

Tubing bender

Flaring tool

Pipe joint compound

Crescent wrench

Leak detection spray

How to Make a Flared Connection

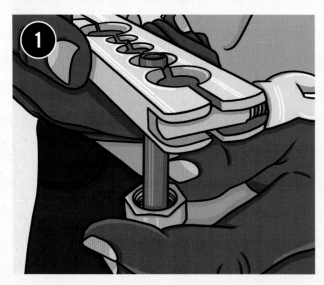

Cut and deburr the tubing to size and make any necessary bends. Slide the flare fitting nut onto the end to be flared. Slip the end into the proper flaring tool opening with about ³⁄₃₂" of tubing projecting above the face of the tool. Tighten the wing nuts on the tool.

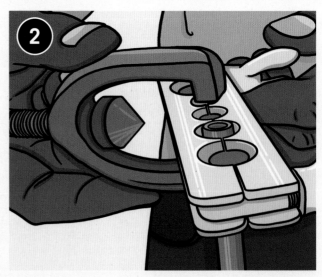

With the tool's wing nuts tightened, slide the flaring yoke onto the body of the tool.

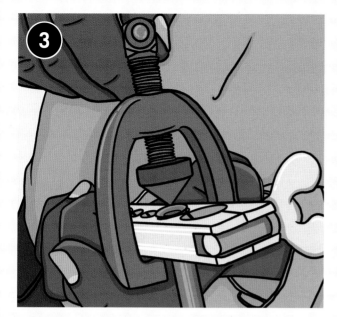

Line the point of the flaring tool head over the end of the tubing. Slowly and steadily screw down the head. Stop once the end is flared out to the edges of the hole. Remove the flaring tool and check that the pipe end seats securely inside the flare nut.

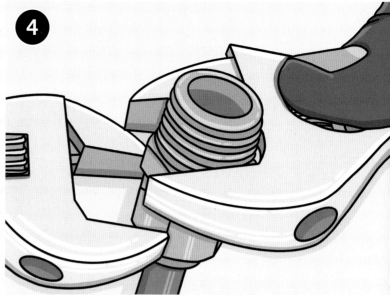

Tighten the flare fitting onto the flared end. Use two crescent or combination wrenches, one on the fitting and one on the nut. Hold the flare nut in place and snug the fitting tight.

NOTE: For an extra layer of protection against leaks, brush pipe joint compound onto the fitting threads before fastening it to the flare nut.

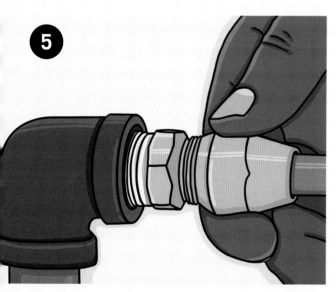

Coat the threads on the opposite end of the fitting with pipe joint compound. Screw the fitting into the supply line fitting (the process is the same for refrigerant, gas, or pressurized water lines). Use a wrench to tighten the flare fitting into the pipe fitting.

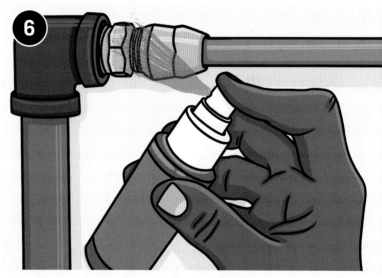

Turn on the gas or refrigerant and check the fitting connections for leaks. Spray bottled leak detector around the connections and check for bubbles. (Or use a homemade half-and-half solution of dish soap and water). If you find a leak, tighten the connection.

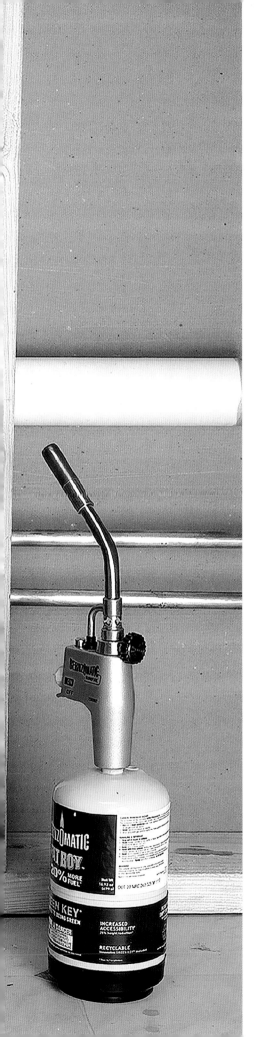

Installing Plumbing Lines

Working on new plumbing can seem even more daunting than making repairs or alterations to existing lines. Actually, though, installing new supply or waste lines has never been easier for the home remodeler, thanks to innovations like PEX and push-fit connectors. Deeper walls that are the result of codes specifying wide studs means more room to work.

Proper planning limits the amount of new pipe and hardware you need. It also reduces effort and time. That's why you should never just launch into even a small and relatively simple plumbing installation. Take detailed measurements and plan exactly where—and how—new lines will go.

Access will be key. If you're not plumbing a newly framed structure, you have to determine how much work you'll need to do to open a wall, floor, or ceiling. Less is always better. Ideally, plan for lines to run in unfinished spaces like basements whenever possible. This ensures easy access in the event of a leak or full-on failure.

The first step must always be consulting local building codes. Many local codes include surprising stipulations, such as prohibiting the use of PEX manifolds within enclosed walls. Most also dictate the size of supply pipe under given circumstances and lengths. That may change how long or short you decide to make a run.

Lastly, don't hesitate to involve a licensed plumber, even if it's just to check your plans and installation strategy, or your work afterward. The modest amount you'll spend will be more than come back to you in peace of mind.

In this chapter:
- Installation Basics
- Planning Plumbing Routes
- Sample Layouts
- Installing Supply Lines
- Installing Drain Lines
- Building a Wet Wall
- New Basement Bath Plumbing
- PEX Stub-outs

Installation Basics

A major plumbing project is a complicated affair that often requires demolition and carpentry skills. Bathroom or kitchen plumbing may be unusable for several days while completing the work, so make sure you have a backup bathroom or kitchen space to use during this time.

To ensure that your project goes quickly, always buy plenty of pipe and fittings—at least 25 percent more than you think you need. Making several extra trips to the building center is a nuisance and can add many hours to your project. Always purchase from a reputable retailer that will allow you to return leftover fittings for credit.

The how-to projects on the following pages demonstrate standard plumbing techniques but should not be used as a literal blueprint for your own work. Pipe and fitting sizes, fixture layout, and pipe routing will always vary according to individual circumstances. When planning your project, carefully read all the information in the planning section. Before you begin work, create a detailed plumbing plan to guide your work and help you obtain the required permits. Don't depend on manufacturer specs to plan the installations of fixtures and the running of pipes; always check local codes. They may vary from the specs and are generally more stringent.

Use 2 × 6 studs to frame "wet walls" when constructing a new bathroom or kitchen. Thicker walls provide more room to run drain pipes and main waste-vent stacks, making installation much easier.

Installing New Plumbing

Use tape to mark the locations of fixtures and pipes on the walls and floors. Read the layout specifications that come with each sink, tub, or toilet, then mark the drain and supply lines accordingly. Position the fixtures on the floor, and outline them with tape, pencil, or marker. Measure and adjust until the arrangement is comfortable to you and meets minimum clearance specifications. If you are working in a finished room, prevent damage to wallpaper or paint by using self-adhesive notes to mark the walls.

Consider the location of cabinets when roughing in the water supply and drain stub-outs. You may want to temporarily position the cabinets in their final locations before completing the drain and water supply runs.

Install control valves at the points where the new branch supply lines meet the main distribution pipes. By installing valves, you can continue to supply the rest of the house with water while you are working on the new branches. These also serve as safety devices to quickly shut off individual lines in the event of a leak or defective fixture.

(continued)

The International Building Code dictates specific limits on notches and holes in framing members, and many local codes follow that guidance. Always consult local codes before altering any framing member. In any case, it's wise to use nailing plates on the framing member edges for any pipes that are closer than 1¼" from the edge. This will protect the pipes from accidental punctures.

NOTCHES

Notches covered by nailing plates were preferred for ease of installation of metal or PVC pipes, but PEX can just as easily be run through stud, joist, and plate holes. The code uses the term "depth", for what most homeowners would think of as "width" (because studs are installed edges out).

- Stud in exterior or load bearing wall: No more than 25 percent of the stud's depth. Examples of maximum notch size:

    2 × 4: ⅞" [1]
    2 × 6: 1⅜" [2]

- Stud in non-load-bearing wall: No more than 40 percent of the stud's depth. Examples of maximum notch size:

    2 × 4: 1⅜" [3]
    2 × 6: 2⅕" [4]

HOLES

Holes in studs should not exceed 60 percent of the stud's depth, the hole must not be closer than ⅝" to an edge, and should not be located in a stud with a notch. If the hole is made in an exterior stud and exceeds 40 percent of the stud's depth, you'll need to sister a stud to that stud (doubling the stud). If two pipes are run through the same stud, the holes should be stacked, not side by side. Examples of maximum hole diameter:

    2 × 4: 2" (int) / 1⅜" (ext) [5]
    2 × 6: 3⅛" (int) / 2⅕" (ext) [6]

JOISTS

Joists are a special case and have their own specific requirements.

- **Notches** should not be more than ⅙ joist depth (width).

- **Holes** should not be more than ⅓ joist depth and should not be closer than 2" from an edge or anywhere in the middle ⅓ of the joist's span.

---

1 .25 × 3.5" (nominal stud width) = .875 or ⅞"
2 .25 × 5.5" (nominal stud width) = 1.375 or 1⅜"
3 .40 × 3.5" (nominal stud width) = 1.4 or 1⅖" (rounded down to ⅜")
4 .40 × 5.5" (nominal stud width) = 2.2 or 2⅕"
5 .60 × 3.5" (nominal stud width) = 2.1 or 2" (rounded down from 2¹⁄₁₀")
6 .60 × 5.5" (nominal stud width) = 3.3 or 3⅛" (rounded down to 3³⁄₁₀")

Access panels are mandated by some codes for critical fixtures like shutoff valves and some other fittings. They are also a best practice anywhere a PEX manifold is enclosed in a wall. The trick is to blend the access panel into the surrounding wall and room. This is usually done by cutting a section of plywood to match the drywall thickness and the size of the opening. Paint it to match the surrounding wall, and trim the opening with modest, simple wood moldings—the more basic, the better. The molding should be painted to match the wall in cases where the existing wall molding has been painted a different color or sheen. Use evenly spaced drywall screws to hold the panel in place (paint their heads to match the surface).

Test-fit materials before cementing or soldering joints. Test-fitting ensures that you have the correct fittings and enough pipe to do the job, and it can help you avoid lengthy delays during installation.

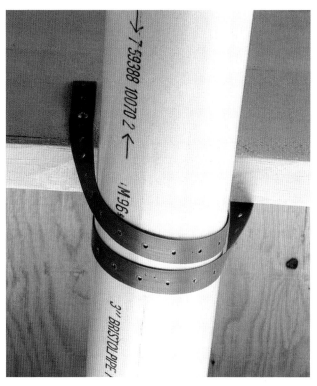

Support pipes adequately. Horizontal and vertical runs of DWV and water supply pipe must be supported at minimum intervals, which are specified by your local plumbing codes. A variety of metal and plastic materials are available for supporting plumbing pipes.

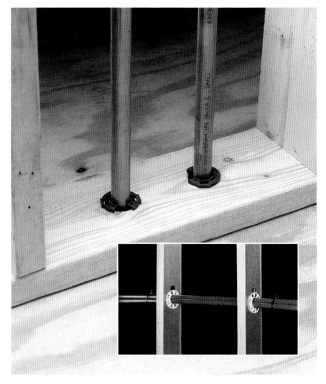

Use plastic bushings to help hold plumbing pipes securely in holes bored through wall plates, studs, and joists. Bushings can help to cushion the pipes, preventing wear and reducing rattling. Always use manufacturer-recommended bushings with metal wall studs (inset).

Install extra tee fittings on new drain and vent lines so that you can pressure-test the system when the building inspector reviews your installation. A new DWV line should have these extra tee fittings near the points where the new branch drains and vent pipes reach the main waste-vent stack.

Planning
Plumbing Routes

The first, and perhaps most important, step when replacing old plumbing is to decide how and where to run the new pipes. Since the stud cavities and joist spaces are often covered with finished wall surfaces, finding routes for running new pipes can be challenging.

When planning pipe routes, choose straight, easy pathways whenever possible. Rather than running water supply pipes around wall corners and through studs, for example, it may be easiest to run them straight up wall cavities from the basement. Instead of running a bathtub drain across floor joists, run it straight down into the basement, where the branch drain can be easily extended underneath the joists to the main waste-vent stack.

In some situations, it is most practical to route the new pipes in wall and floor cavities that already hold plumbing pipes, since these spaces are often framed to provide long, unobstructed runs. A detailed map of your plumbing system can be very helpful when planning routes for new plumbing pipes.

The most complicated part of new plumbing service is often the venting for the DWV system. All fixtures must be vented in a code-approved manner, and these codes are at times daunting to learn. Where possible, run vent lines through walls or up to the attic to tie into existing vents. If that is not allowed, you may need to run a vent pipe up through the roof. In some cases you can use air admittance valves instead of vent pipes.

Plumbing contractors generally try to avoid opening walls or changing wall framing when installing new plumbing. But the do-it-yourselfer does not have these limitations. Faced with the difficulty of running pipes through enclosed spaces, you may find it easiest to remove wall surfaces or to create a newly framed space for running new pipes.

On these pages, you will see some common methods used to create pathways for replacing old pipes with new plumbing.

Build a framed chase. A chase is a false wall created to provide space for new plumbing pipes. It is especially effective for installing a new main drainage stack. On a two-story house, chases can be stacked one over the other on each floor in order to run plumbing from the basement to the attic. Once plumbing is completed and inspected, the chase is covered with wallboard and finished to match the room.

Planning Pipe Routes

Use existing access panels to disconnect fixtures and remove old pipes. Plan the location of new fixtures and pipe runs to make use of existing access panels, minimizing the amount of demolition and repair work you will need to do.

Convert a laundry chute into a channel for running new plumbing pipes. The door of the chute can be used to provide access to control valves, or it can be removed and covered with wall materials, then finished to match the surrounding wall.

Run pipes inside a closet. If they are unobtrusive, pipes can be left exposed at the back of the closet. Or, you can frame a chase to hide the pipes after the installation is completed.

Remove suspended ceiling panels to route new plumbing pipes in joist cavities. Or, you can route pipes across a standard plaster or wallboard ceiling, then construct a false ceiling to cover the installation, provided there is adequate height. Most building codes require a minimum of 7' from floor to finished ceiling.

(continued)

Use a drill bit extension and spade bit or hole saw to drill through wall plates from unfinished attic or basement spaces above or below the wall.

Look for "wet walls." Walls that hold old plumbing pipes can be good choices for running long vertical lengths of new pipe. These spaces are usually open, without obstacles such as fireblocks and insulation.

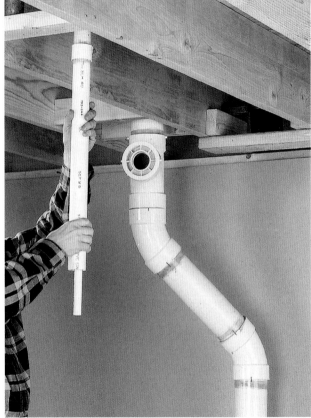

Probe wall and floor cavities with a long piece of plastic pipe to ensure that a clear pathway exists for running new pipe (left). Once you have established a route using the narrow pipe, you can use the pipe as a guide when running larger drain pipes up into the wall (right).

Remove flooring when necessary. Because replacing toilet and bathtub drains usually requires that you remove sections of floor, a full plumbing replacement job is often done in conjunction with a complete bathroom remodeling project.

Remove wall surfaces when access from above or below the wall is not possible. This demolition work can range from cutting narrow channels in plaster or wallboard to removing the entire wall surface. Remove wall surfaces back to the centers of adjoining studs; the exposed studs provide a nailing surface for attaching repair materials once the plumbing project is completed.

Create a detailed map showing the planned route for your new plumbing pipes. Such a map can help you get your plans approved by the inspector, and it makes work much simpler. If you have already mapped your existing plumbing system, those drawings can be used to plan new pipe routes.

Sample Plumbing Layouts

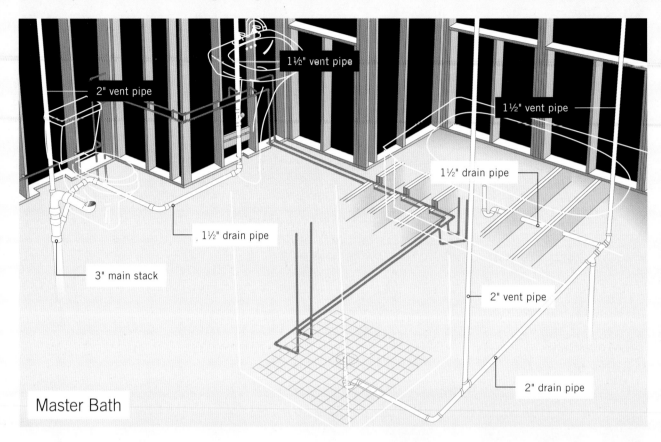

2" vent pipe

1½" vent pipe

1½" vent pipe

1½" drain pipe

1½" drain pipe

3" main stack

2" vent pipe

2" drain pipe

Master Bath

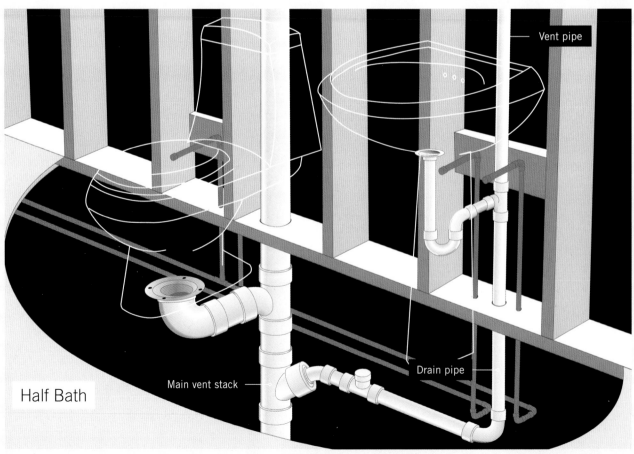

Vent pipe

Drain pipe

Main vent stack

Half Bath

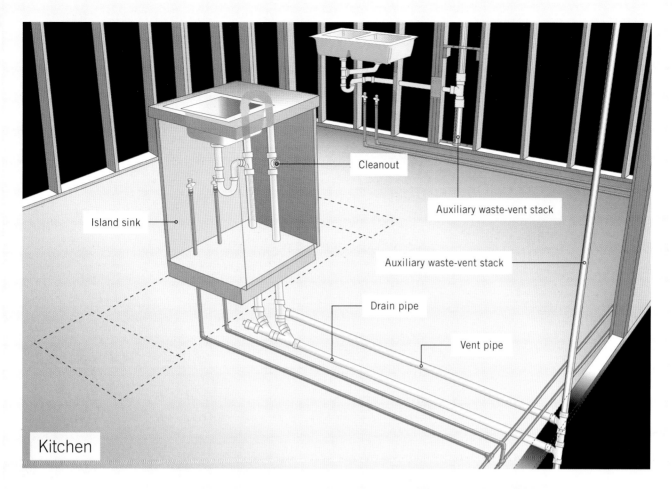

Island sink

Cleanout

Auxiliary waste-vent stack

Auxiliary waste-vent stack

Drain pipe

Vent pipe

Kitchen

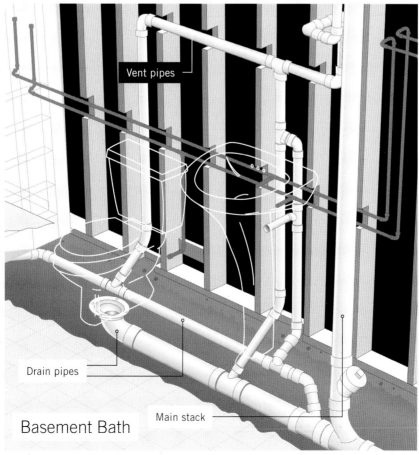

Vent pipes

Drain pipes

Main stack

Basement Bath

How to Install New Supply Lines

Remove the subfloor completely in the installation area if you are running new supply lines inside the floor cavity. Among other advantages, this allows you to dry-fit the complete layout before soldering or cementing.

Support supply risers with a ¾"-thick backer board installed between floor joists. Secure the horizontal supply tubes to the backer with pipe straps. Risers should extend at least 6" above the finished floor.

When soldering copper, tack a piece of metal flashing between wall studs behind the work area to serve as a heat shield. If you'll be doing a lot of soldering, it makes sense to invest in a fiber heat sheild.

Use ¾"-to-½" reducing tees to tap into ¾" branch supply lines. Most plumbing fixtures require only a ½"-dia. supply tube.

Use a tubing cutter to remove sections of branch supply lines.

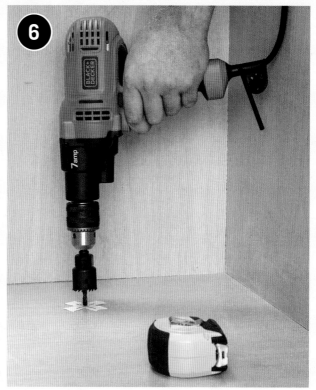

Drill access holes directly into a cabinet base to allow supply risers to enter the cabinet. The holes should align with access holes for the risers in the subfloor.

Use a torpedo level to make sure unattached riser pipes are plumb when marking cutting lines on mating horizontal branch lines. If you're using PEX, you only need a 90° bracket attached to the joist face to run the PEX up to the fixture without a fitting.

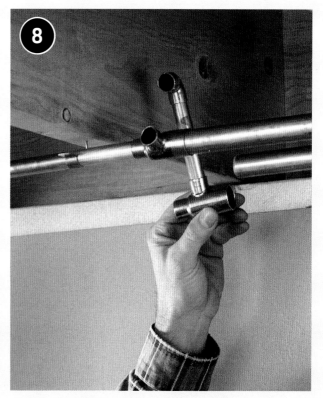

Dry-fit copper or CPVC lines as much as possible. Dry-fitting yields more reliable results for the home DIYer than taking measurements as you go. There is no need to dry-fit PEX, because you should leave ample slack in the lines as you work, which will accommodate any imprecise measurements.

Drain and vent lines may be located in exterior walls, but if you live in a cold climate the walls must be well insulated with ample insulation between the pipes and the exterior. Avoid running supply lines in an exterior wall in cold climates.

If installing a large whirlpool tub, cut away the subfloor to expose the full length of the joists under the tub, then screw or bolt a second joist, called a sister, against each existing joist. Make sure both ends of each joist are supported by load-bearing walls.

Lay large sections of plywood across the joists to create a stable work surface when installing plumbing lines in an open floor.

Use levels to check your work when installing new lines. This is especially important for meeting minimum slope requirements. It's also good practice to ensure that visible lines stay parallel.

If a floor joist interferes with the toilet drain, cut away a short section of the joist and box-frame the area with double headers. The framed opening should be just large enough to install the toilet and sink drains.

Install cleanouts at the ends of branch drain lines to create access points for augers in the event you need to remove a clog.

 ## CONNECTING NEW VENT PIPES TO A MAIN STACK

In the attic, cut into the main waste-vent stack and install a vent tee fitting using banded couplings. The side outlet on the vent tee should face the new 2" vent pipe running down to the bathroom. Attach a test tee fitting to the vent tee.

NOTE: If your stack is cast iron, make sure to adequately support it before cutting into it.

Use elbows, vent tee fittings, reducers, and lengths of pipe as needed to link the new vent pipes to the test tee fitting on the main waste-vent stack. Vent pipes can be routed in many ways, but you should make sure the pipes have a slight downward angle to prevent moisture from collecting in the pipes. Support the pipes every 4' or as required by local codes.

Working with Gas Pipe

Running gas supply lines and making gas hookups are similar jobs to working with drain and supply plumbing. Given the extremely dangerous nature of handling natural gas and propane, however, you should approach these jobs with extreme caution. In fact, many jurisdictions do not allow homeowners to install gas pipe unless they happen to be certified in that area of expertise. Making the hookup from supply lines to gas fixtures is less regulated, but still dangerous. The availability of new flexible gas connectors has made the task simpler and eliminated some of the most troublesome aspects, including the use of flare fittings. If you choose to attempt any projects with gas connections, be sure to pay attention to the materials you'll use. Whether it is the copper supply tubes or the tape used to lubricate threaded connections, gas lines employ an entirely different set of gas-rated pipes, fittings, and materials.

Gas Consumption of Household Appliances

APPLIANCE	AVG. BTU PER HOUR	GAS CONSUMPTION PER HOUR*
Clothes dryer	35,000	35 cu. ft.
50-gallon water heater	50,000	50 cu. ft.
Range/oven	65,000	65 cu. ft.
Furnace	200,000	200 cu. ft.

*Based on output rate of 1,000 BTU per cubic foot of fuel per hour. Your actual rate will likely differ. Check with your energy company.

Determine the flow rate for a branch line by adding the gas consumption per hour (use above data only if specific information is not printed on your appliance label) of each appliance. Although appliances may not run concurrently, it is advisable to select pipe size based on 100% flow rate. Note that distance traveled also plays an important role in selecting pipe size diameter (½", ¾", 1", 1¼", or 1½").

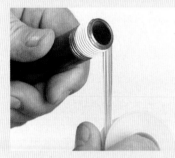

Wrap the male pipe threads with gas-rated Teflon tape before joining to fittings. Wind the tape clockwise (as you face the hole in the pipe), and wrap two or three windings. Alternatively, apply pipe joint compound to the threads.

Turn off the gas at the gas meter using an adjustable wrench. The valve does not have a stop, so it can rotate indefinitely. The gas is off when the bar is perpendicular to the pipe.

Disconnect the existing appliance. If a flexible stainless-steel connector was used, discard it, as they can only be installed once. Remove the gas stub-out or flexible copper line back to the supply line.

Attach a male-threaded-to-flare adapter to the valve. Use two adjustable wrenches—one holding the valve in place and one tightening the fitting.

Attach the appliance connector tube to the valve. Make sure to buy a connector with ends that match the valve and the appliance port. In most cases, you may now use flexible stainless-steel connectors instead of soft copper tubing that requires flaring. But soft copper is allowed if you have the equipment to make a flare fitting joint and want to save a few dollars.

Hook up the appliance by attaching the other flare nut to the threaded gas inlet port on the appliance. Plug in the appliance's power cord. Turn on gas at the main meter and at the stop valve, and test the flare fittings for leaks. Once you're certain all the joints are good, carefully slide the appliance into place.

How to Install New Basement Bath Plumbing

Score cutting lines into the concrete surfaces of the basement foundation floor before attempting to break out the concrete with a jackhammer (recommended) or cold chisel and mallet. This helps prevent cracks outside of the work area and makes for an overall neater job.

Use a jackhammer to break up and remove the basement foundation floor in the installation area so you can run new drain/sewer pipelines from the bathroom to the main drain. Wear a dust mask, hearing protection, and eye protection.

Cleanout

Replace the entire sweep elbow where the drain stack joins the sewer line. The union in the new sweep should have an opening to accommodate the new drain line.

After you've made all your new drain line connections, test the line by dumping water down the risers to make sure there are no leaks.

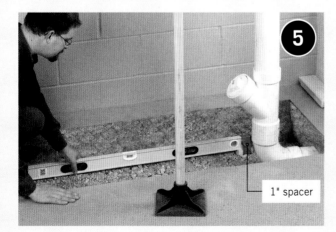

1" spacer

Before enclosing the pipe, check one last time that the drain line runs at a slope of at least ¼" per foot.

Then, cover the new drain lines with a course of drainage rock followed by a layer of fresh concrete that's at least 4" thick.

Building a Wet Wall

A wet wall is simply a wall that contains plumbing for water supply and drainage. To accommodate the drain and vent pipes, which range from 1½ to 3 inches in diameter for branch lines, the wall framing needs to be built with 2 × 6 or larger dimensional lumber. You can also attach furring strips (usually 2 × 2) to existing 2 × 4 framing members to increase wall thickness. The chart on the next page describes how deeply you are allowed to notch wall-framing members under various load conditions, as well as the maximum-diameter holes you may drill for running plumbing and wiring.

Building a new wet wall or converting an existing wall to house new plumbing requires a building permit and an onsite inspection once all of the hookups are made. Do not install any wall coverings until after your plumbing has been inspected and approved.

Measure and mark wall plates, and use a hole saw to drill holes for pipes. The most common for PVC pipes is a 2" diameter; PEX can usually accommodate smaller holes, depending on the service provided.

Use a reciprocating saw or similar saw to cut out squared notches for edge-mounting pipes. See page 70 for maximum stud pipe notches and holes. In any case, ensure that notches are clean and free of jagged edges—especially important if you're running PEX lines.

FIXTURE UNIT TABLE FOR DETERMINING WATER PIPE SIZES

STREET SERVICE	BUILDING SUPPLY + BRANCHES	MAXIMUM ALLOWABLE LENGTH (FEET)					
		40	60	80	100	150	200
30-45 PSI							
¾	½	6	5	4	3	2	1
¾	¾	16	16	14	12	9	6
¾	1	29	25	23	21	17	15
1	1	36	31	27	25	20	17
¾	1¼	36	33	31	28	24	23
1	1¼	54	47	42	38	32	28
1½	1¼	78	68	57	48	38	32
1	1½	85	84	79	65	56	48
1½	1½	150	124	105	91	70	57
2	1½	151	129	129	110	80	64
46-60 PSI							
¾	½	7	7	6	5	4	3
¾	¾	20	20	19	17	14	11
¾	1	39	39	36	33	28	23
1	1	39	39	39	36	30	25
¾	1¼	39	39	39	39	39	39
1	1¼	78	78	76	67	52	44
1½	1¼	78	78	78	78	66	52
1	1½	85	85	85	85	85	85
1½	1½	151	151	151	151	128	105
2	1½	151	151	151	151	150	117
OVER 60 PSI							
¾	½	7	7	7	6	5	4
¾	¾	20	20	20	20	17	13
¾	1	39	39	39	39	35	30
1	1	39	39	39	39	38	32
¾	1¼	39	39	39	39	39	39
1	1¼	78	78	78	78	74	62
1½	1¼	78	78	78	78	78	74
1	1½	85	85	85	85	85	85
1½	1½	151	151	151	151	151	151
2	1½	151	151	151	151	151	151

PIPE HANGERS + SUPPORTS

MATERIAL	JOINTS	HORIZONTAL	VERTICAL
Cast Iron Hub-and-Spigot	Lead-and-oakum	5' (except 10' where 10' pipe is installed)	Base and each floor, not to exceed 15'
Cast Iron Hub-and-Spigot	Compression	Every other joint, unless more than 4', then every joint	Base and each floor, not to exceed 15'
Cast Iron Hubless	Shielded coupling	Every other joint, unless more than 4', then every joint	Base and each floor, not to exceed 15'
Copper	Soldered, threaded, mechanical	1½" or smaller: 6' 2" or larger: 10'	Each floor, not to exceed 10'
Steel (gas)	Threaded or welded	½": 6'; ¾" or 1": 8'; 1¼" up: 10'	½": 6'; ¾"or 1": 8'; 1¼" every floor level
PVC	Solvent cement	All sizes: 4'; allow for expansion every 30'	Base and each story; provided mid-story guides; allow for expansion every 30'
CPVC	Solvent cement	Less than 1": 3' 1¼" or larger: 4'	Base and each story; provided mid-story guides
PEX	Mechanical	Less than 1": 32" 1¼" or larger: 4'	Base and each story; provided mid-story guides; allow for expansion every 30'

PEX Stub-Outs

Stub-outs are supply lines routed out of a wall to service fixtures such as sinks and toilets. Traditionally, copper has been used for stub-outs. Even after PEX gained in popularity and use, plumbers usually connected PEX supply lines to copper stub-outs, reasoning that the copper would a sturdier support for stop valves.

Now, though, many professionals and DIYers are simply extending the PEX water supply lines out of the wall, to be used as stub-outs. This cuts down on the fabrication and connections you would have to make with copper stub-outs, and is just as durable. There's also another reason for transition to all-PEX stub-outs. Some copper stub-outs include impurities from recycled copper, which can shorten the lifespan of the stub-out. This isn't the case with all copper stub-outs, but why take the risk of having to replace the stub-out in a decade or less?

In fact, manufacturers have created whole lines of stub-out supports to make this process even easier. There are a large number of mounting options for PEX stub-outs. Individual brackets can be attached to a stud, or to the top of a wood brace run between studs. More commonly, independent stub-out brackets are used with a metal strap that is fastened edge to edge, between studs. These allow for a lot of flexibility in positioning the stub-outs.

Regardless of material, stub-outs are meant to be installed into an exposed wall cavity. If you're retrofitting an existing bathroom, you need to remove enough drywall to access the studs. If you use PEX, be careful to match the type of pipe you buy to the stub-out hardware and mounts. Although you can find stop valves in many different connection styles, the easiest will be push-fit stop valves. They are a bit more expensive, but have proven to be durable and reliable.

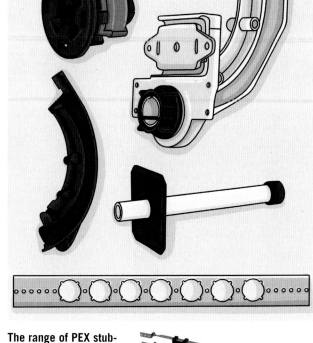

The range of PEX stub-out mounts and brackets means you can find an option for any situation or fixture. These are all as easy—or easier—to use than traditional copper stub-outs.

The innovative nature of today's stub-out brackets and guides means that PEX can be used for the entire stub-out, as shown here. A metal bracket with lock-in guides is strong, durable, and code-compliant in most municipalities.

TOOLS + MATERIALS

Stub-out hardware

PEX stud isolators (optional)

Drill + bits

Tape measure

2' level

Carpenter's pencil

Push-fit angle stop valves

PEX depth gauge

Marker

PEX cutter

How to Install PEX Sink Stub-Outs

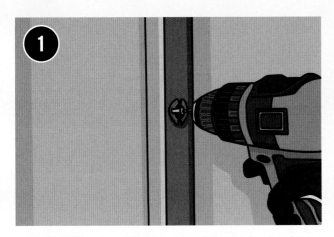

Route the PEX to the stub-out location following local codes. Ensure the integrity of the PEX pipe by installing a plastic isolator at any hole through a stud. Measure and mark the hole location and drill an oversized hole (usually 1⅜"). Screw the isolator flange to the stud face with the supplied screws, and run the pipe through the plastic channel.

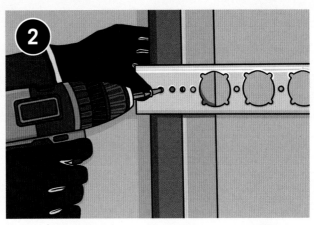

Determine the location and height of the stub-outs. Mark the position of the stub-out support bracket, and check for level. Screw the bracket to the studs.

Slip the cold-water PEX stub-out bend support into the proper opening of the bracket, and lock it in place. Depending on the support, this usually involves simply turning it to click it in place, although some types are two pieces and screwed together. Repeat with the second, hot supply, bend support.

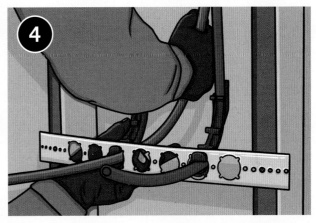

Secure the hot and cold PEX lines into their respective bend supports (cold on right, hot on left). Make sure that the PEX lines extend out further than the length you'll need.

Cut the lines to the appropriate length (usually 6") being sure to account for the wall surface. If you're not sure the length you'll need, you can leave the PEX uncut until you're ready to install the angle stop valve.

How to Install PEX Stub-Outs on Blocking

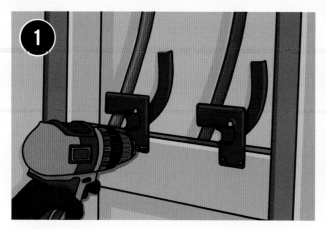

Measure and mark for placement of the nail-plate bend support. Screw the flange plate to the blocking at the marks.

Snap the PEX lines into the bend support channels, leaving a sufficient length of pipe for the angle-stop valve assembly.

How to Finish PEX Stub-Outs: Push-Fit Stop Valve

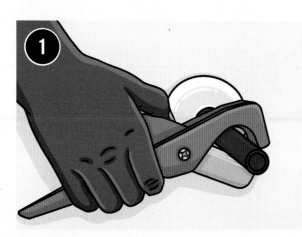

Install the drywall with holes cut for the stub-out pipes. Slide the chrome escutcheon over the end of the PEX pipe and snug to the wall. Cut the pipe, leaving about 2" sticking out (be careful to make a clean, square cut).

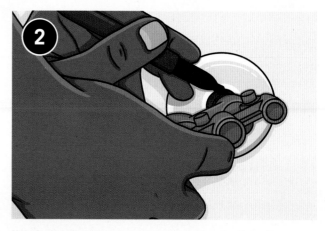

Use the depth gauge to mark the insertion depth for the angle stop.

Note: With careful cutting, you can cut back so that the stop valve fitting will be flush with the escutcheon.

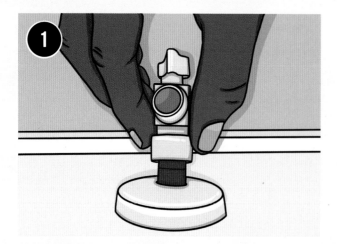

Push the stop valve onto the PEX pipe to the insertion mark, making sure it is oriented correctly. Attach the braided stainless steel fixture supply line to the stop valve's outlet. Turn on the water and check for leaks.

How to Finish PEX Stub-Outs: Compression Stop Valve

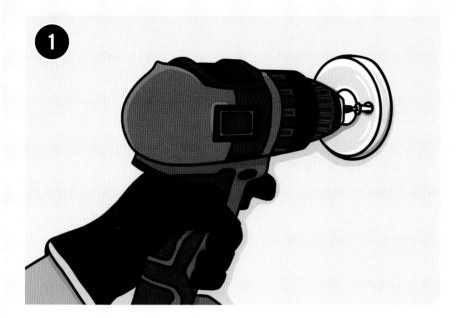

Slide the escutcheon base onto the PEX pipe and mark the holes for the screw anchors. Remove the escutcheon and drill the holes. Tap the anchors into the holes, and screw the escutcheon base to the wall.

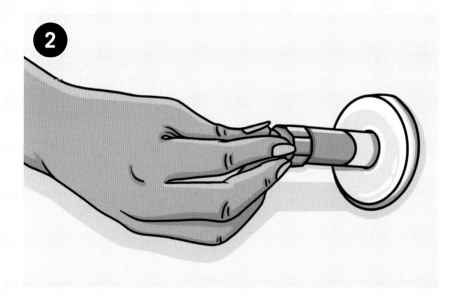

Secure the escutcheon face plate over the base. Cut the PEX pipe back to 1" from the end of the escutcheon pipe. Slide the compression nut over the PEX pipe and then slide the compression sleeve onto the end of the pipe.

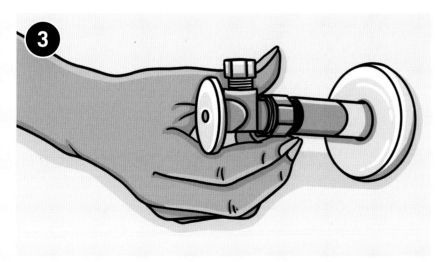

Slide the end of the threaded stop valve into the end of the PEX pipe. Hand-tighten the compression nut onto the threads of the stop valve. Connect the fixture supply line to the stop-valve outlet. Turn on the water and check for leaks.

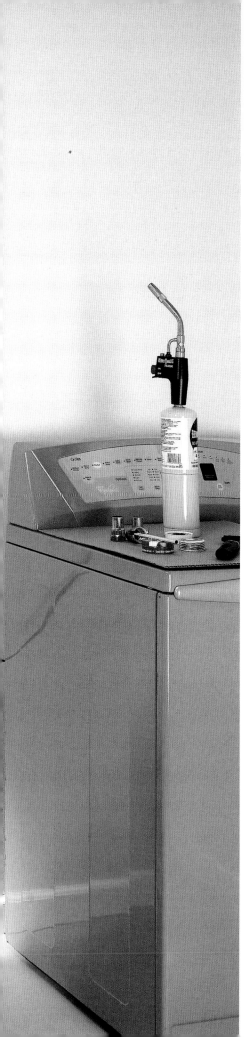

Fixtures, Faucets, Drains + Appliances

A home's plumbing fixtures are key to making the house livable. Your water heater ensures a steady supply of hot water for showers and dishwashing, showers and tubs provide comfort and an essential personal-care function, and toilets keep your home sanitary. Fortunately, installing any home fixture is achievable for even a fairly inexperienced home craftsperson. The same goes for plumbing appliances, like a dishwasher.

The projects in this chapter range from the exceedingly easy, such as replacing a bathroom faucet, to the more challenging, like installing a toilet. The secret to success in any of these projects is proper preparation. Make sure you have all the tools and hardware you need, understand what the manufacturer recommends for installation steps, and give yourself plenty of time to tackle the project. The result will be long-lasting fixtures and plumbing that operates trouble-free—along with the sense of satisfaction from mastering useful plumbing skills.

In this chapter:
- Toilets
- Bidet Toilets
- Kitchen Faucets
- Kitchen Drains + Traps
- Dishwashers
- Garbage Disposals
- Water Heaters
- Tankless Water Heaters
- Lavatory Faucets
- Touchless Faucets
- Lavatory Drains
- Showers
- Wet Rooms
- Bathtubs
- Jetted Tubs
- Water Softeners
- Bathroom Sinks
- Bathroom Vanities
- Kitchen Sinks
- Standpipe Drains
- Whole-House Water Filters

Toilets

Even though the basic function hasn't changed, toilet technology continues to evolve—specifically in the areas of comfort and water conservation.

Water is an increasingly precious commodity in regions throughout the country. Because toilets consume so much water, even small improvements in efficiency pay big environmental dividends, not to mention lowering your water bill.

Comfort may not be as important an issue globally, but it plays a huge part in any homeowner's life. Toilet manufacturers know this. That's why there is a wider range of comfort options from which to choose than ever before. However, this also means many more decisions when equipping a new bathroom or replacing an existing older toilet. Here are key options you'll need to consider on a trip down the toilet aisle of any large home center.

Two-piece toilets remain the most popular option among homeowners. Fortunately, there is a model to match any home design style, from colonial classic to mid-century modern, to contemporary and beyond. Whatever toilet catches your eye, be sure to check measurements and actually sit on it to verify that it will fit into your available space and be as comfortable as possible.

TOOLS + MATERIALS

Adjustable wrench	Supply tube
Bucket + sponge	Teflon tape
Channel pliers	Toilet seat bolts
Hacksaw	Toilet seat
Penetrating oil	Towels
Pliers	Utility knife
Putty knife	Wax ring with or
Rubber gloves	without flange
Screwdriver	

THRONE SPACING

The size of any new toilet will be dictated to one degree or another by the space needed for reasonable movement around the toilet. The measurements below are ideal minimums; these are often the measurements listed in local codes. Keep in mind the key word here is "minimum." Usually, the more space around a toilet, the more comfortable it will be to use.

• 24" from the front edge of the seat to any wall or obstruction.

• 15" from toilet center to nearest surface on either side.

• 30" from center to center of any adjacent "sanitary" fixture.

Choosing a New Toilet

The first choice in shopping for a new toilet is deciding between a traditional one-function model, or opting for one with a built-in bidet function. Although bidet-toilets are quickly growing in popularity, if you don't find one that meets your needs or style, you can always buy a traditional model and outfit it with a bidet seat later. Beyond the primary function, here are other key requirements that will guide your search.

• **Fit.** Any toilet you're considering must fit the space you have available. The critical measurement is "rough-in" space—the distance from the wall surface to the center of the drain. This is usually a standard 12 inches in modern homes, and 10 or 14 inches in older structures. You'll probably find it handier to measure from the wall to a rear bolt. This should match the distance from back of tank to back bolt hole on any toilet you want to buy.

• **Bowl shape.** Toilet bowls come in two shapes: oval and round. Round is the more traditional shape, is better for smaller spaces, and costs less. Oval toilets are easier to keep clean, can have a stronger flush than round bowls, and many people find them more comfortable. They are, however, pricier and take up more space than round models (although a few new oval toilets are designed to fit in the same space as a round model).

• **Tankless versus tank.** Tankless toilets are more expensive, a sleeker look, less likely to break down, and save water. The flush is power assisted so there is less chance of needing a second flush. Tankless models

This contemporary two-piece, side-handle toilet features a pleasingly simple appearance with modern water-saving function.

take less room and are often wall mounted, but are also often much more difficult to install.

• **Flush style.** Traditional flush toilets are gravity fed and use the same amount of water per flush. *Dual flush* models were designed to save water, using a short flush for liquid waste and more water for solids. They have fallen in popularity because of clogs and confusion in how the flush mechanism works. *Assisted flush* uses a powered pump to create a strong, efficient flush with little water. These are much more expensive.

 ## USING GOOD WATERSENSE

Federal law requires that new toilets not use more than 1.6 gallons of water per flush. Some high-efficiency toilets use less. The U.S. Environmental Protection Agency (EPA) awards their WaterSense label to manufacturers for models that are particularly water-conserving while maintaining flush efficiency. The label is an indicator that the toilet uses at least 20 percent less than 1.6 gallons per flush. This becomes even more important as many areas in the country experience drought conditions on a regular basis. Highly efficient toilets featuring this label are widely available at competitive prices.

How to Remove a Toilet

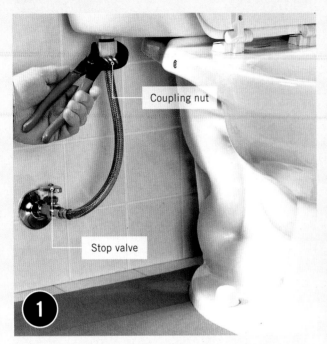

Remove the old supply tube. First, turn off the water at the stop valve. Flush the toilet, holding the handle down for a long flush, and sponge out the tank. Use a wet/dry vac to clear any remaining water out of the tank and bowl. Unthread the coupling nut for the water supply below the tank using channel pliers.

Coupling nut

Stop valve

1

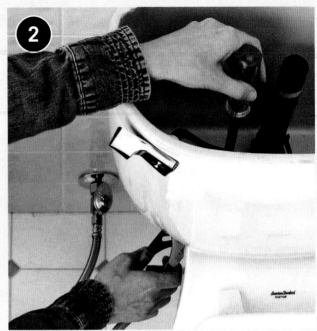

2

Grip each tank bolt nut with a box wrench or pliers and loosen it as you stabilize each tank bolt from inside the tank with a large slotted screwdriver. If the nuts are stuck, apply penetrating oil to the nut and let it sit before trying to remove them again. You may also cut the tank bolts between the tank and the bowl with an open-ended hacksaw. Remove and discard the tank.

3

Remove the nuts that hold the bowl to the floor. First, pry off the bolt covers with a screwdriver. Use a socket wrench, locking pliers, or your channel pliers to loosen the nuts on the tank bolts. Apply penetrating oil and let it sit if the nuts are stuck, then take them off. As a last resort, cut the bolts off with a hacksaw by first cutting down through one side of the nut. Tilt the toilet bowl over and remove it.

 PRYING UP WAX RINGS

Removing an old wax ring is one of the more disgusting jobs you'll encounter in the plumbing universe (the one you see here is actually in relatively good condition). Work a stiff putty knife underneath the plastic flange of the ring (if you can) and start scraping. In many cases, the wax ring will come off in chunks. Discard each chunk right away—they stick to everything. If you're left with a lot of residue, scrub with mineral spirits. Once clean, stuff a rag in the drain opening to block sewer gas.

How to Install a Bidet Toilet

A bidet toilet can be a pleasure to use and just as stylish as a traditional model. You will, however, need a nearby GFCI power plug for the bidet function and any seat heater.

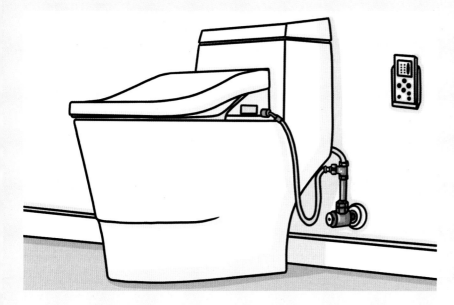

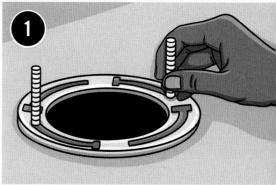

Thoroughly clean the flange and replace if damaged. Repair any floor damage. Clean wax-ring residue with a rag and mineral spirits, and stuff a towel in the opening to block sewer gasses. Fasten the new closet bolts into the flange, sliding them in their channels so that the align.

Lay the supplied template (if your toilet has one, otherwise skip this step) in place and trace around it with a carpenter's or grease pencil. Make sure you can see the outline for positioning the toilet on the flange. Remove and discard the template.

Put on latex gloves. Ensure that the wax ring is room temperature and carefully lay the toilet on its side, on a soft towel. Install the wax ring over the toilet discharge horn without touching the wax. Remove the towel from the hole.

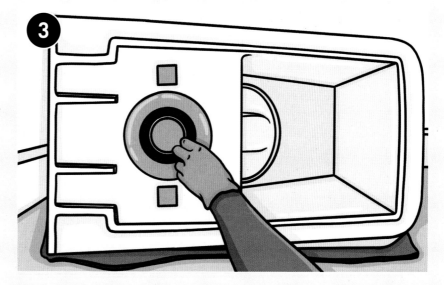

(continued)

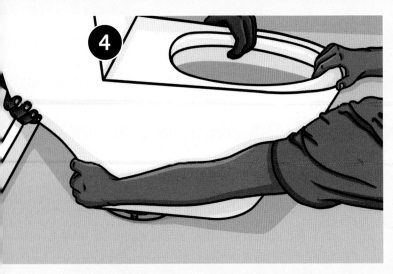

Lift the toilet, using a helper as needed for stability. Following the template outline, set the toilet in position, sliding the holes over the closet bolts. As you do, press down firmly, twisting slightly with your full body weight. This will ensure an even, level seal of the wax ring. Check for level and press down where necessary, but do not rock or tilt the toilet, or you risk breaking the wax ring seal.

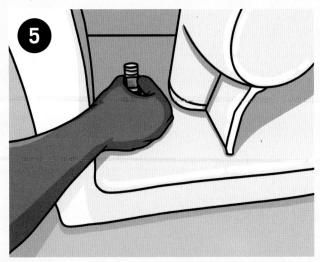

Slip washers on the closet bolts and tighten the nuts down on the bolts. Use a box wrench or the supplied wrench. Tighten until snug, but do not overtighten to avoid cracking the porcelain base.

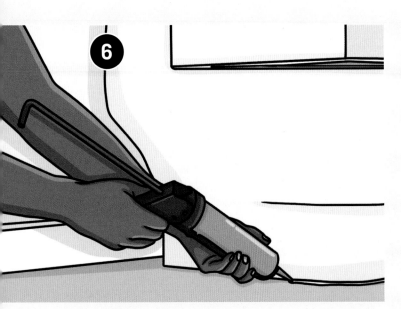

Lay a thin bead of silicone caulk around the base of the toilet. Let it dry for 24 hours before using the toilet.

Push the expansion nuts into the seat holes at the back edge of the bowl. Slip the bolts through the washers, plastic retaining plates, and the baseplate (oriented correct side forward according the manufacturer's instructions). Tighten the bolts snug to the bowl.

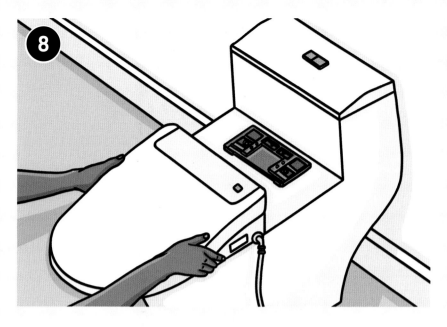

Align the seat with the toilet and slide it back into the base, steadily. You should hear a "click" as the seat locks into place. Give it a gentle tug to ensure it's secure.

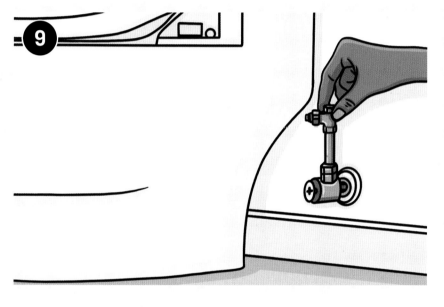

Fasten the three-way valve to the angle stop valve, and connect the bidet hose to the valve T outlet. Connect the tank hose to the straight outlet on the valve.

Turn the water on and let the toilet tank and bidet reservoir fill. Check the tank, connections, and bidet seat for any leaks. Follow the initial setup and self-check for the unit you've purchased, including heating the reservoir water. Determine the location of the remote, if any, and screw the remote holder to the wall using wall anchors or screwing directly into a stud.

Kitchen Faucets

Most new kitchen faucets feature single-handle control levers and washerless designs that rarely require maintenance. Additional features include brushed metallic finishes, detachable spray nozzles, and push-button or touch controls. Some new models are wall-mounted, but they require much more involved installation and are a unique look not to everyone's taste.

If your faucet has a separate sprayer, install the sprayer first. Pull the sprayer hose through the sink opening and attach it to the faucet body before installing the faucet.

A wide selection of extensions and angle fittings lets you easily plumb any sink configuration. Manufacturers offer kits that contain all the fittings needed for attaching a garbage disposal or dishwasher to the sink drain system. You'll need a special installation kit if you choose one of the new touchless kitchen faucets.

TOOLS + MATERIALS

Adjustable wrench

Basin wrench
    or channel pliers

Hacksaw

Faucet

Putty knife

Screwdriver

Silicone caulk

Scouring pad

Scouring cleaner

Plumber's putty

Flexible vinyl or braided steel
    supply tubes

Drain components

Penetrating oil

Modern kitchen faucets tend to be single-handle models, often with useful features such as a pull-out head that functions as a sprayer. Most models come with an optional mounting plate that conceals sink holes when mounted on a predrilled sink flange.

Choosing a New Kitchen Faucet

The best place to start your search for a new faucet is with your sink. In the past, most faucets were mounted directly to the sink deck, which had three or four predrilled holes to accommodate the faucet, spout, sprayer, and perhaps a liquid soap dispenser or an air gap for your dishwasher. Modern kitchen faucets don't always conform to this setup, with many of them designed for a single hole in the sink deck or in the countertop. If you plan to keep your old sink, look for a faucet that won't leave empty holes. Generally, it's best to replace like for like, but unfilled stainless sink holes can be filled with snap-in plugs or a soap dispenser.

The two most basic kitchen faucet categories are single-handle and two-handle. Single-handle models are much more popular now because you can adjust the water temperature easily with just one hand. Another difference is in the faucet body. Some faucets have the taps and the spout mounted onto a faucet body so the spacing between the tailpieces is preset. Others, called widespread faucets, have independent taps and spouts that can be configured however you please, as long as the tubes connecting the taps to the spouts reach. This type is best if you are installing the faucet in the countertop (a common way to go about it with new countertops, such as solid surface, quartz, or granite).

In the past, kitchen faucets almost always had a remote pull-out sprayer. The sprayer was attached to the faucet body with a hose directly below the mixing valve. While this type of sprayer is still fairly common, many faucets today have an integral pull-out spout that is very convenient and less prone to failure than the old-style sprayers.

A single-handle, high arc faucet with traditional remote sprayer. The mounting plate is decorative and optional.

Two-handled faucets are less common but remain popular choices for traditional kitchens. The gooseneck spout also has a certain elegance, but avoid this type if you have a shallow sink that's less than 8" deep.

A single-handle faucet with pull-out spray head requires only one hole in your sink deck or countertop—a real benefit if your sink is not predrilled or if it is an undermount model. Touchless versions are even handier and come in the same variety of styles.

How to Remove an Old Faucet

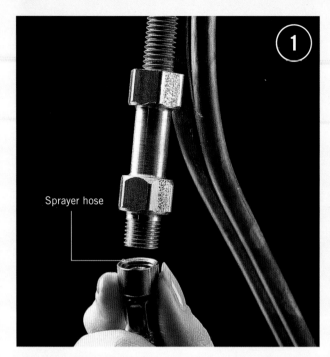

Sprayer hose

To remove the old faucet, start by clearing out the cabinet under the sink and laying down towels. Turn off the hot and cold stop valves and open the faucet to make sure the water is off. Detach the sprayer hose from the faucet sprayer nipple and unscrew the retaining nut that secures the sprayer base to the sink deck. Pull the sprayer hose out through the sink deck opening.

Spray the mounting nuts that hold the faucet or faucet handles (on the underside of the sink deck) with penetrating oil for easier removal. Let the oil soak in for a few minutes. If the nut is rusted and stubbornly stuck, you may need to drill a hole in its side, then tap the hole with a hammer and screwdriver to loosen it.

Mounting nut

Unhook the supply tubes at the stop valves. Don't reuse old chrome supply tubes. If the stops are missing or unworkable, replace them. Then remove the coupling nuts and the mounting nuts on the tailpieces of the faucet with a basin wrench or channel pliers.

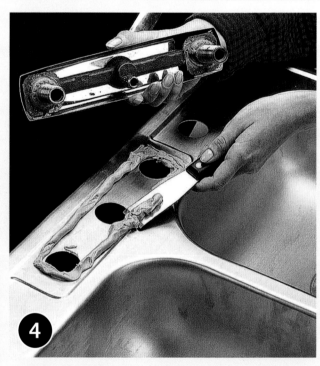

Pull the faucet body from the sink. Remove the sprayer base if you wish to replace it. Scrape off any putty or caulk with a putty knife, and clean off the sink with a scouring pad and a nonabrasive cleaner.

How to Install a Pulldown Kitchen Sink Faucet

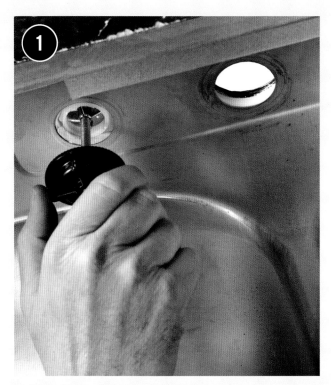

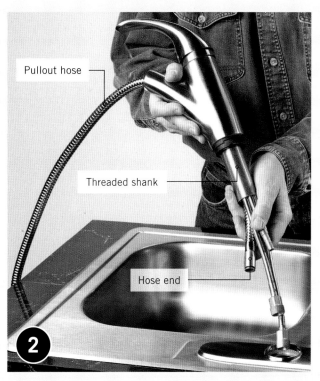

Install the base plate (if your faucet has one) onto the sink flange so it is centered. Have a helper hold it straight from above as you tighten the mounting nuts that secure the base plate from below. Make sure the plastic gasket is centered under the base plate. These nuts can be adequately tightened by hand.

Retract the hose by drawing it out through the faucet body until the fitting at the end of the hose is flush with the bottom of the threaded faucet shank. Insert the shank and the supply tubes down through the top of the deck plate.

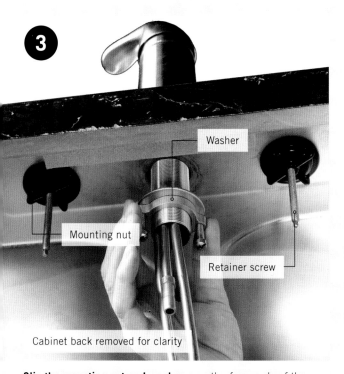

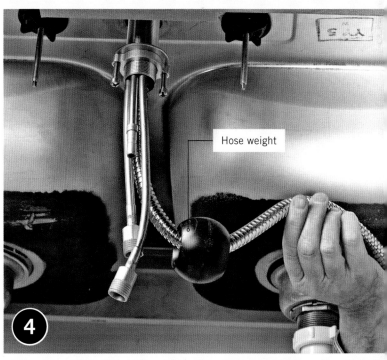

Slip the mounting nut and washer over the free ends of the supply tubes and hose, then thread the nut onto the threaded faucet shank. Hand tighten. Tighten the retainer screws with a screwdriver to secure the faucet.

Slide the hose weight onto the pullout hose (the weight helps keep the hose from tangling, and it makes it easier to retract).

(continued)

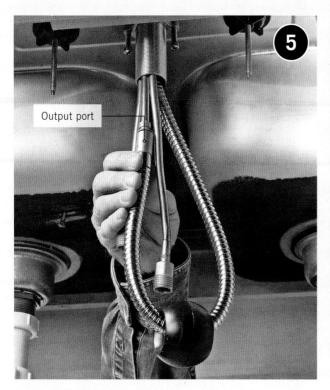

Connect the end of the pullout hose to the outlet port on the faucet body using a quick connector fitting.

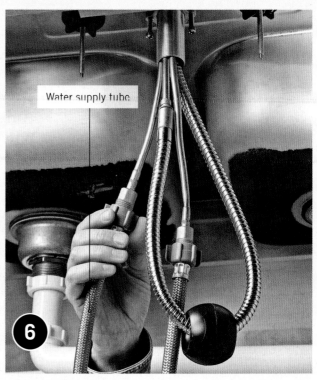

Hook up the water supply tubes to the faucet inlets. Make sure the tubes are long enough to reach the supply risers without stretching or kinking.

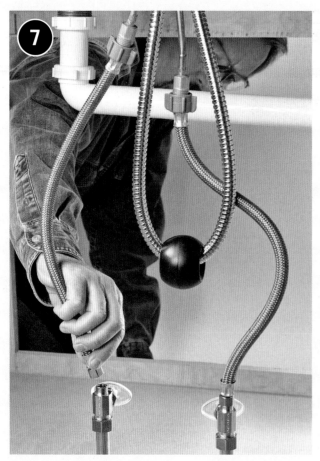

Connect the supply tubes to the supply risers at the stop valves. Make sure to get the hot lines and cold lines attached correctly.

Attach the spray head to the end of the hose and turn the fitting to secure the connection. Turn on the water supply and test.

TIP: Remove the aerator in the tip of the spray head and run hot and cold water to flush out any debris.

Friction washer

Mounting nut

Clean around the sink holes and slip the faucet's washer onto the base. Place the faucet and, working from underneath, slip a friction washer onto each tailpiece. Hand-tighten the mounting nuts. Tighten the nuts fully with channel pliers. Wipe up any squeeze-out on the sink deck with a wet rag.

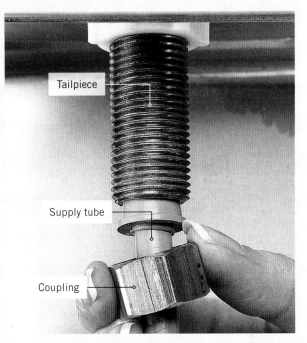

Tailpiece

Supply tube

Coupling

Connect the supply tubes to the tailpieces. Make sure the tubes are long enough to reach the stop valves and that the coupling nuts will fit over the tubes and tailpieces.

Sprayer tailpiece

Apply a ¼" bead of plumber's putty to the underside of the sprayer base. With the base threaded onto the hose, insert the tailpiece through the sink deck opening. From underneath, slip the friction washer over the sprayer tailpiece and screw the mounting onto the tailpiece.

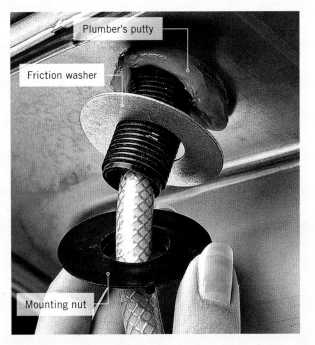

Plumber's putty

Friction washer

Mounting nut

Tighten the sprayer tailpiece mounting nut with channel pliers, and clean up any excess putty. Screw the sprayer hose onto the nipple on the bottom of the faucet. Hand-tighten and then give a quarter turn more with channel pliers. Turn on the water, remove the faucet's aerator, and flush out any debris.

Kitchen Drains + Traps

Kitchen traps, also called sink drains or trap assemblies, are made of 1½-inch pipes, slip washers, and nuts, so they can be easily assembled and disassembled. Most plastic types can be tightened by hand, with no wrench required. Pipes made of chromed brass will corrode in time, and rubber washers will crumble, meaning they need to be replaced. Plastic pipes and plastic washers last virtually forever. All traps are liable to get bumped out of alignment; when this happens, they should be taken apart and reassembled.

A trap's configuration depends on how many bowls the sink has, whether or not you have a garbage disposal and/or a dishwasher drain line, and local codes. On this page we show three of the most common assembly types. Tee fittings on these traps often have a baffle, which reduces the water flow somewhat. Check local codes to make sure your trap is compliant.

TOOLS + MATERIALS

Flathead screwdriver	Teflon tape
Spud wrench	Washers
Trap arm	Waste tee fitting
Mineral spirits	P-trap
Cloth	Saw
Strainer kit	Miter box
Plumber's putty	

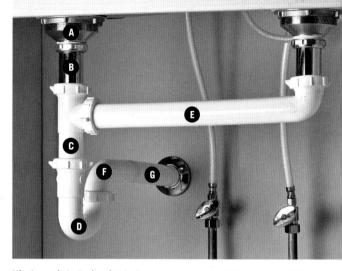

Kitchen sink drains include a strainer body (A), tailpiece (B), waste tee (C), P-trap (D), outlet drain line (E), trap arm (F), and wall stub-out with coupling (G).

In this arrangement, the dishwasher drain hose (A) attaches to the garbage disposal (B), and a trap arm (C) leads from the disposal to the P-trap (D).

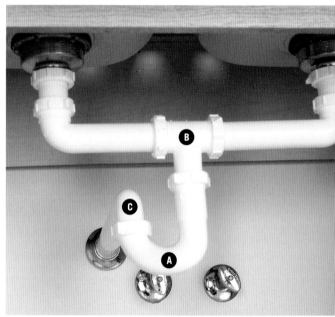

A "center tee" arrangement has a single P-trap (A) that is connected to a waste tee (B) and the trap arm (C).

DRAIN KITS

Kits for installing a new sink drain include all the pipes, slip fittings, and washers you'll need to get from the sink tailpieces (most kits are equipped for a double bowl kitchen sink) to the trap arm that enters the wall or floor. For wall trap arms, you'll need a kit with a P-trap. Both drains normally are plumbed to share a trap. Chromed brass or PVC with slip fittings let you adjust the drain more easily and pull it apart and then reassemble if there is a clog. Some pipes have fittings on their ends that eliminate the need for a washer. Kitchen sink drains and traps should be 1½" o.d. pipe—the 1¼" pipe is for lavatories and doesn't have enough capacity for a kitchen sink.

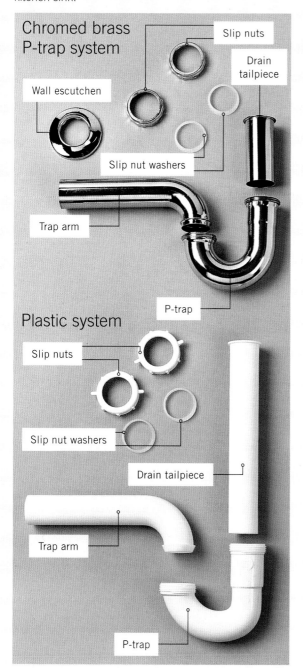

Chromed brass P-trap system

- Slip nuts
- Drain tailpiece
- Wall escutchen
- Slip nut washers
- Trap arm
- P-trap

Plastic system

- Slip nuts
- Slip nut washers
- Drain tailpiece
- Trap arm
- P-trap

TIPS FOR CHOOSING DRAINS

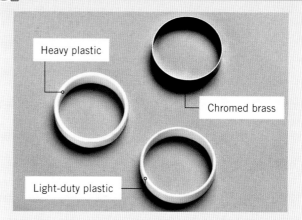

- Heavy plastic
- Chromed brass
- Light-duty plastic

Wall thickness varies in sink drain pipes. The thinner plastic material is cheaper and more difficult to obtain a good seal with than the thicker, more expensive tubing. The thin product is best reserved for lavatory drains, which are far less demanding.

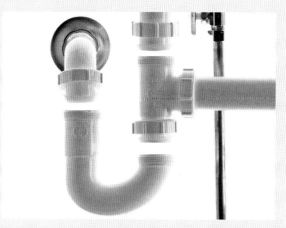

Slip joints are formed by tightening a male-threaded slip nut over a female-threaded fitting, trapping and compressing a beveled nylon washer to seal the joint.

Use a spud wrench to tighten the strainer body against the underside of the sink bowl. Normally, the strainer flange has a layer of plumber's putty to seal beneath it above the sink drain and a pair of washers (one rubber, one fibrous) to seal below.

How to Hook Up a Kitchen Sink Drain

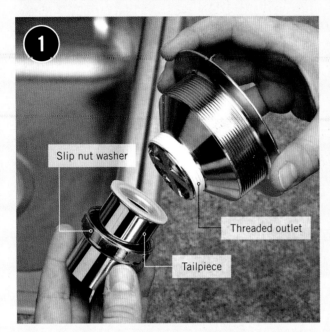

1

Slip nut washer

Threaded outlet

Tailpiece

If you are replacing the sink strainer body, remove the old one and clean the top and bottom of the sink deck around the drain opening with mineral spirits. Attach the drain tailpiece to the threaded outlet of the strainer body, inserting a non-beveled washer between the parts if your strainer kit includes one. Lubricate the threads or apply Teflon tape so you can get a good, snug fit.

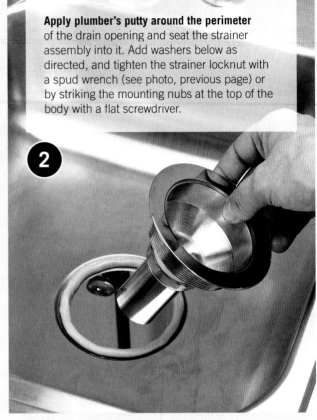

Apply plumber's putty around the perimeter of the drain opening and seat the strainer assembly into it. Add washers below as directed, and tighten the strainer locknut with a spud wrench (see photo, previous page) or by striking the mounting nubs at the top of the body with a flat screwdriver.

2

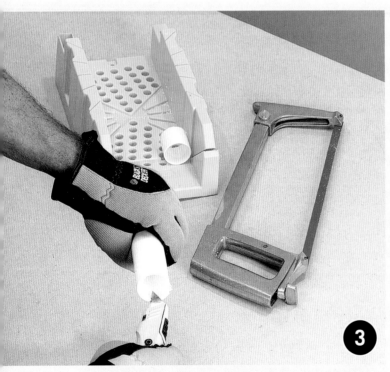

3

You may need to cut a trap arm or drain tailpiece to length. Cut metal tubing with a hacksaw. Cut plastic tubing with a handsaw, power miter saw, or a hand miter box and a backsaw or hacksaw. You can use a tubing cutter for any material. Deburr the cut end of plastic pipe with a utility knife.

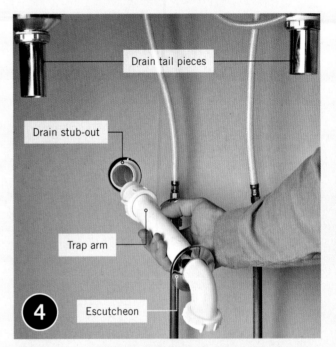

Drain tail pieces

Drain stub-out

Trap arm

4

Escutcheon

Attach the trap arm to the male-threaded drain stub-out in the wall using a slip nut and beveled compression washer. The outlet for the trap arm should point downward.

NOTE: The trap arm must be lower on the wall than any of the horizontal lines in the set-up, including lines to dishwasher, disposal, or the outlet line to the second sink bowl.

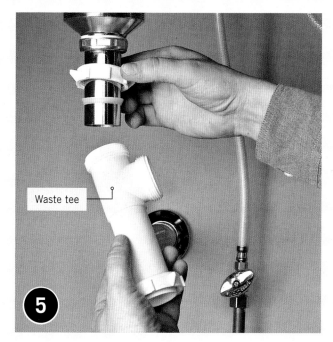

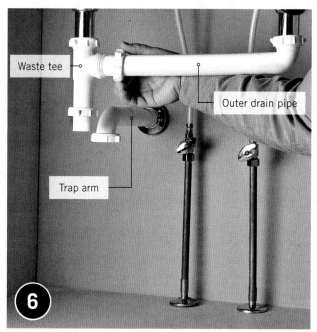

Attach a waste tee fitting to the drain tailpiece, orienting the opening in the fitting side so it will accept the outlet drain line from the other sink bowl. If the waste tee is higher than the top of the trap arm, remove it and trim the drain tailpiece.

Join the short end of the outlet drain pipe to the tailpiece for the other sink bowl, and then attach the end of the long run to the opening in the waste tee. The outlet tube should extend into the tee ½"—make sure it does not extend in far enough to block water flow from above.

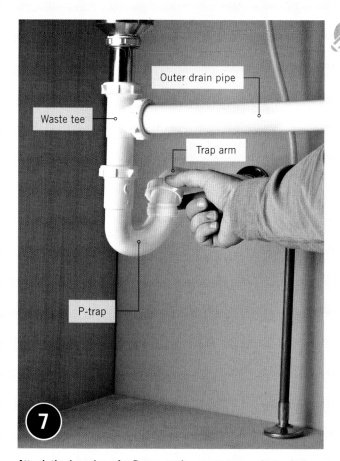

VARIATION: DRAIN IN FLOOR

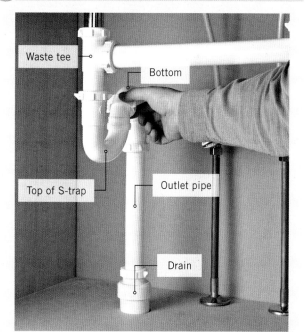

Attach the long leg of a P-trap to the waste tee and attach the shorter leg to the downward-facing opening of the trap arm. Adjust as necessary and test all joints to make sure they are still tight, and then test the system.

If your drain stub-out comes up out of the floor or cabinet base instead of the wall, you probably have a two-part S-trap instead of a P-trap in your drain line. This arrangement is illegal in some areas, because a heavy surge of waterflow from a nearby fixture can siphon the trap dry, rendering it unable to block gases. Check with your local plumbing inspector to learn if S-traps are allowed in your area.

Dishwashers

A dishwasher that's past its prime may be inefficient in more ways than one. If it's an old model, it probably wasn't designed to be very efficient to begin with. But more significantly, if it no longer cleans effectively, you're probably spending a lot of time and hot water pre-rinsing the dishes. This alone can consume more energy and water than a complete wash cycle on a newer machine. So even if your old dishwasher still runs, replacing it with an efficient new model can be a good green upgrade.

In terms of sizing and utility hookups, dishwashers are generally quite standard. If your old machine is a built-in and your countertops and cabinets are standard sizes, most full-size dishwashers will fit right in. Of course, you should always measure the dimensions of the old unit before shopping for a new one to avoid an unpleasant surprise at installation time. Also be sure to review the manufacturer's instructions before starting any work.

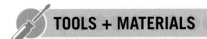

TOOLS + MATERIALS

Screwdrivers
Adjustable wrench
2' level
¾" discharge tube
½" flexible supply tubing
Cable connector
Teflon tape
Hose clamps
Wire connectors
Carpet scrap
Bowl

Replacing an old, inefficient dishwasher is a straightforward project that usually takes just a few hours. The energy and water savings start with the first load of dishes and continue with every load thereafter. Newer units also do a better job of cleaning your dishware and glassware.

How to Replace a Dishwasher

Disconnect old plumbing connections. First unscrew the front access panel. Once the access panel is removed, disconnect the water supply line from the L-fitting on the bottom of the unit. This is usually a brass compression fitting, so just turning the compression nut counterclockwise with a box or adjustable wrench should do the trick. Use a bowl to catch any water that might leak out when the nut is removed.

L-fitting

❷

❶

Start by shutting off the electrical power to the circuit at the main service panel. Also, turn off the water supply at the shutoff valve, usually located directly under the floor or in the cabinet beneath the kitchen sink.

NOTE: Most local codes now require that dishwashers be on a GFCI-protected circuit. If yours is not, it's always a good idea to replace the regular receptacle with a GFCI-protected model or to replace the circuit breaker at the main panel with a GFCI breaker.

Disconnect old wiring connections. The dishwasher has an integral electrical box at the front of the unit where the power cable is attached to the dishwasher's fixture wires. Take off the box cover and remove the wire connectors that join the wires together.

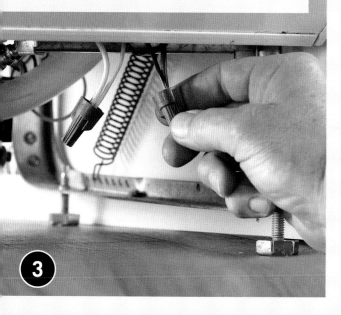

❸

❹

Disconnect the discharge hose, which is usually connected to the dishwasher port on the side of the garbage disposal. To remove it, just loosen the screw on the hose clamp and pull it off. You may need to push this hose back through a hole in the cabinet wall and into the dishwasher compartment so it won't get caught when you pull out the dishwasher.

(continued)

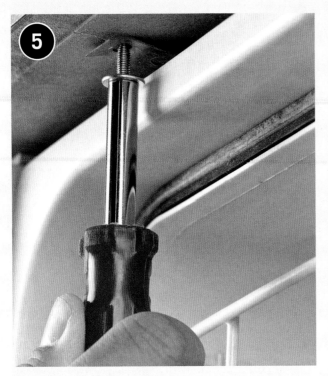

Detach the unit from the cabinets. Remove the screws that hold the brackets to the underside of the countertop. Then put a piece of cardboard or old carpet under the front legs to protect the floor from getting scratched, and pull the dishwasher out.

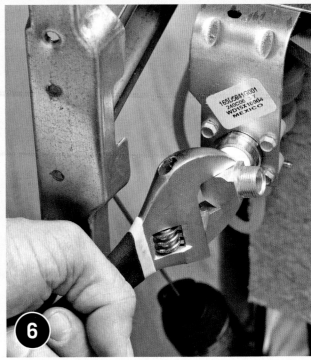

First, read the appliance's installation instructions carefully, and then prepare the new dishwasher to be installed. Tip it on its back and attach the new L-fitting into the threaded port on the solenoid. Apply Teflon tape to the fitting threads to allow the coupling to be tightened fully.

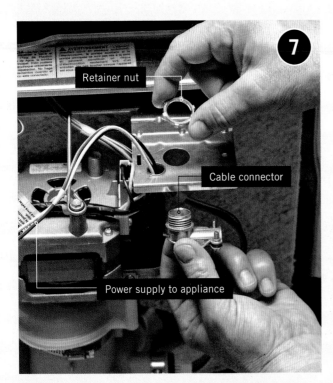

Retainer nut

Cable connector

Power supply to appliance

Prepare for the wiring connections. Like the old dishwasher, the new one will have an integral electrical box for making the wiring connections. Remove the box cover. Then install a cable connector on the back of the box and bring the power cable from the service panel through this connector.

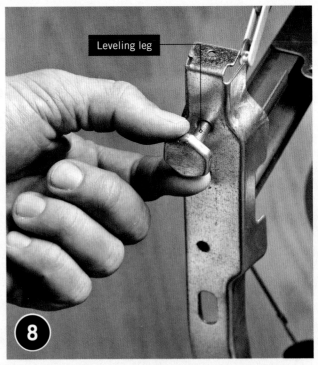

Leveling leg

Install a leveling leg at each of the four corners while the new dishwasher is still on its back. Leave about ½" of each leg projecting from the bottom of the unit. These will have to be adjusted later to level the appliance. Tip the appliance up onto the feet, and slide it into the opening. Check for level in both directions and adjust the feet as required.

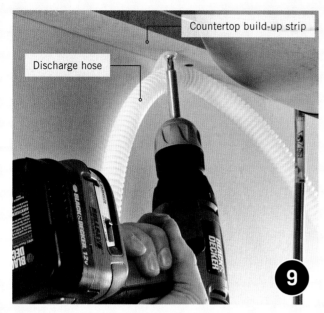

Countertop build-up strip

Discharge hose

9

Push an adapter over the disposal's discharge nipple and tighten it in place with a hose clamp. If you don't have a disposal, replace one of the drain tailpieces with a dishwasher tailpiece, and clamp the discharge tube to its fitting.

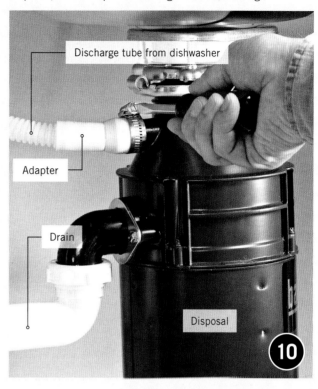

Discharge tube from dishwasher

Adapter

Drain

Disposal

10

Once the dishwasher is level, attach the brackets to the underside of the countertop to keep the appliance from moving. Then pull the discharge hose into the sink cabinet and install it so there's a loop that is attached with a bracket to the underside of the countertop. This loop prevents waste water from flowing from the disposal back into the dishwasher.

NOTE: Some codes require that you install an air gap fitting for this purpose. Check with your local building department.

TUBE CHOICES

Codes still allow flexible copper supply tubes such as the one shown in the next step, but a flexible dishwasher supply tube, such as reinforced, braided stainless steel, is a better choice in just about any situation. Copper tubes may crimp and either burst or restrict water flow when you move the dishwasher.

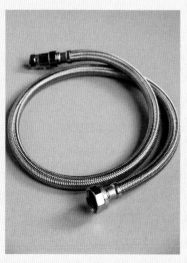

11

Brass bushing

Compression nut

Supply tube

L-fitting

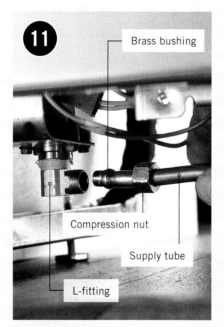

Adjust the L-fitting on the dishwasher's water inlet valve until it points directly toward the water supply tubing. Then lubricate the threads slightly with a drop of dishwashing liquid and tighten the tubing's compression nut onto the fitting, keeping the brass bushing between the nut and the L-fitting. Use an adjustable wrench to turn the nut clockwise.

12

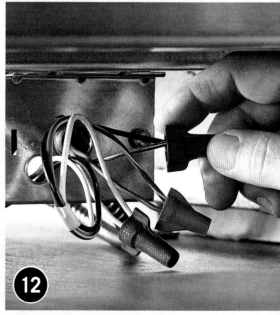

Complete the electrical connections by clamping the cable and joining the wires with wire nuts, following the manufacturer's instructions. Replace the electrical cover, usually by hooking it onto a couple of prongs and driving a screw. Restore power and water, and test. Replace the toe-kick panel.

Garbage Disposals

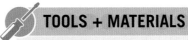

TOOLS + MATERIALS

Screwdriver	Mineral spirits
Channel pliers	Plumber's putty
Spud wrench (optional)	Wire caps
Hammer	Hose clamps
Hacksaw or tubing cutter	Threaded wye fitting
Drain auger	Electrical tape
Putty knife	

A garbage disposal is a useful luxury in any kitchen. The appliance can grind through food waste with ease, making meal prep and clean-up simple and fast. Although you can choose from ⅓-, ½-, ¾-, or 1-horsepower models, ¾ hp is the most common because it is the ideal balance between grinding power and energy conservation for most households.

The other basic choice you'll make in selecting a disposal is between batch feed and continuous feed. Batch feed disposals are triggered by a lid that is put in place in the drain, ensuring that the blades spin only when there is a safety measure in place. These units don't need a separate switch and are, consequently, less expensive. Continuous feed are the more popular style. The unit is turned on or off by way of a wall or sink-top switch or button, and the disposal runs as long as the switch is left on.

You can choose from other options, as well. A supplied power cord will allow you to plug the unit into a GFCI undersink outlet, making installation far easier than hardwiring the unit into an electrical line. (Of course, you'll need an outlet under the sink.)

Look for an auto-reverse feature, which is the best way to clear jams. If you don't like the noise a disposal makes, shop for a model with "quiet" construction; these include extra insulation to silence motor noise. If you're installing the disposal yourself, it's wise to find one with a quick-mount feature that will make installation simpler.

If you're replacing an older disposal, you only need to remove the old and install the new—you can use the existing hook-ups in most cases. However, if you're installing a disposal where there has never been one, you'll want to check local codes. Some still prohibit the use of garbage disposals, due to the added burden on local sewer lines.

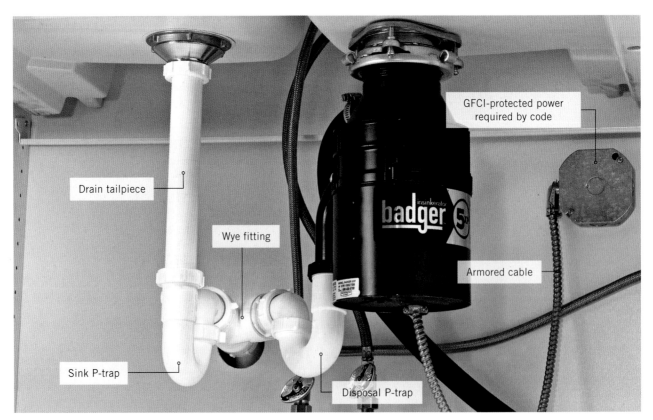

A properly functioning garbage disposal that's used correctly can help reduce clogs. Some plumbers use separate P-traps for the disposal and the drain outlet tube, as shown here. Others contend that configuring the drain line with a single P-trap minimizes the chance that a trap will have its water seal broken by suction from the second trap.

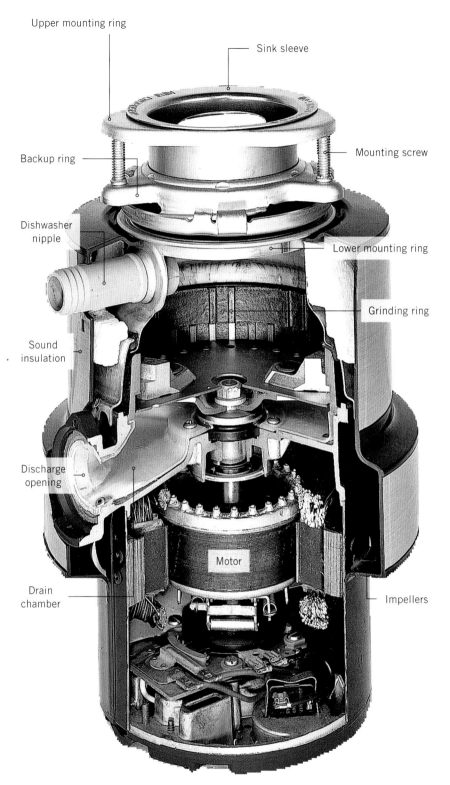

Upper mounting ring

Sink sleeve

Backup ring

Mounting screw

Dishwasher nipple

Lower mounting ring

Grinding ring

Sound insulation

Discharge opening

Motor

Drain chamber

Impellers

A garbage disposal grinds food waste so it can be flushed away through the sink drain system. A quality disposal has a ½-horsepower or larger self-reversing motor. Other features to look for include sound insulation, a grinding ring, and overload protection that allows the motor to be reset if it overheats. Better garbage disposals have a five-year manufacturer's warranty.

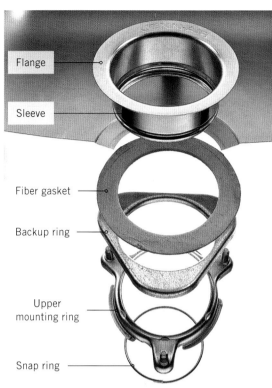

Flange

Sleeve

Fiber gasket

Backup ring

Upper mounting ring

Snap ring

The disposal is attached directly to the sink sleeve, which comes with the disposal and replaces the standard sink strainer. A snap ring fits into a groove around the sleeve of the strainer body to prevent the upper mounting ring and backup ring from sliding down while the upper mounting ring is tightened against the backup ring with mounting screws. Use a fiber gasket compressor when the mounting screws are tightened to create a better seal under the flange.

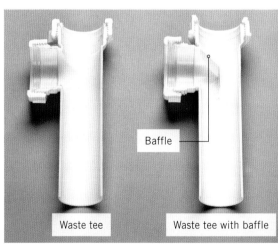

Waste tee

Baffle

Waste tee with baffle

Kitchen and drain tees are required to have a baffle if the tee is connected to a dishwasher or disposal. The baffle is intended to prevent discharge from finding its way up the drain and into the sink.

How to Replace a Garbage Disposal

Remove the old disposal if you have one. You'll need to disconnect the drain pipes and traps first. If your old disposal has a special wrench for the mounting lugs, use it to loosen the lugs. Otherwise, use a screwdriver. If you do not have a helper, place a solid object directly beneath the disposal to support it before you begin removal. **Important: Shut off electrical power at the main service panel before you begin removal.** Disconnect the wire leads, cap them, and stuff them into the electrical box.

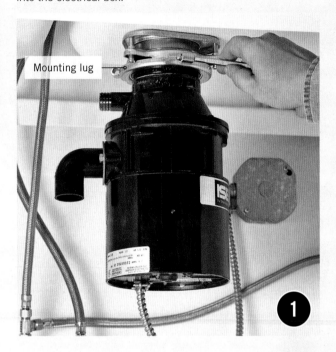

Mounting lug

❶

❷

Clear the drain lines all the way to the branch drain before you begin the new installation. Remove the trap and trap arm first.

❸

Upper mounting ring

Lower mounting ring

Snap ring

3/4 HP
5XP
3-Year

Disassemble the mounting assembly, and then separate the upper and lower mounting rings and the backup ring. Also remove the snap ring from the sink sleeve. See photo, previous page.

❹

Sink sleeve

Press the flange of the sink sleeve for your new disposal into a thin coil of plumber's putty that you have laid around the perimeter of the drain opening. The sleeve should be well-seated in the coil.

Slip the fiber gasket and then the backup ring onto the sink sleeve, working from inside the sink base cabinet. Make sure the backup ring is oriented the same way it was before you disassembled the mounting assembly.

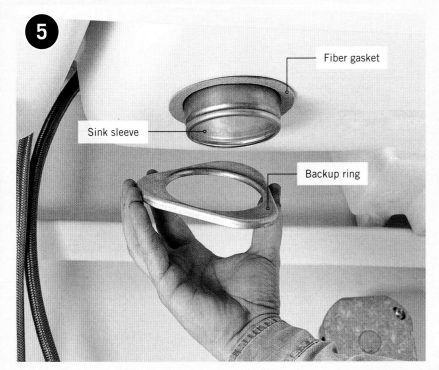

5

Fiber gasket

Sink sleeve

Backup ring

6

Insert the upper mounting ring onto the sleeve with the slotted ends of the screws facing away from the backup ring so you can access them. Then, holding all three parts at the top of the sleeve, slide the snap ring onto the sleeve until it snaps into the groove.

7

Tighten the three mounting screws on the upper mounting ring until the tips press firmly against the backup ring. It is the tension created by these screws that keeps the disposal steady and minimizes vibration.

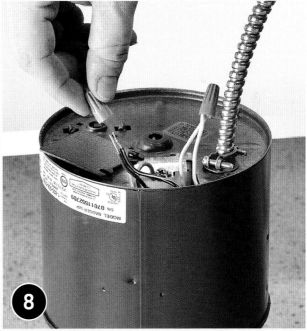

8

Make electrical connections before you attach the disposal unit on the mounting assembly. Shut off the power at the service panel if you have turned it back on. Remove the access plate from the disposal. Attach the white and black branch circuit wires from the electrical box to the white and black wires (respectively) inside the disposal. Twist a small wire cap onto each connection and wrap it with electrical tape for good measure. Also attach the green ground wire from the box to the grounding terminal on your disposal.

(continued)

Knock out the plug in the disposal port if you will be connecting your dishwasher to the disposal. If you have no dishwasher, leave the plug in. Insert a large flathead screwdriver into the port opening and rap it with a mallet. Retrieve the knock-out plug from inside the disposal canister.

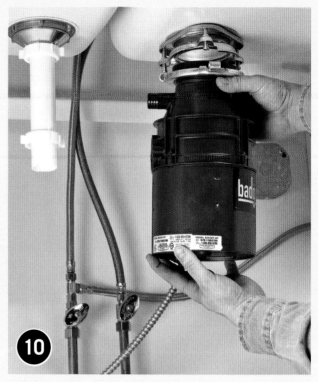

Hang the disposal from the mounting ring attached to the sink sleeve. To hang it, simply lift it up and position the unit so the three mounting ears are underneath the three mounting screws, and then spin the unit so all three ears fit into the mounting assembly. Wait until after the plumbing hookups have been made to lock the unit in place.

Attach the discharge tube to the disposal according to the manufacturer's instructions. It is important to get a very good seal here or the disposal will leak. Go ahead and spin the disposal if it helps you access the discharge port.

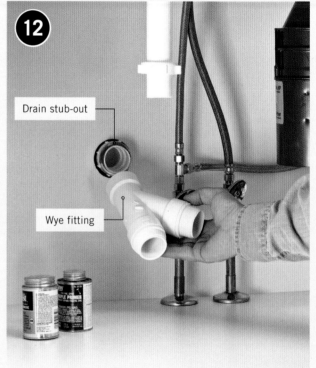

Drain stub-out

Wye fitting

Attach a wye fitting at the drain stub-out. The wye fitting should be sized to accept a drain line from the disposal and another from the sink. Adjust the sink drain plumbing as needed to get from the sink P-trap to one opening of the wye.

Install a trap arm for the disposal in the open port of the wye fitting at the wall stub-out. Then, attach a P-trap or a combination of a tube extension and a P-trap so the trap will align with the bottom of the disposal discharge tube.

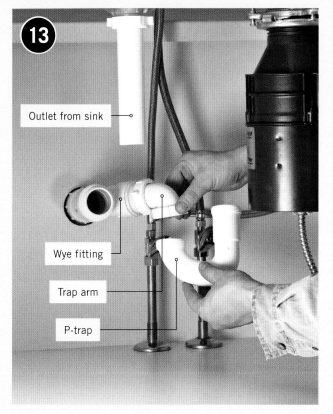

Outlet from sink

Wye fitting

Trap arm

P-trap

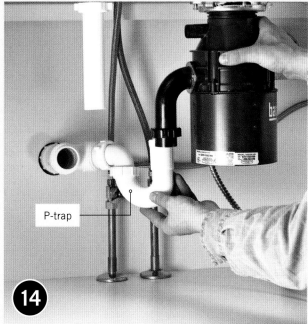

P-trap

Spin the disposal so the end of the discharge tube is lined up over the open end of the P-trap, and confirm that they will fit together correctly. If the discharge tube extends down too far, mark a line on it at the top of the P-trap and cut at the line with a hacksaw. If the tube is too short, attach an extension with a slip joint. You may need to further shorten the discharge tube first to create enough room for the slip joint on the extension. Slide a slip nut and beveled compression washer onto the discharge tube and attach the tube to the P-trap.

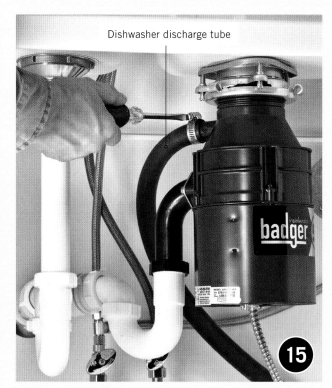

Dishwasher discharge tube

Connect the dishwasher discharge tube to the inlet port located at the top of the disposal unit. This may require a dishwasher hookup kit. Typically, a hose clamp is used to secure the connection.

Lock the disposal into position on the mounting ring assembly once you have tested to make sure it is functioning correctly and without leaks. Lock it by turning one of the mounting lugs until it makes contact with the locking notch.

Water Heaters

Although it may seem daunting, replacing your water heater is not much more complicated than replacing a garbage disposal or kitchen faucet. Even if you decide to upgrade your unit, or go to an entirely new technology, the plumbing is still relatively simple and doable. You should keep in mind that the modern equivalent of your existing water heater may be a very different size; always measure before swapping a water heater out and before shopping for a new one.

The best long-term value for your money can be found in an Energy Star–rated unit. Because the water heater runs so much in any home, a little energy cost savings over the long haul will add up to more than the higher cost when you buy the unit. And think to the future when you're shopping. You can now choose from among "smart" water heaters that can be connected and controlled via Wi-Fi and your smartphone or home control console. You can also consider the energy-conserving option of a tankless unit, which offers greater longevity.

Expect a water heater to last around 8 to 12 years. The longevity depends on many factors, including quality, levels, maintenance, and other factors, such as water hardness. The best time to replace a water heater is before it leaks and fills your basement with water. It's a bit of a gamble, but once your old heater starts showing signs of wear and perhaps even acting up a bit, go ahead and make the change.

Water heaters for primary duty in residences range in size from 30 gallons to 65 gallons. For a family of four, a 40- or 50-gallon model should be adequate. While you don't want to run out of hot water every morning, you also don't want to pay to heat more water than you use. Base your choice on how well your current water heater is meeting your demand.

Follow local codes when choosing the pipe and fittings for both gas and water. Make sure there is a gas shutoff within 5 feet of the water heater. Also, there should be a union between the shutoff and the water heater so pipes can be easily dismantled for service.

A water heater is one of the most important and heavily used plumbing appliances in any house. Professionals recommend replacing a water heater that is more than ten years old.

TOOLS + MATERIALS

Tubing cutter	Discharge tube
Hacksaw	Garden hose
Pipe wrenches	Drain pan
Adjustable wrench	Pipe thread lubricant
Channel pliers	Vent pipe elbow
Screwdriver	Gas supply pipe + fittings
MAPP torch kit	Copper soldering supplies
Appliance dolly	Leak detector solution
Water heater	Ball-type water
T + P relief valve	shutoff valve

Use armored cable or wires housed in metal conduit to bring electrical power to electric water heaters. The armored cable or conduit should enter the top of the unit through a conduit clamp.

The nameplate on the side of a water heater lists tank capacity, insulation R-value, and working pressure (pounds per square inch). More efficient water heaters have an insulation R-value of 7 or higher. The nameplate for an electric water heater includes the voltage and the wattage capacity of the heating elements and thermostats. New water heaters also have a yellow energy guide label that lists typical yearly operating costs.

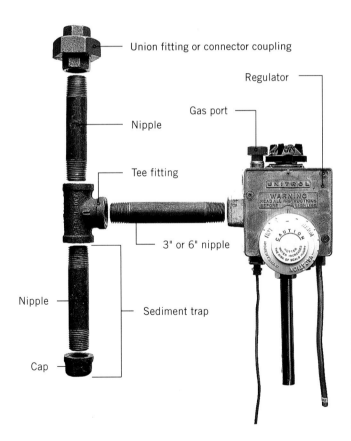

Union fitting or connector coupling

Regulator

Gas port

Nipple

Tee fitting

3" or 6" nipple

Sediment trap

Nipple

Cap

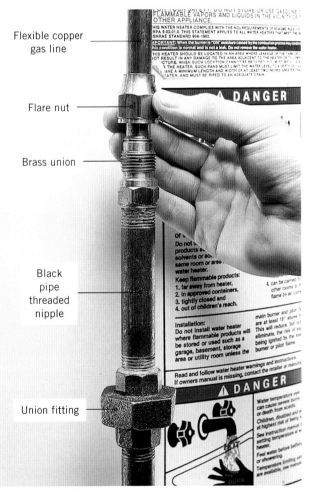

Flexible copper gas line

Flare nut

Brass union

Black pipe threaded nipple

Union fitting

Install a sediment trap between the gascock and the gas port on your gas water heater. A sediment trap is simply a vertical pipe nipple that is installed at the base of the union to allow any impurities in the fuel to collect rather than being drawn into the combustion chamber through the port. In most cases it is easier to locate the sediment trap at the water heater connection point, not the gascock fitting on the supply pipe.

If your house has soft copper gas supply lines, use a flare fitting to connect an additional threaded nipple from the black pipe assembly that connects to the water heater regulator. If you have black pipe supply lines, use a union fitting.

Gas Water Heater

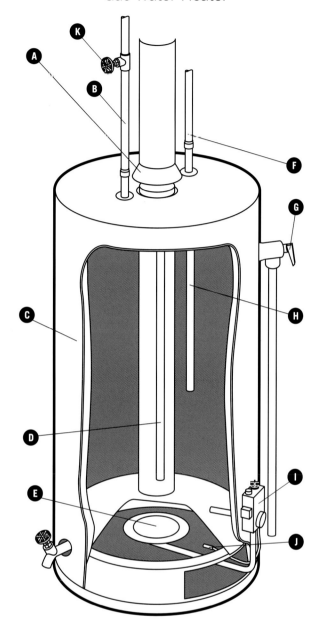

Electric Water Heater

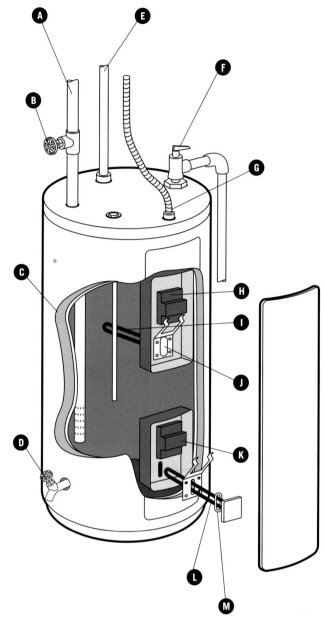

Gas water heater parts include:
(A) Draft hood and vent
(B) Cold water inlet pipe
(C) Tank
(D) Dip tube
(E) Gas burner
(F) Hot water outlet
(G) Temperature/pressure relief valve
(H) Anode rod
(I) Thermostat
(J) Thermocouple
(K) Cold water inlet valve

Electric water heater parts can include:
(A) Cold water inlet pipe
(B) Cold water inlet valve
(C) Insulation
(D) Draincock
(E) Hot water outlet pipe
(F) Temperature/pressure relief valve
(G) Power cable
(H) Upper heating element thermostat
(I) Upper heating element
(J) Bracket
(K) Lower heating thermostat
(L) Lower heating element
(M) Gasket

Gas water heaters operate on either propane or natural gas and are generally very economical to run. They do cost a bit more than electric heaters up front. The installation on the next page features a gas water heater. Check with your local building department to find out if homeowners are allowed to install gas appliances in your municipality.

Electric water heaters require 240-volt service, which might overload your service panel if you are replacing a gas heater with an electric model. Their primary advantages are that they are cheaper to purchase (but not to operate) and they do not require that you make gas connections.

How to Remove a Water Heater

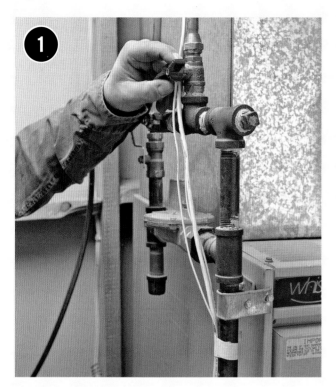

Shut off the gas supply at the stopcock installed in the gas line closest to the water heater. The handle of the stopcock should be perpendicular to the gas supply pipe. Also shut off the water supply. Shut off power to the water heater if it is electric.

Drain the water from the old heater by hooking a garden hose up to the sillcock drain and running it to a floor drain. If you don't have a floor drain, drain the water into buckets. For your personal safety, wait until the water heater has been shut off for a couple of hours before draining it.

Disconnect the gas supply from the water heater. To do so, loosen the flare fitting with two wrenches or pliers in a soft copper supply line, or loosen the union fitting with two pipe wrenches for black pipe supply lines (right).

(continued)

Unscrew the vent pipe from the draft hood. Also remove vent pipes up to and including the elbow to inspect them for corrosion, and replace if needed.

Cut the water supply lines. Prior to cutting, shut off the cold water supply either at the stop valve downline from the heater or at the water meter. Replace the shutoff valve with a new ball-type shutoff valve.

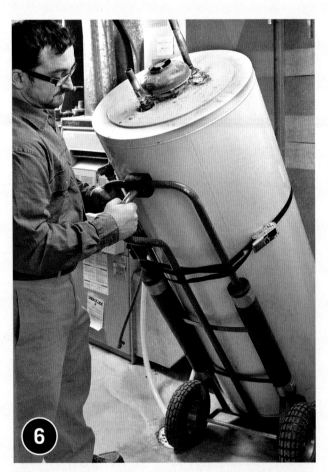

Remove the old water heater and dispose of it properly. Most trash collection companies will haul it away for a modest fee. Don't simply leave it out at the curb unless you know that is allowed by your municipal waste collection department. A two-wheel dolly is a big help here. Water heaters usually weigh around 150 pounds.

INSTALL A RELIEF VALVE

Prepare the new water heater for installation. Before you put the water heater in place, install a T + P relief valve in the valve opening. Make sure to read the manufacturer's instructions and purchase the recommended valve type. Lubricate the threads and tighten the valve into the valve opening with a pipe wrench.

How to Install a Gas Water Heater

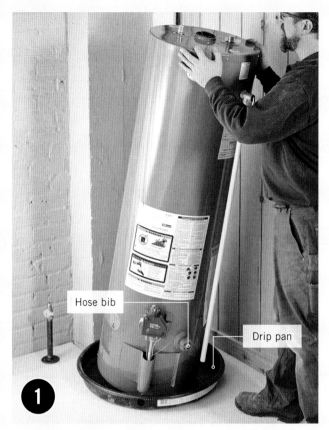

Hose bib

Drip pan

1

Remove the old unit and position the new unit in the installation area. A drip pan is required if the water heater is installed where a leak could cause damage. This usually means anywhere except a crawlspace or an unfinished basement. If the water heater is not level, level it by shimming under the bottom with a metal or composite shim.

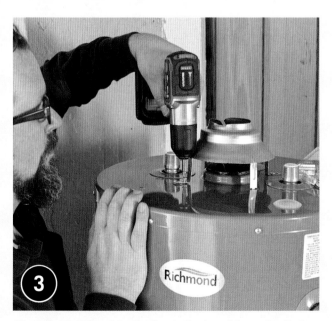

Richmond

3

Attach the draft hood for the flue to the top of the unit with the provided hardware. Attach any other connector parts that are not preattached according to the manufacturer's instructions.

Attach a discharge tube to the T + P relief valve. You may use either copper pipe or CPVC drain pipe. Cut the tube so the free end is between 1½ and 6" above the floor. If you have floorcoverings you wish to protect, add a 90° elbow and a copper drain tube that leads from the discharge tube to a floor drain.

2

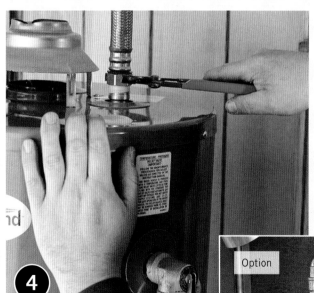

4

Option

Attach approved supply connectors to the inlet and outlet ports at the top of the appliance. Flexible connectors are much easier to work with, but you may use copper tubing if you prefer. If using copper, you'll need a red-coded copper nipple for the outlet port and a blue-coded copper nipple for the inlet port (inset).

(continued)

Join the supply connectors to the supply tubing with approved couplings. If the supply line feeding the water heater has no shutoff valve nearby, it is recommended that you add one. As long as there is a shutoff on the incoming supply side you do not need one on the outgoing (hot water) line.

Assemble the vent and attach the end to the draft hood for the flue.

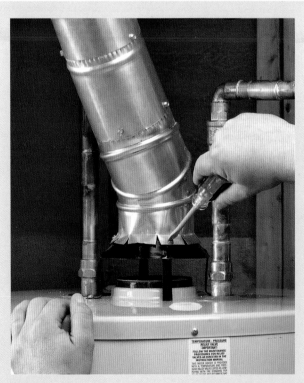

OPTION: If you are running a new vent, you will most likely need to use an elbow fitting and adjustable fittings to achieve the configuration you need. The new vent should be inspected and approved by your local building department.

Begin making the gas connections. Working with gas pipes and tubing is dangerous, and you should only attempt it if you have considerable experience in this skill area. If you are not comfortable working with gas pipe, hire a plumber to take on this part of the job. Begin by screwing the male-threaded union securely into the gas regulator port. Wrap gas-approved lubricating tape around the threads first. Tighten with channel pliers, taking care not to overtighten or cause undue pressure on the regulator.

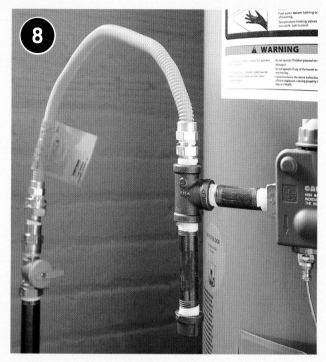

Connect a flexible gas supply tube to the port on a shutoff valve on the gas supply line. The shutoff must be within six feet of the appliance. Connect the other end to the union at the regulator. Wrap the threads in each threaded connection with three or four tight courses of gas-rated lubricating tape first. Include a sediment trap in the hook-up (see page 119).

Turn on the gas supply and test the gas connections with testing solution (inset) to make sure there are no leaks—do not use dish soap or any other products that may contain chlorides. Make sure the tank drain valve is closed, then turn on the water supply and check for water leaks. Once you have determined there are no plumbing leaks, light the pilot light (the instructions are always printed on a label near the pilot light).

HOOKING UP ELECTRIC WATER HEATERS

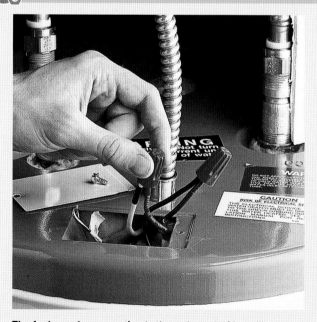

The fuel supply connection is the only part of installing an electric water heater that differs from installing a gas heater, except that electric heaters do not require a vent. The branch circuit wires (240 volts) are twisted together with mating wires in the access panel located at the top of the unit.

Temperature adjustments on electric water heaters are made by tightening or loosening a thermostat adjustment screw located near the heating element. Always shut off power to the unit before making an adjustment. In this photo you can see how close the live terminals for the heating element are to the thermostat.

How to Drain and Flush a Water Heater Tank

You can extend the life of your water heater, and keep energy costs as low as possible, by regularly flushing out the sediment that accumulates in any water heater tank.

 ## TOOLS + MATERIALS

Garden hose

Flathead screwdriver

White bucket (optional)

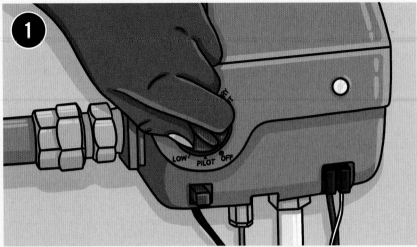

Turn off the water heater at the source. Flip the breaker for an electric heater, or shut off the gas for a gas water heater.

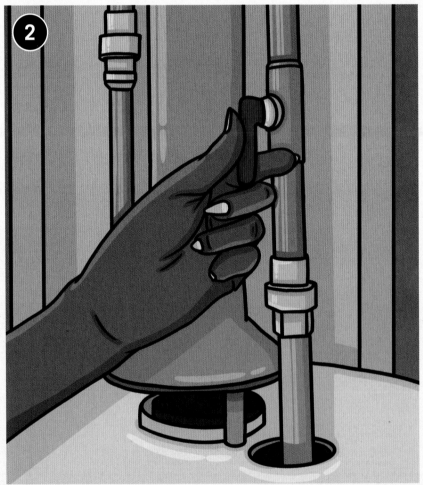

Turn off the cold-water supply at the shutoff valve for the line supplying the water heater. Connect one end of a garden hose to the drain bib at the base of the water heater. The hose should be snug enough not to leak, but not so tight that it will be difficult to get off or would damage the bib threads.

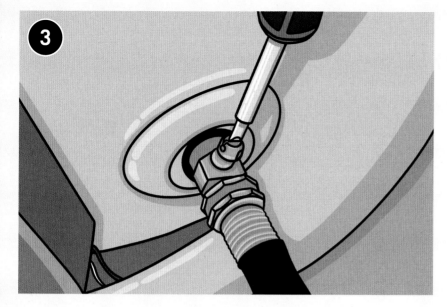

3

Turn on the hot water at any faucet in the house, to create air pressure that will drain the water heater. Use a screwdriver to open the drain bib valve by turning it about a quarter turn counterclockwise. If the water doesn't drain, you may have a backflow preventer valve in your system. In that case, release the T + P relief valve that is located on the side of the water heater, near the top.

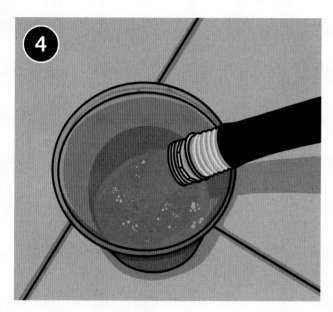

4

Let the tank drain entirely. Drain the water directly into a waste line, either inside or outside. Once the heater is completely drained, open the cold water shutoff valve for about 30 seconds. Shut it off and let the water flush out sediment in the bottom of the tank. You should be able to see some in the water coming out of the hose. Repeat the flushing process several times, until no sediment flushes.

NOTE: To help detect sediment coming out the hose, drain the flush water into a clean, light-colored 5-gallon bucket.

5

Close the water heater's drain bib valve and remove the hose. Open the water supply valve and begin filling the water heater. Leave a faucet or the T + P relief valve open until the tank is halfway filled, then close the tap or valve. Turn the power or gas back on.

Tankless Water Heater

A tankless water heater, as its name indicates, does not keep a tankful of hot water at all times. It heats water only when a hot-water faucet is opened, and so is also called an "on-demand" water heater. A tankless unit can cost a good deal more initially than a standard tank unit, but it typically saves enough in energy costs to pay back the investment within three to five years. Another advantage: you'll never run out of hot water.

Consult with your salesperson to choose a unit large enough to supply all the hot water you may simultaneously need. The model shown, for instance, is rated at nearly 200,000 BTU and can supply up to 9.5 gallons per minute (GPM), enough hot water for two or three faucets (including shower faucets) or appliances at a time. In addition to a whole-house unit such as this, you may also purchase a smaller "point-of-use" unit to supply hot water for, say, a single bathroom. Many of these units are small enough to fit inside a cabinet.

The following pages show installing a gas-fired condensing tankless water heater, which is more efficient than non-condensing units. It requires running two PVC vent pipes out the wall or roof.

This is a pretty ambitious project but within reach of a do-it-yourselfer with good plumbing skills. Consult with your local building department and get a permit before starting work. You will likely need to have the project inspected.

Select a suitable location, perhaps right where the old tank unit was. Always read and follow the manufacturer's installation instructions. It should be near the main cold-water supply pipe and a hot-water pipe leading to the house's faucets and appliances. You will need an electrical receptacle and gas supply line to run vent pipes out the wall or up through the roof.

A tankless water heater can be installed near the old water heater's location to minimize new water and gas pipe runs. It takes up far less space than a standard tank heater. The unit shown on the following pages is a gas-fired condensing unit, which requires two vent pipes; non-condensing units have only one vent pipe. Vent pipes run outside the house at a downward slope. There are connections and valves for a gas supply, a cold-water supply, and a hot-water line to the house, and the unit can simply be plugged into a 120-volt electrical receptacle.

TOOLS + MATERIALS

Tankless water heater with thermostat	Tubing cutter	Screws	Black gas pipe with pipe dope
Drill with screwdriver bit + hole saw	Saw for cutting PVC pipe	PVC pipe	Shutoff valves for water + gas
Channel pliers	Propane torch	PVC primer + cement	
Pipe wrench	Level	Copper supply pipe	
	Pipe straps	Solder + flux	

How to Install a Tankless Water Heater

Position the water heater away from combustible materials and where it can be easily accessed for servicing. Mount the unit securely to a wall using the brackets provided, driving screws into studs. If the wall is masonry, use masonry screws or lag screws with shields.

1

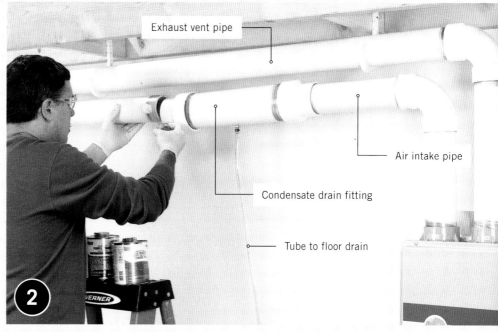

2

Exhaust vent pipe

Air intake pipe

Condensate drain fitting

Tube to floor drain

Plan the path for the exhaust vent pipe and the air intake pipes, which must exit the house at a recommended location (if the exit location is a house wall, the distance from windows and eaves must meet manufacturers' requirements). Cut PVC pipe and assemble with fittings using primer and cement. If you live in a cold climate, install a condensate drain fitting on the air intake pipe at a convenient point for running the drain tube to a floor drain.

3

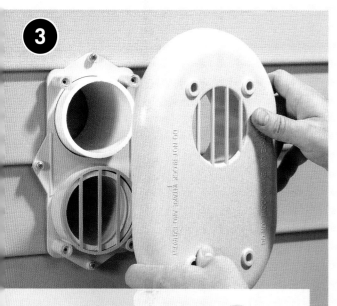

Run the pipes out of the house. Make sure all horizontally run pipes slope slightly downward, and support pipes with straps. Using the parts from a "termination kit," cut two holes for the pipes, slip on interior flanges, and run the pipes through the flanges and out the wall. On the outside, attach a termination cap with screws, and caulk the edges.

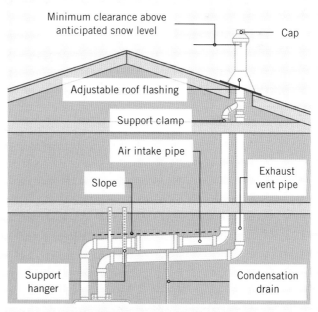

Minimum clearance above anticipated snow level

Cap

Adjustable roof flashing

Support clamp

Air intake pipe

Slope

Exhaust vent pipe

Support hanger

Condensation drain

If venting out a wall is not feasible, you may need to run the pipes up and out the roof. In this case, all horizontal runs should be sloped upward, so condensed water runs back into the water heater. In the attic, join the two pipes together with a wye fitting. Run the pipe out the roof, slip on adjustable roof flashing, cut the pipe to the approved height above the roof, and add an approved cap to the top of the pipe.

(continued)

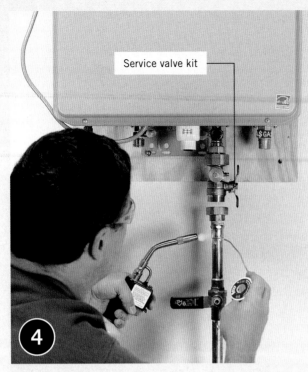

Service valve kit

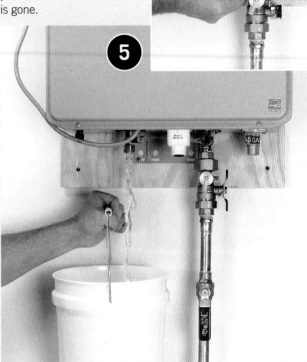

Turn on the valves and run cold water briefly through the unit to be sure water flows freely. Close the unit's shutoff valve, then remove and clean the water heater's internal filter (inset). If there is a good deal of debris, repeat this process until the debris is gone.

5

4

Hook up the cold-water connections. If your house has copper piping, do not use heat to sweat pipes or fittings that are connected to the tankless heater, or you could damage internal parts. Buy the service valve kit made for your unit. Install a cold-water shutoff valve prior to the connection parts. Connect the cold-water parts. Allow them to cool (if you sweated copper), then connect to the unit's valve.

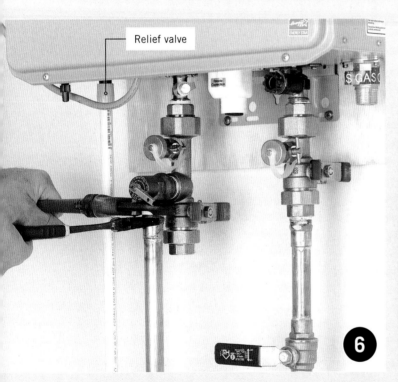

Relief valve

6

Connect the other parts of the service valve kit. This includes another valve for the hot water, as well as a relief valve. Extend the relief valve's pipe down to a point near where it can run to a floor drain. Also run a drain tube from the unit to a floor drain or utility sink.

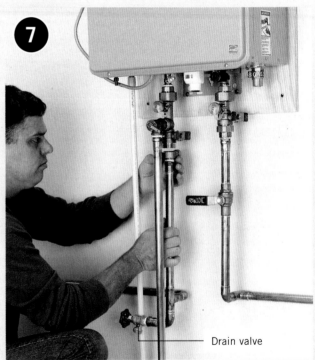

7

Drain valve

Connect to the house's hot-water line. Provide for a drain valve as shown, so you can drain the tank for service. As with the cold-water line (step 4), if the pipes are copper, do not heat any pipes or fittings while they are connected to the heater.

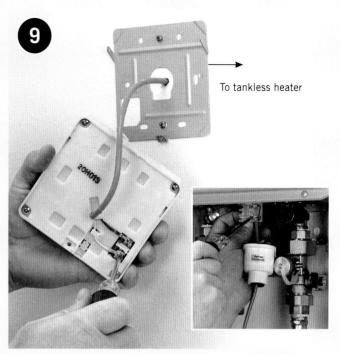

To tankless heater

Hook up the gas connection. Working with black gas pipe, install a gas shutoff valve just below the unit, then install a union so you can easily disconnect the pipes for servicing. Connect the other pipes as shown; make sure to include a vertical sediment trap. Turn on the gas and test with leak detector solution to make sure there are no leaks.

Connect the thermostat. Connect two-wire thermostat cable to the unit (inset) and run it to a convenient location for controlling the water heater. Attach the thermostat's plate to the wall and run the cable through it. Attach the wires to the back of the thermostat's cover, and snap on the cover.

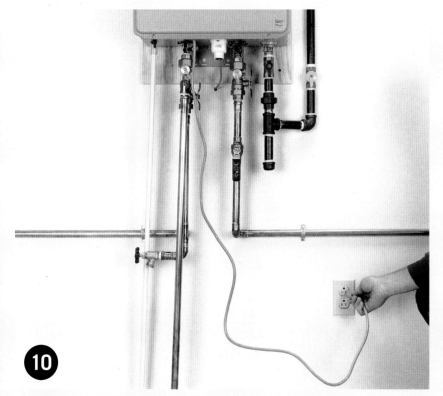

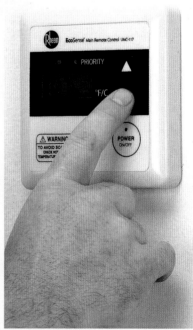

Test the water heater. Turn on the water supply and plug the unit into an electrical receptacle. Make sure you know which circuit breaker controls the water heater. When there is a demand for hot water (from a faucet or appliance), the water heater will turn on automatically and an electric spark will ignite the gas.

Program the thermostat. Turn off the gas and water to the water heater by closing the shutoff valves, and follow the manufacturer's instructions for setting the water temperature.

Lavatory Faucets

Bathroom faucets (often sold as "lavatory" faucets) are manufactured with one of three mounting styles: centerset, widespread, or single hole. Centerset are the least expensive. They are constructed of a single body containing handles and spout; they require three holes in the sink or counter.

Widespread faucets also require three mounting holes, one each for the handles and spout—but they can be spaced as needed or desired. Single-hole faucets are sleeker, with a spout and handle in one thin construction, which is attached through a single hole in the vanity deck or sink. A fourth type, wall-mount, is rare because it's the hardest to plumb or replace.

All bathroom faucets come in a full range of finishes, including matte and shiny versions. They are also offered in an incredible selection of styles, from Victorian reproductions to modern works of art.

The choice of faucet may be limited if you're replacing an existing unit and keeping your sink; you'll have to choose based on the holes. However, single-

hole models often come with a plate to cover any additional holes in the sink. In any case, it's wise to measure hole spacing before shopping for a faucet. A 4-inch handle spread is the most common centerset distance, followed by an 8-inch spread. Also measure from the mounting holes to the center (deepest part) of the sink. The spout of any faucet you choose should ideally direct water down into the center of the sink, to avoid excess splashing.

TOOLS + MATERIALS

Widespread or centerset faucet + hardware	Adjustable wrench
Phillips screwdriver	Box wrench
Basin wrench	Plumber's putty
	Teflon tape

Touchless faucets, like the one pictured, have become increasingly popular. Not only do they make it easier for children and anyone with mobility issues to use a bathroom sink, they are also more hygienic than other options.

Lavatory Faucet Guide

Every bathroom needs a faucet. When it comes to bathroom faucets, spending a little bit more can be the difference between a trouble-free unit that lasts a decade or more, and a problem fixture that you have to replace in a year or two. Even after you've chosen a mounting style from those described on page 132, you'll need to decide on the type of material and valve used in the faucet.

• **Finishes.** Faucet materials include chrome, brass, bronze, copper, gold, nickel, and stainless steel. Some of those are offered in matte, brushed, or polished appearances. Shiny finishes show fingerprints and water marks more than matte surfaces will, and darker surfaces will show toothpaste, creams, or lotion spots more obviously. The most appealing look matches faucet to drain components.

• **Valve type.** You'll choose from four basic types of faucet valves.

Compression: The oldest, least expensive, and most prone to leaking. A valve stem raises and lowers, compressing a rubber washer. The washer eventually deteriorates and must be replaced.

Ball: As it sounds, the valve is an actual ball in a single-handle faucet. The valve rotates so that an opening allows water flow. Uses O-rings, springs, and washers, any of which can be fouled or break.

Cartridge: Reliable, durable, and easy to replace, cartridge valves are the preferred choice for those looking to balance cost and durability.

Ceramic disc: The most recent development and most expensive technology, this valve is two ceramic discs that are cut with channels that align when the faucet is opened.

• **Valve construction.** Brass is the most durable, followed by brass-coated, corrosion resistant metal, and plastic, in that order.

• **Luxury features.** Looking for a faucet upgrade? Consider LED lights in the spout or handles, which can make the faucet easier to use in the middle of the night, decorative handle insets, or a waterfall design in which the spout is actually an open channel that routes the flow of water to the sink.

Even though many use older compression valves, centerset faucets remain popular for their low prices, ease of installation, and full range of elegant designs.

Called "vessel faucets", special taller versions are used with vessel sinks, to minimize splashing and to effectively reach over the edge of higher vessel sinks.

Made explicitly for use in existing 4" centerset holes in sink and vanity decks, "mini-widespread" faucets like this one offer the same style as their larger cousins, but in a more compact package meant as a direct upgrade from a traditional centerset faucet.

NOTE: Shown from behind with backsplash cut away for clarity.

Shut off the water to the existing faucet and open the valves to drain the water. Disconnect the water supply tubes from the faucet, and remove the old faucet by unscrewing the mounting nuts.

Clean off any existing plumber's putty or sealant from the surface of the sink, then lay a new bead of plumbers putty around each of the three openings. Install the two valves into the sink openings by inserting the spout and valves and then threading the mounting screws onto the tailpieces from below the sink.

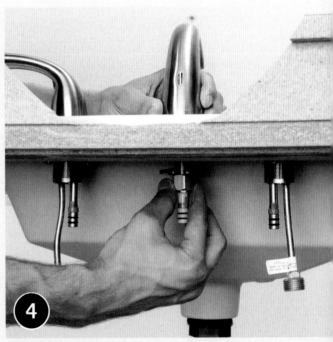

Exact mounting procedures vary; our faucet has retainer screws that are tightened after the mounting nut is threaded over the tailpieces. This secures the valves and spout tightly to the sink.

Repeat this procedure to install the center spout. Make sure the spout is aligned correctly to be perpendicular to the back of the sink.

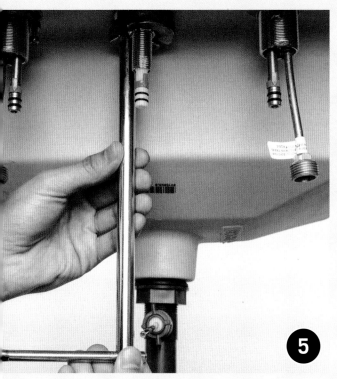

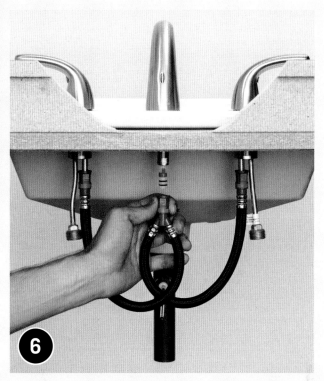

Tighten the spout mounting nut securely. A basin wrench will make this easier, since access to the mounting nut may be difficult.

Attach the water connection tubes from the valve tailpieces to the spout tailpiece. Thread the mounting nuts by hand, then tighten slightly with channel pliers or an adjustable wrench (in tight quarters, this can also be done with a basin wrench).

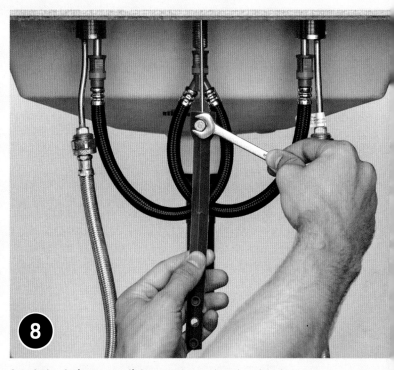

Connect water-supply tubes from the water shutoff valves to the water-supply tubes on the faucet-valve tailpieces using an adjustable wrench (or basin wrench, where access is limited). The hot water normally connects to the left faucet valve and the cold water to the right. Turn on the water and test the faucet. If any fittings leak, tighten them slightly until they are watertight.

Attach the drain-stopper linkage to the push rod and to the stopper pivot lever.

Most modern faucets come with flexible plastic gaskets that create a durable watertight seal on the bottom of the faucet. However, an inexpensive faucet may have a flimsy-looking foam seal that doesn't seal well. If that is the case with your faucet, discard the seal and press a ring of plumber's putty into the sealant groove on the underside of the faucet body.

Insert the faucet tailpieces through the holes in the sink. From below, thread washers and mounting nuts over the tailpieces, then tighten the mounting nuts with a basin wrench until snug. Wrap the the threads of the stop valves with Teflon tape and thread the metal nuts of the flexible supply risers to these. Wrench tighten about a half-turn past hand tight. Overtightening these nuts will strip the threads. Now tighten the coupling nuts to the faucet tailpieces with a basin wrench.

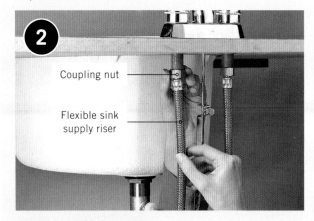

Coupling nut

Flexible sink
supply riser

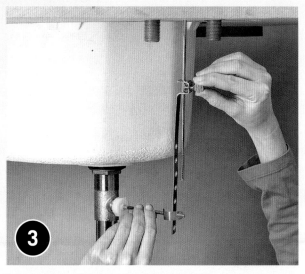

Slide the lift rod of the new faucet into its hole behind the spout. Thread it into the clevis past the clevis screw. Push the pivot rod all the way down so the stopper is open. With the lift rod also all the way down, tighten the clevis to the lift rod.

Tighten the handle screws firmly, so they won't come loose during operation. Cover each handle screw with the appropriate index cap—Hot or Cold.

Unscrew the aerator from the end of the spout. Turn the hot and cold water taps on full. Turn the water back on at the stop valves and flush out the faucet for a couple of minutes before turning off the water at the faucet. Check the riser connections for drips. Tighten a compression nut only until the drip stops. Replace the aerator.

Touch-Activated Bathroom Faucets

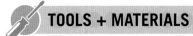
TOOLS + MATERIALS

Faucet + hardware	Flashlight
Adjustable wrenches	Eye protection
Channel pliers	Work gloves
Teflon tape	

If you've ever washed your hands in an airport bathroom, chances are you've already come across a touchless faucet. Developed to conserve water and stop the spread of disease, these faucets have quickly become ubiquitous in commercial facilities across the country and around the world.

But now homeowners can enjoy the benefits of hands-free faucets in their own bathrooms. Widely available in home centers and hardware stores nationwide, these feature varying technologies depending on the manufacturer.

The most common type of commercial hands-free bathroom faucet relies on an infrared motion sensor, much like those in home-security systems. When something solid passes within the sensor's range, the faucet turns on for a predetermined period of time. Home units operate a little differently. They include motion-sensing and "touch-on, touch-off" units. The model we selected for this installation project uses an electrical field sensor that reacts to the stored charge in every human body, called *capacitance*. Whether motion or touch activated, these home faucets rely on an electrical field created by a solenoid connected to the faucet body. When a human hand disrupts the electrical field, the faucet turns on or off. Touch faucets operate the same, but the faucet body itself is the electrical field.

For most of these types of faucets, water temperature and flow rate are set manually before the faucet is "programmed." Then it's a case of tapping the faucet body or waving a hand near it to start or stop the flow.

Although these faucets are pricier than standard manual models, they represent a leap forward for people with motor-skill difficulties or for preventing disease spread between family members using a busy bathroom in a crowded house. The good news is that they are not much more challenging to install than a standard faucet—with the exception of units that are hardwired into the home's electrical system. Hardwired units should be installed by a licensed professional.

A touch-activated faucet such as this can save water, make life easier for children and physically challenged users, and they come in a nice selection of style and finish options.

How to Install a Touch-Activated Faucet

Check the parts in the box against the instruction-sheet part list. Remove the center from the base gasket as necessary, and thread the base's LED wire through the hole in the gasket. Seat the gasket into the groove in the insulator base and ensure that it is snug and level.

NOTE: Sink shown here unmounted for clarity. If your vanity deck has multiple holes, you'll need to use the supplied escutcheon plate. Run the LED wire through the escutcheon hole and seat the insulator base on top of the escutcheon (make sure the LED light is facing forward).

Slide the mounting bracket into place under the sink, on the mounting post. Be sure that the LED wire and supply lines are not crimped by the bracket. The mounting bracket needs to be oriented correctly; check the manufacturer's instructions to ensure it's situated in the correct direction and secured with the metal side down.

Ensure the LED wire is not crimped, and thread the mounting-post nut on the mounting post. Hand-tighten. Check again that the faucet body is positioned correctly on the top of the sink and the LED light is facing forward. Tighten the mounting nut with a wrench or with the tool supplied by the manufacturer, as shown here.

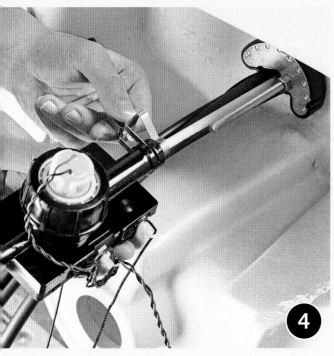

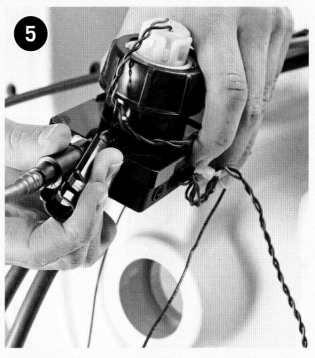

Insert the outlet tube into the top of the solenoid until it is snugly attached. Secure the tube in place with the metal clip provided. These clips can often be attached more than one way, so check the instructions to make sure you've installed the clip correctly. Then, lightly pull on the solenoid to ensure the tube is firmly attached and won't come free under pressure.

Slide the feeder hose into the bottom of the solenoid until it is snug. Snap the attachment clip in place to secure the hose, and again pull gently on the hose to make sure the clip is secure.

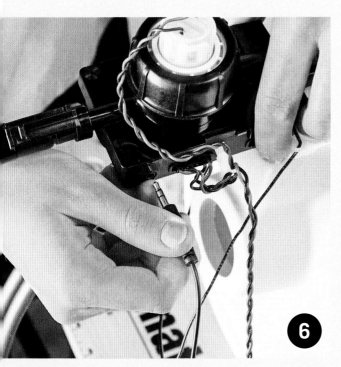

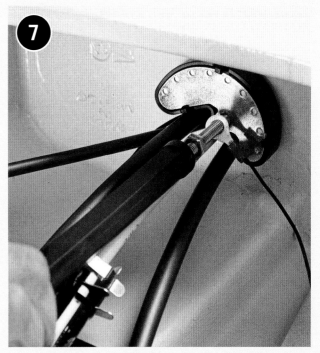

Touch the cold supply knob or another ground with your hand to dissipate any residual static charge. Remove the protective cap or endpiece from the end of the LED wire hanging from the faucet. Plug the prong of the wire into the hole in the solenoid. Make sure it is all the way in (on this model, you push until you hear a click).

Slide the solenoid ground wire onto the mounting post and secure it in place with a nut. Tighten the nut with a wrench, ensuring that the wires don't twist together. Put the batteries in the battery box, and then connect the wire from the solenoid to the connection on the battery box. Secure the battery box to the cabinet floor, wall, or underside of the sink. Set up the faucet touch feature and water temperature following the manufacturer's instructions.

Lavatory Drains

Pop-up stoppers are chrome-plated, long-legged plugs in bathroom sinks that are opened and closed with a knob behind the spout. The stopper itself is just the visible part of a behind-the-scenes assembly that makes sure the stopper sits and stands on cue. New faucets come with their own pop-up stopper assemblies, assuming they use one, but you may also purchase one by itself. This will include everything from the stopper to the pipe that drops into the trap. Choose a pop-up stopper assembly that's heavy brass under the chrome finish. This will hold up better to time and abuse than a plastic or light-gauge metal model.

TOOLS + MATERIALS

Channel pliers
Screwdriver
Plumber's putty

Teflon tape
Hacksaw or tin snips
(optional)

Installing a lavatory drain is a bit trickier than installing a kitchen-sink drain because most have a pop-up stopper with linkage.

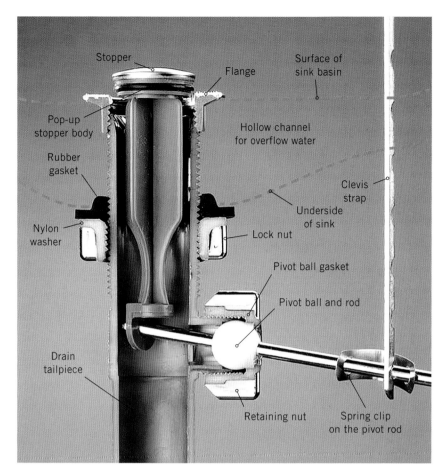

Stopper

Flange

Surface of sink basin

Pop-up stopper body

Hollow channel for overflow water

Rubber gasket

Clevis strap

Nylon washer

Underside of sink

Lock nut

Pivot ball gasket

Pivot ball and rod

Drain tailpiece

Retaining nut

Spring clip on the pivot rod

Pop-up stoppers keep objects from falling down the drain, and they make filling and draining the sink easy. When you pull up on the lift rod, the clevis strap is raised, which raises the pivot rod, which seesaws on the pivot ball and pulls the pop-up stopper down against the flange. This blocks water through the sink drain, but water may still overflow into the overflow channel drain through overflow ports in the pop-up body. This is a nice feature if you leave the water running in a plugged basin by mistake.

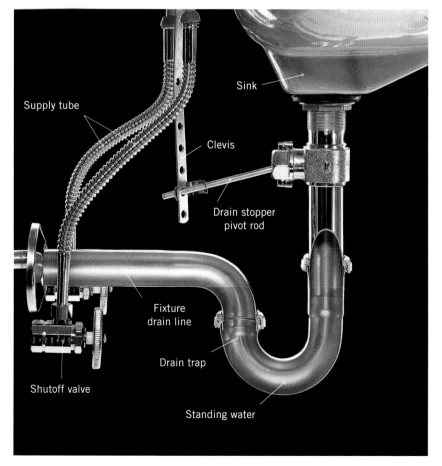

Supply tube

Sink

Clevis

Drain stopper pivot rod

Fixture drain line

Drain trap

Shutoff valve

Standing water

The lavatory drain trap holds water that seals the drain line and prevents sewer gases from entering the home. Each time a drain is used, the standing trap water is flushed away and replaced by new water. The shape of the trap and fixture drain line resembles the letter P, so sink traps are called P-traps.

How to Replace a Pop-Up Stopper

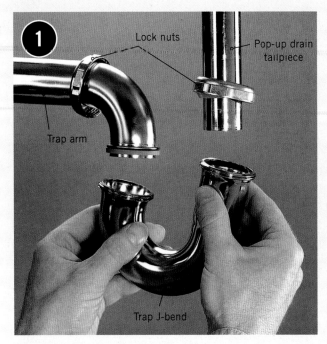

Put a basin under the trap to catch water. Loosen the nuts at the outlet and inlet to the trap J-bend by hand or with channel pliers, and remove the bend. The trap will slide off the pop-up body tailpiece when the nuts are loose. Keep track of washers and nuts and their up/down orientation by leaving them on the tubes.

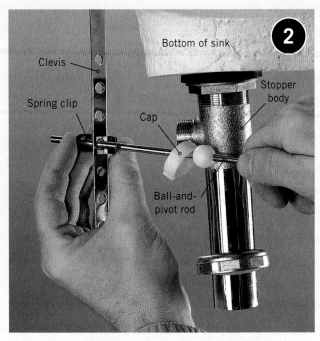

Unscrew the cap holding the ball-and-pivot rod in the pop-up body and withdraw the ball. Compress the spring clip on the clevis, and withdraw the pivot rod from the clevis.

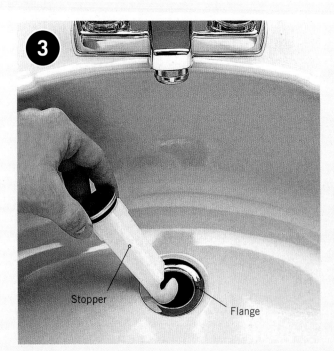

Remove the pop-up stopper. Then, from below, remove the lock nut on the stopper body. If needed, keep the flange from turning by inserting a large screwdriver in the drain from the top. Thrust the stopper body up through the hole to free the flange from the basin, and then remove the flange and the stopper body.

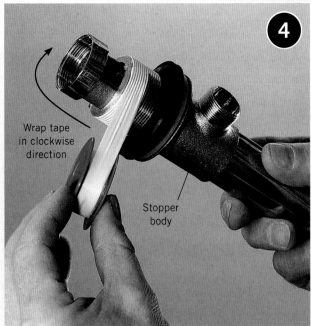

Clean the drain opening above and below, and then thread the locknut all the way down the new pop-up body followed by the flat washer and the rubber gasket (beveled side up). Wrap three layers of Teflon tape clockwise onto the top of the threaded body. Make a ½"-diameter snake from plumber's putty, form it into a ring, and stick the ring underneath the drain flange.

⑤

From below, face the pivot-rod opening directly back toward the middle of the faucet and pull the body straight down to seat the flange. Thread the locknut/washer assembly up under the sink, then fully tighten the locknut with channel pliers. Do not twist the flange in the process, as this can break the putty seal. Clean off the squeezeout of plumber's putty from around the flange.

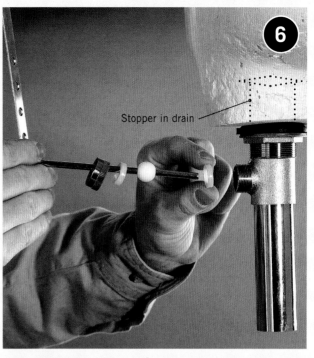

⑥

Stopper in drain

Drop the pop-up stopper into the drain hole so the hole at the bottom of its post is closest to the back of the sink. Put the beveled nylon washer into the opening in the back of the pop-up body with the bevel facing back.

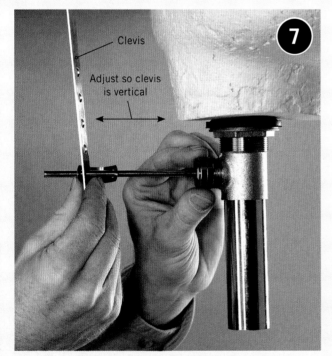

⑦

Clevis

Adjust so clevis is vertical

Put the cap behind the ball on the pivot rod, as shown. Sandwich a hole in the clevis with the spring clip and thread the long end of the pivot rod through the clip and clevis. Put the ball end of the pivot rod into the pop-up body opening and into the hole in the stopper stem. Screw the cap onto the pop-up body over the ball.

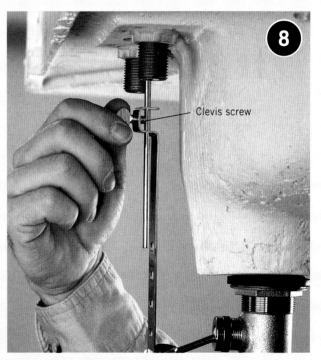

⑧

Clevis screw

Loosen the clevis screw holding the clevis strap to the lift rod. Push the pivot rod all the way down (which fully opens the pop-up stopper). With the lift rod also all the way down, tighten the clevis screw to the rod. If the clevis runs into the top of the trap, cut it short with a hacksaw or tin snips. Reassemble the J-bend trap.

Plumber's putty

Shower Kits

The fastest and easiest way to create a new shower in your bathroom is to frame in the stall area with lumber and drywall and then install a shower enclosure kit. Typically consisting of three fiberglass or plastic walls, these enclosure kits snap together at the corners and nestle inside the flanges of the shower pan (also called the receptor) to create nearly foolproof mechanical seals. Often, the walls are formed with shelves, soap holders, and other conveniences.

Although for purposes of this installation project, the version shown here is a plain, flat surface, you can choose from colored, textured, and faux surfaces that convincingly mimic the look of marble, ceramic tile, and other surfaces.

If you are on a tight budget, you can find extremely inexpensive enclosure kits to keep costs down. Some kits are sold with the receptor (and even the door) included. The kit shown here is designed to be attached directly to wall studs, but others require a backer wall for support. The panels are attached to the backer with high-tack panel adhesive.

A paneled shower surround is inexpensive and easy to install. Designed for alcove installations, they often are sold with matching shower pans (called receptors). A shower surround requires a minimum of 80" of clear ceiling height and 24" of clear opening area in front of the shower.

TOOLS + MATERIALS

Tape measure	Strap wrench	Hacksaw	Showerhead	Jigsaw
Pencil	Adjustable wrench	Masking tape	Faucet	Duct tape
Hammer	Pliers	Silicone caulk + caulk gun	Plumbing supplies	Miter box
Carpenter's square	Drill/driver		Panel adhesive	Eye protection
Screwdrivers	Center punch	Shower enclosure kit	Spud wrench	Work gloves
Pipe wrench	File	Pan (receptor)	Large-head roofing nails	
Level	Utility knife	Shower door		

How to Install a Shower Enclosure

Mark out the location of the shower on the floor and walls. Most kits can be installed over cementboard, but you can usually achieve a more professional-looking wall finish if you remove the wallcovering and floor covering in the installation area. Dispose of the materials immediately, and thoroughly clean the area.

Sill plate

If you are adding a wall to create the alcove, lay out the locations for the studs and plumbing on the new wood sill plate. Also lay out the stud locations on the cap plate that will be attached to the ceiling. Refer to the enclosure kit instructions for exact locations and dimensions of studs. Attach the sill plate to the floor with deck screws and panel adhesive, making sure it is square to the back wall and the correct distance from the side wall.

New wall stud

Install the 2 × 4 studs at the outlined locations. Check with a level to make sure each stud is plumb, and then attach them by driving deck screws toenail style into the sill plate and cap plate.

Align a straight 2 × 4 right next to the sill plate and make a mark on the ceiling. Use a level to extend that line directly above the sill plate. Attach the cap plate at that point.

(continued)

5

Cut an access hole in the floor for the drain, according to the installation manual instructions. Drill openings in the sill plate of the wet wall (the new wall in this project) for the supply pipes, also according to the instructions.

6

Install a drain pipe and branch line, and then trim the drain pipe flush with the floor. If you are not experienced with plumbing, hire a plumber to install the new drain line.

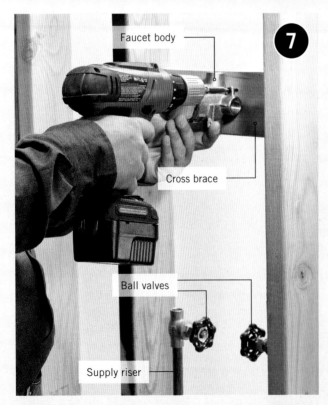

7

Faucet body

Cross brace

Ball valves

Supply riser

Install new supply risers as directed in the instruction manual (again, have a plumber do this if necessary). Also install cross braces between the studs in the wet wall for mounting the faucet body and shower arm.

8

If the supply plumbing is located in a wall (old or new) that is accessible from the non-shower side, install framing for a removable access panel.

9

Attach the drain tailpiece that came with your receptor to the underside of the unit, following the manufacturer's instructions precisely. Here, an adjustable spud wrench is being used to tighten the tailpiece.

OPTION: To stabilize the receptor, especially if the floor is uneven, pour a layer of self-leveling floor compound into the installation area, taking care to keep it out of the drain access hole.

10

Set the receptor in place, check to make sure it is level, and shim it if necessary. Secure the receptor with large-head roofing nails driven into the wall stud so the heads pin the flange against the stud. Do not overdrive the nails.

Lay out the locations for the valve hole or holes in the end wall panel that will be installed on the wet wall. Check your installation instructions. Some kits come with a template marked on the packaging carton. Cut the access hole with a hole saw and drill or with a jigsaw and fine-tooth blade. If using a jigsaw, orient the panel so the good surface is facing down.

11

(continued)

Clip connectors

Position the back wall so there is a slight gap (about ⅟₃₂") between the bottom of the panel and the rim of the receptor—set a few small spacers on the rim if need be. Tack a pair of roofing nails above the top of the back panel to hold it in place (or use duct tape). Position both end walls and test the fits. Make clip connections between panels (inset) if your kit uses them.

Remove the end walls so you can prepare the installation area for them. If your kit recommends panel adhesive, apply it to the wall or studs. In the kit shown here, only a small bead of silicone sealant on the receptor flange is required.

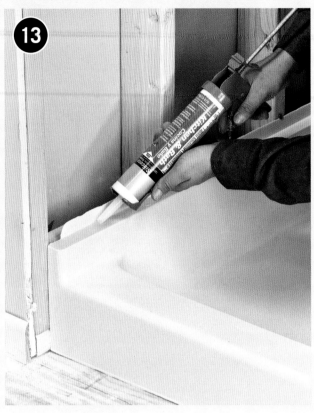

Reinstall the end panels, permanently clipping them to the back panel according to the kit manufacturer's instructions. Make sure the front edges of the end panels are flush with the front of the receptor.

Once the panels are positioned correctly and snapped together, fasten them to the wall studs. If the panels have predrilled nail holes, drive roofing nails through them at each stud at the panel tops.

Install wallcovering material above the enclosure panels and anywhere else it is needed. Use cementboard, and maintain a gap of ¼" between the shoulders of the top panel flanges and the wallcovering.

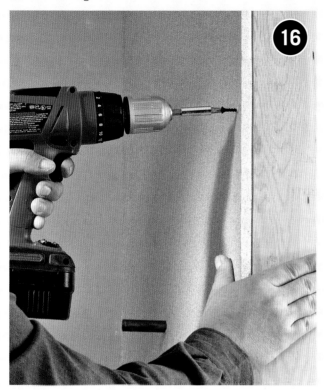

Finish the walls, and then caulk between the enclosure panels and the wallcoverings with tub-and-tile caulk.

Install the faucet handles and escutcheon, and caulk around the escutcheon plate. Install the shower arm escutcheon and showerhead.

You can make an access panel out of plywood framed with mitered case molding or buy a ready-made plumbing panel. Attach the panel to the opening created in step 8.

How to Install a Hinged Shower Door

Measure the width of the shower opening. If the walls of the shower slope inward slightly before meeting the base, take your measurement from a higher point at the full width of the opening so you don't cut the door base too short. Cut the base piece to fit using a hacksaw and a miter box. File the cut ends if necessary to deburr them.

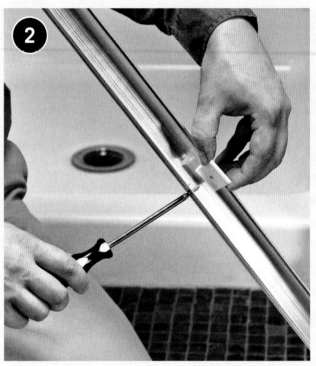

Place the base jamb on the curb of the shower base. If the joint where the wall meets the curb is sloped, you'll need to trim the corners of the base piece to follow the profile. Place a jamb carefully onto the base, and plumb it with a level. Then, mark a drilling point by tapping a centerpunch in the middle of each nail hole in each jamb. Remove the jambs, drill pilot holes, and then attach the jambs with the provided screws.

Identify which side jamb will be the hinge jamb and which will be the strike jamb according to the direction you want your hinged door to swing. Prepare the jambs for installation as directed in your instructions.

Remove the bottom track and prepare the shower base curb for installation of the base track, following the manufacturer's directions. Permanently install the bottom track. Bottom tracks (not all doors have them) are usually attached to the side jambs or held in place with adhesive. Never use fasteners to secure them to the curb.

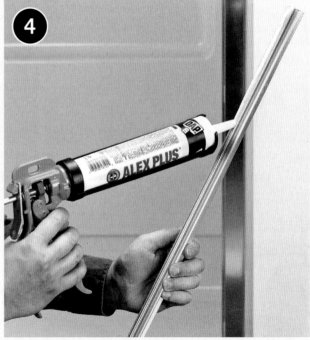

5

Working on the floor or another flat surface, attach the door hinge to the hinge jamb, if required. In most systems, the hinge is fitted over the hinge jamb after you attach it to the wall.

6

Attach the hinge to the door panel, according to the manufacturer's instructions. Attach any cap fitting that keeps water out of the jamb.

7

Fit the hinge jamb over the side jamb and adjust it as directed in your instruction manual. Once the clearances are correct, fasten the jambs to hang the door.

Sweep

8

Install the magnetic strike plate and any remaining caps or accessories, such as towel rods. Also attach the sweep that seals the passage, if provided.

Neo-Angle Shower

A neo-angle shower kit is a quick and simple solution for installing a shower in a smaller bathroom. This type of shower tucks into any corner with a wet wall, and most include the walls, doors, and even the shower pan. You may need to build a base pan for less expensive kits, but it's still an achievable DIY option that can transform a half-bath.

The kit used for this installation includes the shower pan, three wall pieces (two flat panels and a corner shelf/connector unit), and the glass panels and frames for the sliding door. All connectors and hardware are included, but this isn't the case with all such kits. When buying a shower kit, always examine the components and read the instructions carefully to see if additional parts and materials are needed.

The key to smooth installation with a wall-kit shower is making sure the wall panels, frames, and shower pan fit squarely in the corners and against the existing walls. Walls that are out of square or not perfectly flat can complicate this job, so correcting faulty walls is time well spent if you're installing a neo-angle shower.

Any shower kit will require very diligent and careful sealing of the joints using silicone caulk. Do not rush this step, because it is crucial to achieving a workable, leak-free shower.

TOOLS + MATERIALS

Neo-angle shower kit with shower pan	Straightedge	Carpenter's square	Clean cloths
Tape measure	Utility knife	Hammer	Plastic wall anchors
Pencil or marker	Silicone sealant	Center punch	Eye protection
4' level	Wall (panel) adhesive	Phillips screwdriver	Work gloves
Drill with bits + hole saw	Silicone caulk	Masking tape	
	Caulk gun	Mineral spirits	

How to Install a Neo-Angle Shower

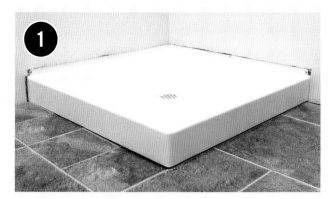

Prepare the floor drain and install a prefabricated shower pan in the corner of the room, following the instructions on steps 5 to 10 on pages 146 to 147. Make sure the outside diameter of the drain pipe matches the requirements of the shower pan (ours required a 2⅜" outside diameter for the drain pipe). The shower pan must sit perfectly level on the floor and tight against the wall studs on the two adjoining walls for the installation to proceed smoothly.

Drill holes and drive plastic wall anchors for the metal shower channels. The plastic wall anchors are included in most shower kits. If the channel falls on a wall stud, forego the anchors and screw it directly to the stud.

Position the wall channels in place and secure them to the wall with mounting screws driven through the mounting holes and into the wall anchors.

Draw centerlines along the top of the outer thresholds of the shower pan. Position one of the metal wall channels vertically against the wall, so the bottom edge is centered on the centerline. Use a level to adjust the wall channel for plumb, then mark the mounting-hole locations on the wall through the holes in the wall channel.

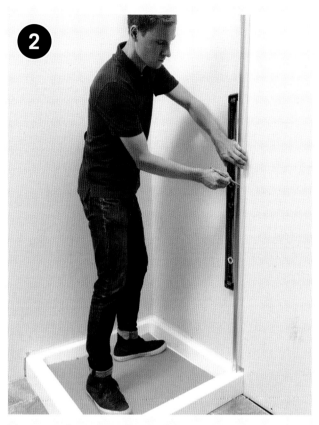

Fill the gaps between the shower base and the wall with silicone latex caulk. Install the other wall channel in the same way, and seal the remaining gap between the shower pan and the wall. Lightly sand the top face of the shower pan curbs with the sandpaper included in the kit. This will create a better bonding surface when you seal the pan at the end of the project. *(continued)*

Prepare the walls in whatever manner recommended by the kit instructions. Test-fit the side panels and the corner panel by taping them in place temporarily with masking tape, with the shiny side of the panels facing out. The wall panels should butt against the wall channels and rest flat against the shower-pan curbs. If the wall panels don't line up correctly, it indicates that the wall channels are out of plumb or the shower pan is not level. The corner panel should slightly overlap the side wall panels, by about ½". Some trimming may be necessary if the overlap is greater.

To prepare the side wall that will contain the plumbing fixtures, cut a cardboard template to the same size as the wall panel and place the template against the wall. Mark the location of the shower and faucet on the template. Make an X against this side of the cardboard for reference. Remove the cardboard template, then use a utility knife to cut openings for the plumbing stub-outs on the template. Test-fit the cardboard template against the wall, making sure the plumbing pipes fit correctly.

Use the template to mark the opening on the wall panel that will hold the shower plumbing fixtures, then use an appropriately sized hole saw to cut openings in the wall panel. Make sure to align the wall panel correctly when marking: the shiny side will face into the shower.

Beginning with the panel without plumbing cutouts, spread a continuous ¼" bead of panel adhesive along the four edges of the back of the wall panel, no closer than 2" to the edges. Leave gaps at the ends so air can escape when you press the panels against the wall. Also apply an S-shaped continuous bead to the center of the panel. Position the panel against the wall so the bottom rests firmly against the shower-pan curb and side edges are against the wall channel and the corner of the room. Press the panel against the wall firmly, and smooth it with even hand pressure until the panel is perfectly flat. Repeat with the wall that has plumbing cutouts, making sure to apply a bead of panel adhesive around the cutouts. Finally, apply panel adhesive to the back of the corner panel and press it into place. (Some shower models may have a connecting rod that joins the corner panel to the shower-pan unit.) If any excess adhesive has squeezed out around the edges of the panel, clean it away with a rag moistened with mineral spirits.

Following the kit instructions, begin assembling the doorframes. With our kit, the first step is to attach the center guide to the bottom rail using the screws included with the kit.

Stand the sliding door panels upright so the hanging brackets are at the top. Install the rollers on the same side of the door panels as the door stops.

Most shower kits have both stationary glass panels and sliding panels. Begin by installing the first stationary panel by inserting it into the wall channel so the roller channel at the side of the top rail is facing inside the shower stall. Now insert the sliding door panel on this side, so that the rollers engage the roller channel inside the top rail. Repeat this step with the opposite-side stationary panel and sliding door panel. Secure the top and bottom rails of the glass panels to the side channels and to one another using the corner connectors included with the kit.

(continued)

Install the seal strips on the back of both sliding door panels, as per the kit instructions. These pliable strips will allow the door to form a watertight seal against the stationary panels.

Make small adjustments to the entire assembly to center it on the top face of the shower pan curbs. Once you've positioned it correctly, so that the entire unit is plumb and the bottoms of the stationary panels are flat and level on the shower pan, drill holes in the frame through the adjustment holes in the glass frames and secure the unit to the wall channels with the provided screws. Test the doors and, if necessary, make small adjustments by loosening and then reattaching the roller screws at the top of the doors. Allow the shower unit to sit in place for 12 hours before beginning the waterproofing step.

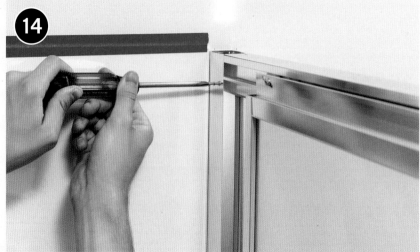

15

Waterproofing the shower requires the use of two different but similar-sounding products: siliconized latex caulk and silicone sealant. First, apply silicone caulk to the seams between the wall panels and corner panel, between the wall panels and the metal wall channels, the seam where the wall panels and corner panel meet the shower pan, and along the tops of the wall panels. Apply silicone sealant to the heads of all screws in the upright panel frames. From inside of the shower, apply silicone sealant along the seams where the bottom rails lie on the shower pan curb and along the bottoms of the wall channels and glass panel upright frames. Also apply silicone sealant around the center guide. Apply silicone sealant around the joint where the bottom rails butt up against the bottom connector. Finally, apply sealant to the heads of any exposed screws.

16

Let the caulked and sealed seams dry completely. To complete your shower, make the plumbing hookups of the shower faucet spray head and the shower valve. Test the shower to check for leaks.

Custom Shower Bases

Building a custom-tiled shower base lets you choose the shape and size of your shower rather than having its dimensions dictated by available products. Building the base is quite simple, though it does require time and some knowledge of basic masonry techniques because the base is formed primarily using mortar. What you get for your time and trouble can be spectacular.

Before designing a shower base, contact your local building department regarding code restrictions and to secure the necessary permits. Code requirements will have a major influence on the size and position of the base.

Custom shower bases are designed to be surfaced with tile: usually ceramic, porcelain, or glass. Choose your tile before finalizing the design of the base so you can minimize cutting where possible. Consider that larger floor tile (6 × 6 inches or longer) is less likely to develop leaks in the grout lines because there are fewer, and it also requires less cleaning and maintenance than smaller tiles, such as mosaic. At the same time, however, the existence of more grout lines makes the surface less slippery when wet.

A custom shower base allows you to create the perfect shower for your particular bathroom, not to mention the luxurious walk-in shower of your dreams.

Cross-Section of a Shower Pan

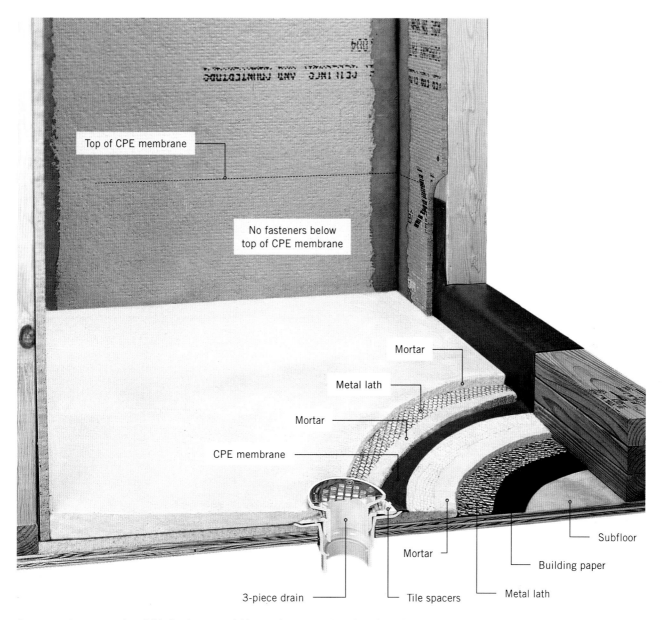

Top of CPE membrane

No fasteners below top of CPE membrane

Mortar

Metal lath

Mortar

CPE membrane

Subfloor

Building paper

Mortar

Tile spacers

Metal lath

3-piece drain

A custom shower pan is a fairly intricate, multi-layered construction, but choosing to build one gives you the ultimate design flexibility.

TIPS FOR BUILDING A CUSTOM SHOWER BASE

A custom-tiled shower base is built in three layers to ensure proper water drainage: the pre-pan, the shower pan, and the shower floor. A mortar pre-pan is first built on top of the subfloor, establishing a slope toward the drain of ¼" for every 12" of shower floor. Next, a waterproof chlorinated polyethylene (CPE) membrane forms the shower pan, providing a watertight seal for the shower base. Finally, a second mortar bed reinforced with wire mesh is installed for the shower floor, providing a surface for tile installation. If water penetrates the tiled shower floor, the shower pan and sloped pre-pan will direct it to the weep holes of the 3-piece drain. One of the most important steps in building a custom-tiled shower base is testing the shower pan after the CPE membrane has been installed. This allows you to locate and fix any leaks to prevent costly damage.

How to Build a Custom Shower Base

1

2

Remove building materials to expose subfloor and stud walls. Cut three 2 × 4s for the curb and fasten them to the floor joists and the studs at the shower threshold with 16d galvanized common nails. Also cut 2 × 10 lumber to size and install in the stud bays around the perimeter of the shower base. Install (or have installed) drain and supply plumbing.

Staple 15# building paper to the subfloor of the shower base. Disassemble the 3-piece shower drain and glue the bottom piece to the drain pipe with PVC cement. Partially screw the drain bolts into the drain piece, and stuff a rag into the drain pipe to prevent mortar from falling into the drain.

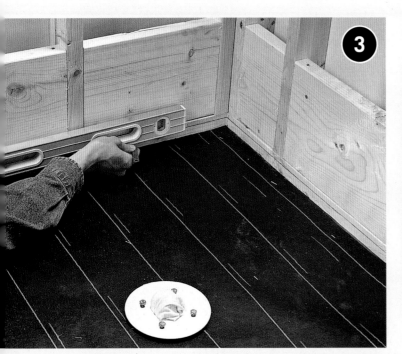

3

4

Mark the height of the bottom drain piece on the wall farthest from the center of the drain. Measure from the center of the drain straight across to that wall, then raise the height mark ¼" for every 12" of shower floor to slope the pre pan toward the drain. Trace a reference line at the height mark around the perimeter of the entire alcove using a level.

Staple galvanized metal lath over the building paper; cut a hole in the lath ½" from the drain. Mix thinset mortar to a fairly dry consistency using a latex additive for strength; mortar should hold its shape when squeezed (inset). Trowel the mortar onto the subfloor, building the pre-pan from the flange of the drain piece to the height line on the perimeter of the walls.

Continue using the trowel to form the pre-pan, checking the slope using a level and filling any low spots with mortar. Finish the surface of the pre-pan with a wood float until it is even and smooth. Allow the mortar to cure overnight.

Measure the dimensions of the shower floor, and mark it out on a sheet of CPE waterproof membrane using a felt-tipped marker (be sure to use a high-quality CPE shower liner; less-expensive PVC liners become brittle in time and can develop leaks). From the floor outline, measure out and mark an additional 8" for each wall and 16" for the curb end. Cut the membrane to size using a utility knife and straightedge. Be careful to cut on a clean, smooth surface to prevent puncturing the membrane. Lay the membrane onto the shower pan.

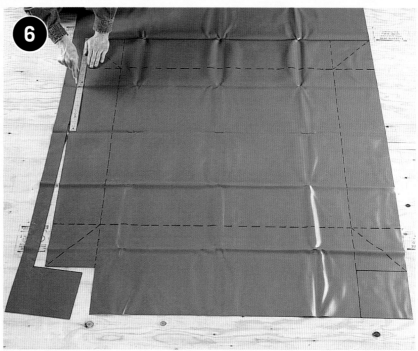

Measure to find the exact location of the drain and mark it on the membrane, outlining the outer diameter of the drain flange. Cut a circular piece of CPE membrane roughly 2" larger than the drain flange, then use CPE membrane solvent glue to weld it into place and reinforce the seal at the drain.

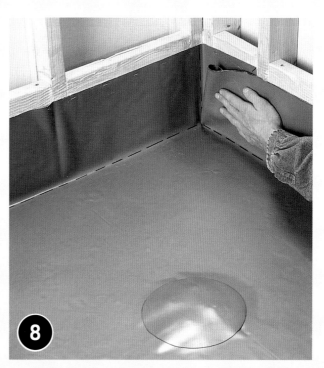

Apply CPE sealant around the drain. Fold the membrane along the floor outline. Set the membrane over the pre-pan so the reinforced drain seal is centered over the drain bolts. Working from the drain to the walls, carefully tuck the membrane tight into each corner, folding the extra material into triangular flaps.

(continued)

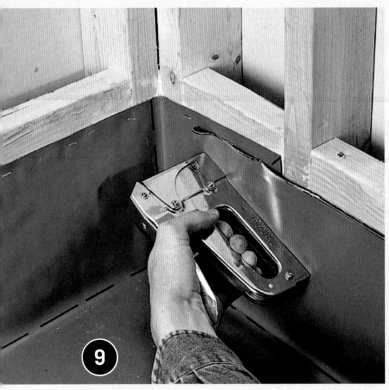

(9)

Apply CPE solvent glue to one side, press the flap flat, then staple it in place. Staple only the top edge of the membrane to the blocking; do not staple below the top of the curb or on the curb itself.

Dam corner

(10)

At the shower curb, cut the membrane along the studs so it can be folded over the curb. Solvent glue a dam corner at each inside corner of the curb. Do not fasten the dam corners with staples.

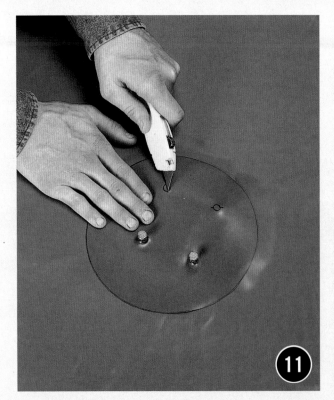

(11)

At the reinforced drain seal on the membrane, locate and mark the drain bolts. Press the membrane down around the bolts, then use a utility knife to carefully cut a slit just large enough for the bolts to poke through. Push the membrane down over the bolts.

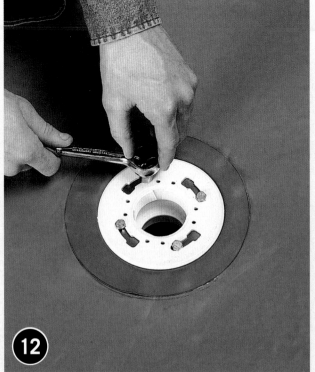

(12)

Use a utility knife to carefully cut away only enough of the membrane to expose the drain and allow the middle drain piece to fit in place. Remove the drain bolts, then position the middle drain piece over the bolt holes. Reinstall the bolts, tightening them evenly and firmly to create a watertight seal.

Test the shower pan for leaks overnight. Plug the drain and fill the shower pan with water, to 1" below the top of the curb. Mark the water level and let the water sit overnight. If the water level remains the same, the pan holds water. If the level is lower, locate and fix leaks in the pan using patches of membrane and CPE solvent.

Install cementboard on the alcove walls using ¼" wood shims to lift the bottom edge off the CPE membrane. To prevent puncturing the membrane, do not use fasteners in the lower 8" of the cementboard. Cut a piece of metal lath to fit around the three sides of the curb. Bend the lath so it tightly conforms to the curb. Pressing the lath against the top of the curb, staple it to the outside face of the curb. Mix enough mortar for the two sides of the curb.

Apply thinset mortar to the edges of the curb, using a straight board as a guide. When the mortar has set, remove the board and apply thinset to the top of the curb.

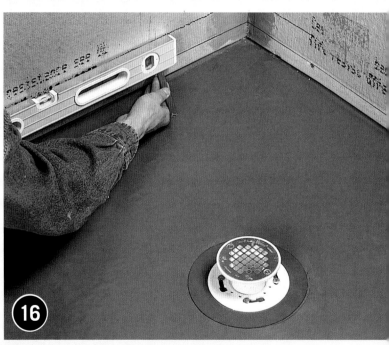

Attach the drain strainer piece to the drain, adjusting it to a minimum of 1½" above the shower pan. On one wall, mark 1½" up from the shower pan, then use a level to draw a reference line around the perimeter of the shower base. Because the pre-pan establishes the ¼" per foot slope, this measurement will maintain that slope.

(continued)

Spread tile spacers over the weep holes of the drain to prevent mortar from plugging the holes. Mix the floor mortar, then build up the shower floor to roughly half the planned thickness of this layer. Cut metal lath to cover the mortar bed, keeping it ½" from the drain (see photo in step 18).

Continue to add mortar, building the floor to the reference line on the walls. Use a level to check the slope, and pack mortar into low spots with a trowel. Leave space around the drain flange for the thickness of the tile. Float the surface until it is smooth and slopes evenly to the drain. When finished, allow the mortar to cure overnight before installing the tiles.

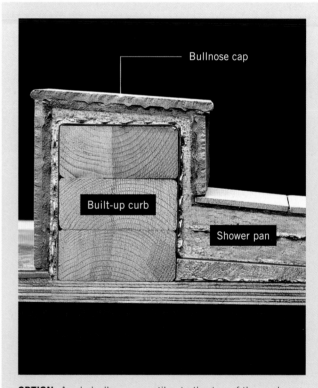

Install the tile. At the curb, cut the tiles for the inside to protrude ½" above the unfinished top of the curb, and cut the tiles for the outside to protrude ⅝" above the top, establishing a ⅛" slope so water drains back into the shower. Use a level to check the tops of the tiles for level as you work.

OPTION: Apply bullnose cap tiles to the top of the curb, sloping them toward the shower slightly. Make sure cap tiles overhang wall tiles.

Textured surfaces improve the safety of tile floors, especially in wet areas such as this shower. The shower floor has been finished with pebble tile that feels as good as it looks.

Mosaic tile, with its mesh backing and small shapes, works well on walls and on curved accents around this shower.

The raised curb on this open shower keeps most of the water headed toward the drain. But no matter, the entire bathroom is tiled, so stray droplets aren't a problem.

Wet Rooms + Curbless Showers

Wet rooms—a bathroom in which all surfaces are waterproof—are a sophisticated bathroom look and are becoming a popular option for American homeowners. They are also easy to clean and forgiving of random splashes and runaway streaming water.

The idea behind a wet room is that moisture doesn't need to be contained in any single area of the room, because the whole room is as waterproof as a shower stall. This alleviates the need for divider walls and enclosures, freeing up space and giving a wet room a seamless, streamlined look. Because of the space-saving aspects, wet rooms are particularly well suited for smaller bathrooms.

Installing a wet room involves laying down layers that work together to provide an impermeable barrier to water, in a process called "tanking." That process is made easy with the use of special rubberized waterproof tape and waterproofing compound that is simply rolled onto wall and floor surfaces. Some companies even provide complete wet room kits. The finished surface can be traditional tile (the most common choice), solid panels, such as the quartz composite surfaces used in contemporary vanity countertops, or sheet flooring, such as vinyl or linoleum.

In practice, the preliminary work is a lot like taping and skim coating a newly drywalled room. The more challenging aspects of wet room installation are making sure all the openings—from drains to water-supply inlets—are properly sealed with special membranes and correctly sloping the floor to a central drain. Normally, a wet room floor is sloped from all four corners for this purpose, but you can opt for a sleeker look with the use of a concealed linear "trench" drain along one edge of the room. This type of drain requires that the floor be sloped in one direction only.

Regardless of the drain used, wet rooms normally include a curbless shower, because there is no need to contain runoff water. Curbless showers present a sleek and sophisticated look, which is why homeowners are choosing to include them in many different

A curbless shower is a natural part of a wet room. A single wall surface material is commonly used on all walls for ease of installation and to unify the look.

bathrooms—including those that are not true wet rooms. Properly installed within an enclosure, a curbless shower can serve a traditional bathroom every bit as well as a raised-pan shower would.

Installing a curbless shower has become a feasible project for even modestly skilled home DIYers thanks to well-thought-out kits that include all the materials you'll need. Wet rooms, on the other hand, usually require professional installation to ensure the leaks never become a problem and that all applicable building codes are met.

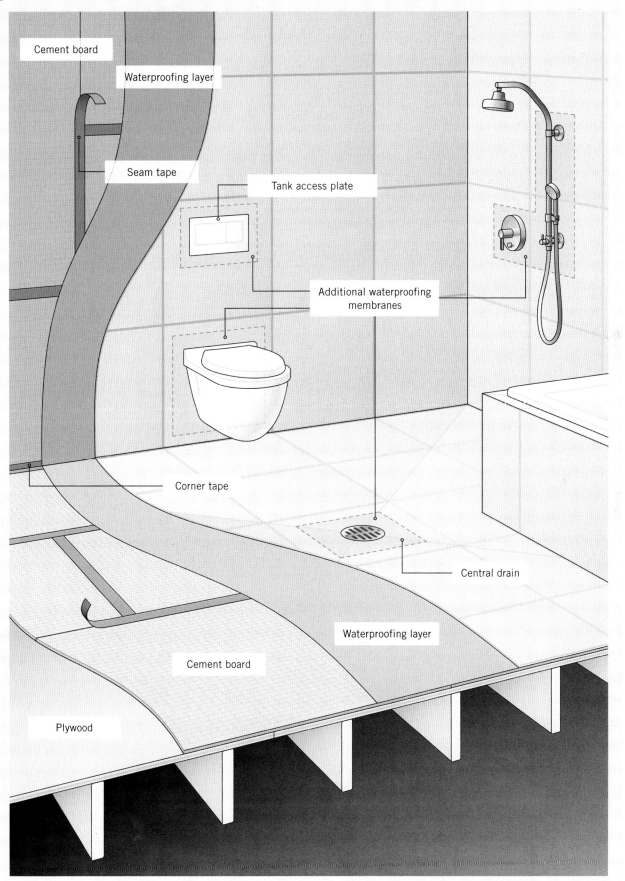

Cement board

Waterproofing layer

Seam tape

Tank access plate

Additional waterproofing membranes

Corner tape

Central drain

Waterproofing layer

Cement board

Plywood

Installing a Curbless Shower

Whether it's part of a complete "wet room" or installed as a standalone feature, a curbless shower combines easy access for those with limited mobility, convenience for other users, and a look that is trendy, sophisticated, and attractive. The trick to installing one of these water features is to ensure the moisture stays inside the shower.

Once upon a time, creating a reliably waterproof enclosure for a curbless shower was no small chore. It meant putting a lot of work into creating a custom shower pan. This kind of project was usually above the skill level or desire of the weekend DIYer, and it generally meant hiring a contractor.

Now you can buy curbless shower pan kits that make installation a breeze. The manufacturers have thought through all the issues that can arise and have developed the kits and shower pans to be as foolproof as possible, while also meeting prevailing codes and best standards and practices. Installing a curbless shower using one of these kits is a realistic project for any home handyperson with even moderate DIY skills and a weekend to spare.

These pans come with preconfigured slopes to ensure optimal drainage away from the shower's edges. The product we used for this project, a kit from AKW Resouce Center, includes an offset drain hole that offers the option of rotating the pan in the event a joist or mechanicals are in the way. This product is offered in many different sizes and can be cut with a circular saw to just about any shape—including more unusual, curvy shapes for a truly custom look.

Curbless shower pan manufacturers also sell pans with trench drains for an even sleeker look. The pan we used for this project is typical of the prefab curbless pan construction; it can support 1,100 pounds even though the pan itself weighs less than 70 pounds, and it sits right on top of floor joists, with the addition of blocking to support the area around the drain and to provide nailing surfaces around the edges.

Kits such as these offer advantages beyond the ease of installation and a thoughtful configuration of parts. Usually, the plumbing can be completely adjusted and connected from above, so you won't need to work in the basement or a crawl space or open up a first-floor ceiling to install a second-floor shower. The kits themselves generally include almost everything you'll need for the installation.

TOOLS + MATERIALS

Circular saw	Palm sander + 120-grit pad
Silicone caulk	Scissors
Torpedo level	Rubber gloves
Drill + bits	Paintbrush
PVC cement + brush	Roller + roller handle
Screwdriver	Eye protection
Speed square	Work gloves
Putty knife	Knee pads

A curbless shower kit includes almost everything you need. All you have to supply are some basic tools, the tile, and a little elbow grease.

WET ROOMS + UNIVERSAL DESIGN

Because a wet room allows the bathroom to be designed with fewer barriers and a single-level floor surface, these rooms are natural partners to a Universal Design approach. If you're thinking about converting a bathroom to a wet room, it's worthwhile to consider a little extra effort to make the space as accessible as possible for the maximum number of users.

Walls. Where codes allow it, consider using thick plywood rather than cementboard for the wall sub-surfaces. Plywood allows for direct installation of grab bars without the need for blocking or locating studs. If you're set on using cementboard, plan out locations for grab bars near toilets, behind and alongside bathtubs, and in showers. Most codes specify that grab bars must be able to support up to 200 pounds—which usually means adding blocking in the walls behind the grab bars.

Shower stall. One of the benefits to adding a curbless shower is easy wheelchair (or walker) access. For maximum accessibility, the shower area should be at least 60" wide by at least 36" deep (60" by 60" is preferable). This allows a wheelchair-bound user to occupy the stall with a helper. And, although the idea is a wide-open shower space, it's always a good idea to add a fold down seat. This allows for transfer from a wheelchair or a place for someone with limited leg strength and endurance to sit.

 How to Install a Waterproof Subbase for a Curbless Shower

Remove the existing flooring material in the area of the shower pan (if you're remodeling an existing bathroom). Use a circular saw to cut out and remove the subfloor in the exact dimensions of the shower pan. Finish the cuts with a jigsaw or handsaw.

Reinforce the floor with blocking between joists as necessary. Toenail bridge blocking in on either side of the drain waste pipe location and between joists anywhere you'll need a nailing surface along the edges of the shower pan. If trusses or joists are spaced more than 16" O.C., add bridge blocking to adequately support the pan.

(continued)

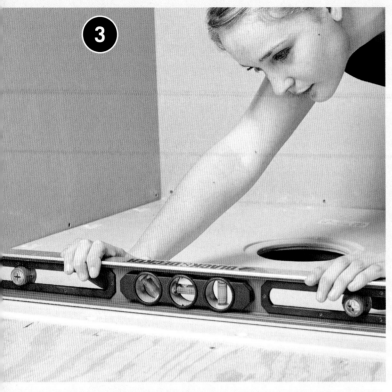

Set the pan in the opening to make sure it fits and is level. If it is not level, screw shims to the tops of any low joists and check again: repeat if necessary until the pan is perfectly level in all directions.

Install or relocate drain pipes as needed. Check with your local building department: if the drain and trap are not accessible from below, you may need to have an on-site inspection before you cover up the plumbing.

Check the height of the drainpipe. Its top should be exactly 2⅜" from the bottom of the pan. Measure down from the top of the joist. If the drainpipe is too high, remove it and trim with a saw. If it is too low, replace the assembly with a new assembly that has a longer tailpiece.

Lay a thick bead of construction adhesive along the contact areas on all joists, nailing surfaces, and blocking.

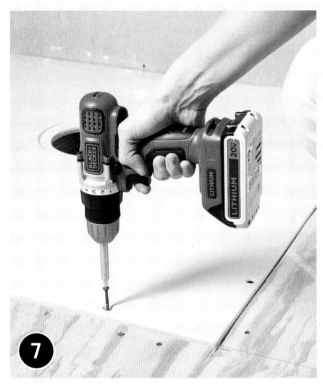

7

Set the pan in place and screw it down using at least 2 screws along each side. Do not overtighten the screws. If you've cut off the screwing flange on one or more sides to accommodate an unusual shape, drill ⅛" pilot holes in the cut edges at joist or blocking locations and drive the screws through the holes.

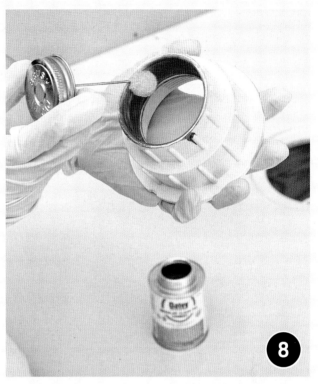

8

Disassemble the supplied drain assembly. Be careful not to lose any of the screws. Place the drain tailpiece on the waste pipe under where the pan's drainhole will be located, and measure to check that it sits at the correct level. Cement the tailpiece to the end of the waste pipe.

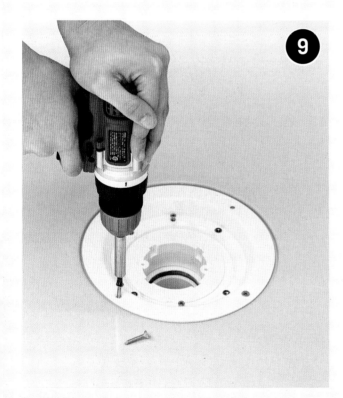

9

Position the supplied gaskets on top of the tailpiece (check the manufacturer's instructions; the gaskets usually need to be layered in the correct order). Set the drain flange piece on top of the tail and into the drain hole in the pan. Drill ⅛" pilot holes through the flange and into the pan. Screw the flange to the pan.

Thread the tail top piece into the tail through the drain flange. Use a speed square or other lever, such as spread channel pliers, to snugly tighten the tail top piece in place.

10

(continued)

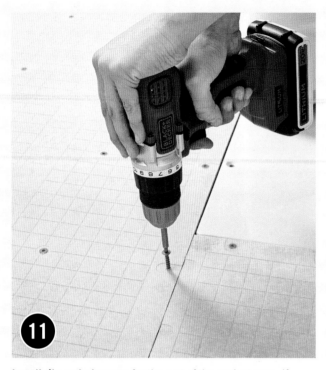

Install tile underlayment for the rest of the project area. If the underlayment is higher than the top of the pan once it is installed, you'll have to sand it to level, gradually tapering away from the pan.

Scrape any stickers or other blemishes off the pan with a putty knife. Lightly sand the entire surface of the pan using 120-grit sandpaper to help the sealant adhere. After you're done sanding, wipe down the sanded pan with a damp sponge. Make sure the entire area is clean.

Seal the edge seams at the wall and between the pan and subfloor with waterproof silicone sealant. Caulk any pan screw holes that were not used.

Cut strips of waterproofing tape to cover all seams in the tile underlayment (both walls and floor). Also cut strips for the joints where walls and floor meet. Open the pail of liquid waterproofing membrane and mix the liquid thoroughly. Beginning at the top and working down, brush a bed of waterproofing liquid over the seams. Before it dries, set the tape firmly into the waterproofing. Press and smooth the tape. Then brush a layer of waterproofing compound over the tape.

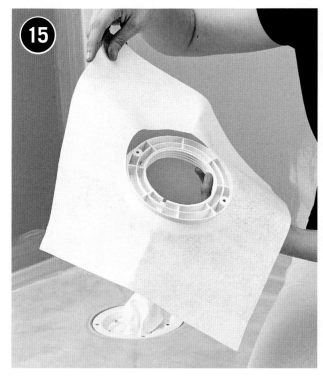

Trace a hole in the center of the waterproof drain gasket using the bottom of the drain clamping donut. Cut the hole out using scissors. Be careful cutting the gasket, because it is a crucial part of the drain waterproofing. Check the fit with the gasket against the underside of the clamping donut top flange.

Apply a thin coat of the waterproofing compound around the drain hole and to the back of the drain gasket. Don't apply too much; if the waterproofing is too thick under the gasket, it may not dry correctly.

Put the gasket in place and brush a coat of the waterproofing over the gasket. Screw the clamping donut in place on the top of the drain and over the membrane. Hand-tighten the bolts and then cover the clamping donut with the waterproofing compound (avoid covering the slide lock for the drain grate).

Use a roller to roll waterproofing compound across the walls and over the entire pan surface. The ideal is 4mm thick (about the thickness of a credit card). Allow this first coat to dry for 2 hours, then cover with a second coat. This should conclude the waterproofing phase of the project, and you're ready to begin laying tile once the waterproofing compound has dried thoroughly.

How to Tile a Curbless Shower

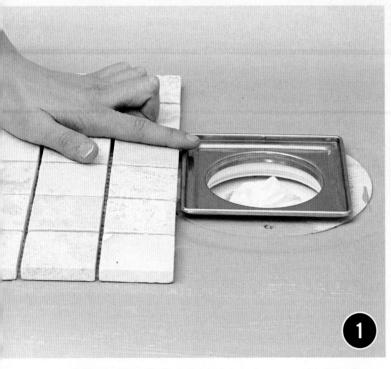

Set the floor tile first. Begin by placing a sample of the floor tile directly next to the drain so you can set the drain grate height to match. The adjustable mounting plate for the grate should be flush with the tops of the tile.

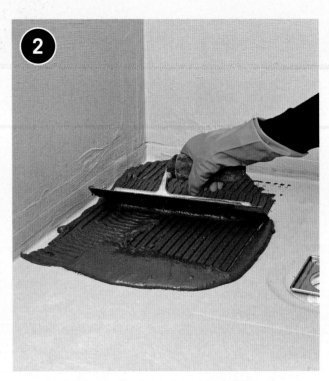

Begin laying floor tile in the corner of the shower. Lay a bed of thinset tile adhesive using a notched trowel. The thinset container should specify the notch size (⅜" square notch is common).

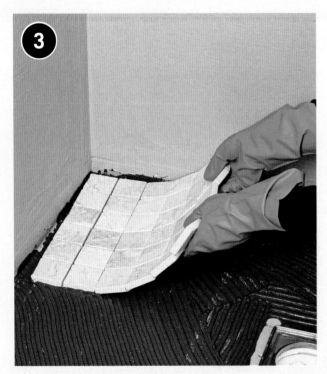

Place the corner tile into the bed of thinset and press it to set it. Don't press down too hard or you will displace too much of the material. Continue laying tile, fanning out from the corner toward the drain opening. Leave space around the drain opening, because you'll likely need to cut tiles to fit.

Install tile so a small square of untiled area is left around the drain opening (which, in the system seen here, is square, making for an easier cutting job).

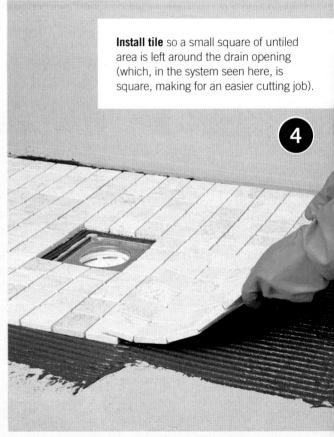

Mark the tiles that surround the drain opening for cutting. Leave a small gap between the tiles next to the drain grate mounting plate.

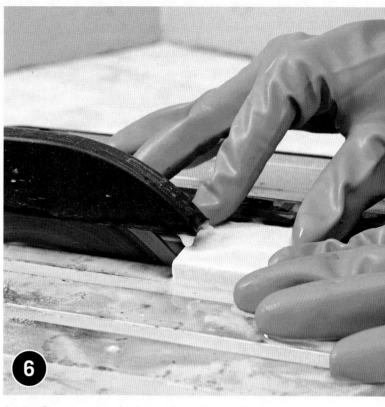

Cut the tiles along the trim lines using a tile saw. If you are not comfortable using a tile saw, score the tiles and cut them with tile nippers.

Apply mortar onto the shower pan, taking care not to get any on the drain grate mounting plate. You may need to use a small trowel or a putty knife to get into small gaps.

Set the cut tiles around the drain opening, doing your best to maintain even gaps that match the gaps in the rest of the floor. Once you've finished tiling around the drain, complete setting floor tile in the rest of the project area.

(continued)

Let the floor tile set overnight, and then apply grout. Using a grout sponge, wipe the grout over the gaps so all are filled evenly. After the grout dries, buff the floor with a towel to wipe up excess residue.

Snap the grate cover into the cover mounting plate (if you've stuffed a rag into the drain opening to keep debris out, be sure to remove it first). The grate cover seen here locks in with a small key that should be saved in case you need to remove the grate cover.

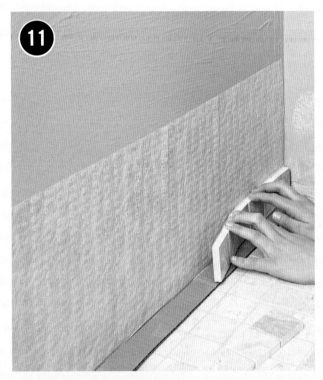

Begin setting the wall tile. Generally, it's easiest if you start at the bottom and work upward. Instead of thinset adhesive, an adhesive mat is being used here. This product is designed for walls and is rated for waterproof applications. It is a good idea to use a spacer (¼" thick or so) to get an even border at the bottoms of the first tiles.

In the design used here, a border of the same mosaic tile used in the floor is installed all around the shower area to make the first course. Dark brown accent tiles are installed in a single vertical column running upward, centered on the line formed by the shower faucet and showerhead. This vertical column is installed after the bottom border.

Next, another vertical column of accent tiles is installed on each side of the large, dark tiles. These columns are also laid using the floor tile, which connects the walls and floor visually in an effective way.

Finally, larger field tiles that match the floor tile used outside the shower area are installed up to the corner and outward from the shower area. Starting at the bottom, set a thin spacer on top of the border tiles to ensure even gaps.

Grout the gaps in the wall tiles. It's usually a good idea to protect any fittings, such as the shower faucet handle escutcheon, with painters tape prior to grouting. If you wish, a clear surround may be installed to visually define the shower area, as in the photo to the right, but because the shower pan is pitched toward the drain it really is not necessary.

Alcove Bathtubs

Most homes are equipped with an alcove tub (usually 60 inches long) that includes a tub surround and shower. Combining the tub and the shower in one fixture is a way to conserve precious bathroom floorspace and simplify the initial installation. Plus, only one fixture needs cleaning.

But because tub/showers are so efficient, they do get a lot of use and tend to have fairly limited lifespans. Pressed steel tubs have enamel finishes that crack and craze; plastic and fiberglass tubs get grimy and stained; even acrylic and composite tubs show wear eventually (and as with other fixtures, styles and colors change too). Fortunately, today's acrylic and fiberglass tubs have more durable finishes than those made a decade or two ago.

If you are not completely remodeling the bathroom, plan to make the new tub fit with its surroundings. For instance, if you have wall tiles, you'll need to remove some of them in order to remove and replace the tub. Make sure you can buy new tiles that exactly match the size and color of the existing tiles. Also check the width of the new tub; if it is narrower than the old tub, it may leave an untiled space on the floor that you will need to fill.

Plumbing an alcove tub is a relatively difficult job because getting access to the drain lines attached to the tub and into the floor is often very awkward.

Although an access panel is required by some codes, the truth is that many tubs were installed without them or with panels that are too small or hard to reach to be of much use. If you are contemplating replacing your tub, the first step in the decision process should be to find the access panel and determine if it is sufficient. If it is not (or there is no panel at all), consider how you might enlarge it. Often, this means cutting a hole in the wall of the adjoining room and also in the ceiling below. This creates more work, of course, but compared to the damage caused by a leaky drain from a subpar installation, making an access opening is little inconvenience.

An alcove tub can be every bit as stylish as any other type of tub, as long as you pay the same attention to the surround as you do to the rest of the room.

Left hand tub

Right hand tub

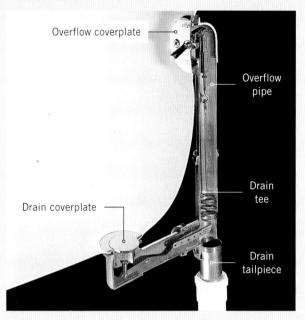

Overflow coverplate

Overflow pipe

Drain coverplate

Drain tee

Drain tailpiece

Choose the correct tub for your plumbing setup.
Alcove-installed tubs with only one-sided aprons are sold as either "left-hand" or "right-hand" models, depending on the location of the predrilled drain and overflow holes in the tub. To determine which type you need, face into the alcove and check whether the tub drain is on your right or your left.

A drain-waste-overflow kit with stopper mechanism must be purchased separately and attached after the tub is set. Available in both brass and plastic types, most kits include an overflow coverplate, an overflow pipe that can be adjusted to different heights, a drain tee fitting, an adjustable drain tailpiece, and a drain coverplate that screws into the tailpiece.

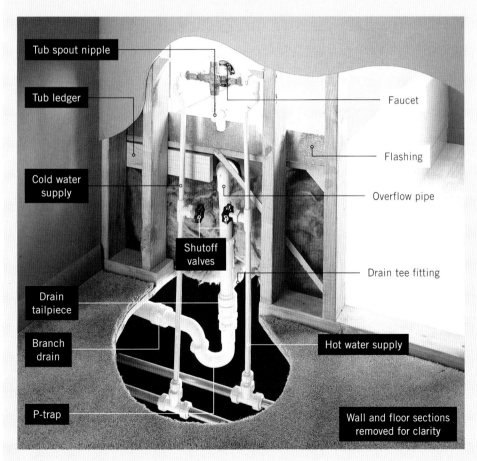

Tub spout nipple

Tub ledger

Cold water supply

Shutoff valves

Drain tailpiece

Branch drain

P-trap

Faucet

Flashing

Overflow pipe

Drain tee fitting

Hot water supply

Wall and floor sections removed for clarity

The supply system for a bathtub includes hot and cold supply pipes, shutoff valves, a faucet and handle(s), and a spout. Supply connections can be made before or after the tub is installed. PEX pipe can make this a much easier task.

The drain-waste-overflow system for a bathtub includes the overflow pipe, drain tee, P-trap, and branch drain. The overflow pipe assembly is attached to the tub before installation.

How to Install a New Alcove Tub

Prepare for the new tub. Inspect and remove old or deteriorated wall surfaces or framing members in the tub area. In just about every case, it makes sense to go ahead and strip off the old alcove wallcoverings and ceiling down to the studs so you can replace them. This also allows you to inspect for hidden damage in the wall and ceiling cavities. Plus, many codes no longer allow the use of moisture-resistant drywall (greenboard) in tub and shower areas. Cementboard should be used instead.

Check the subfloor for level—if it is not level, use pour-on floor leveler compound to correct it (ask at your local flooring store). Make sure the supply and drain pipes and the shutoff valves are in good repair, and correct any problems you encounter. If you have no bath fan in the alcove, now is the perfect time to add one.

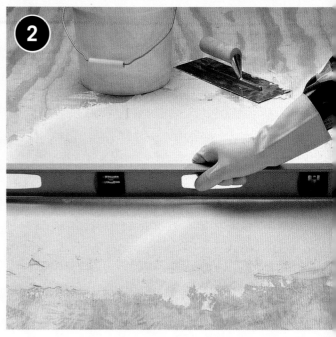

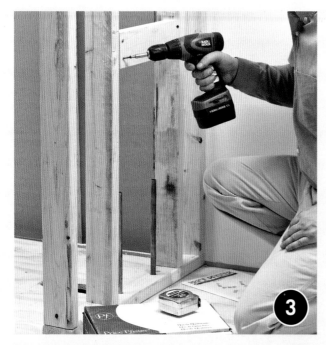

Check the height of the crossbraces for the faucet body and the showerhead. If your family members needed to stoop to use the old shower, consider raising the brace for the showerhead. Read the instructions for your new faucet/diverter and check to see that the brace for the faucet body will conform to the requirements (this includes distance from the surround wall as well as height). Adjust the brace locations as needed.

Begin by installing the new water supply plumbing. Measure to determine the required height of your shower riser tube and cut it to length. Attach the bottom of the riser to the faucet body and the top to the shower elbow.

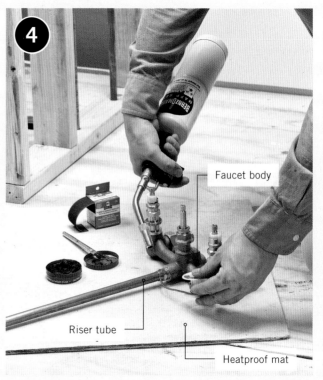

Faucet body

Riser tube

Heatproof mat

5

Attach the faucet body to the cross brace with pipe hanger straps. Then, attach supply tubing from the stop valves to the faucet body, making sure to attach the hot water to the left port and cold to the right port. Also secure the shower elbow to its cross brace with a pipe strap. Do not attach the shower arm yet.

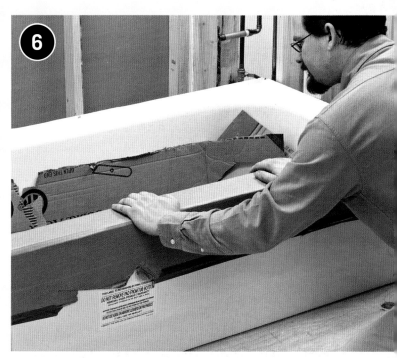

6

Slide the bathtub into the alcove. Make sure the tub is flat on the floor and pressed flush against the back wall. If your tub did not come with a tub protector, cut a piece of cardboard to line the tub bottom and tape pieces of cardboard around the rim to protect the finish from shoes and dropped tools.

7

Mark locations for ledger boards. To do this, trace the height of the top of the tub's nailing flange onto the wall studs in the alcove. Then remove the tub and measure the height of the nailing flange. Measure down this same amount from your flange lines and mark the new ledger board location.

8

Install 1 × 4 ledger boards. Drive two or three 3"-galvanized deck screws through the ledger board at each stud. All three walls should receive a ledger. Leave an open space in the wet wall to allow clearance for the drain-waste-overflow (DWO) kit. Measure to see whether the drain will line up with the tub's DWO. If not, you may need to cut and reassemble the drain.

(continued)

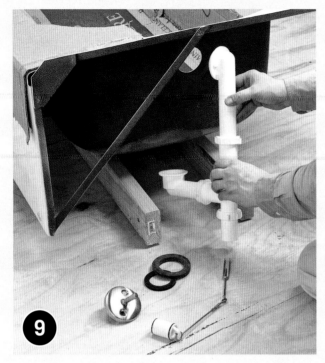

9

Install the DWO pipes before you install the tub. Make sure to get a good seal on the slip nuts at the pipe joints. Follow the manufacturer's instructions to make sure the pop-up drain linkage is connected properly. Make sure rubber gaskets are positioned correctly at the openings on the outside of the tub.

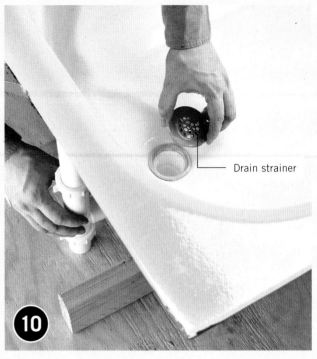

Drain strainer

10

Thread the male-threaded drain strainer into the female-threaded drain waste elbow. Wrap a coil of plumber's putty around the drain outlet underneath the plug rim first. Hand tighten only.

11

Attach the overflow coverplate, making sure the pop-up drain controls are in the correct position. Tighten the mounting screws that connect to the mounting plate to sandwich the rubber gasket snugly between the overflow pipe flange and the tub wall. Then, finish tightening the drain strainer against the waste elbow by inserting the handle of a pair of pliers into the strainer body and turning.

12

Working with a helper, place the tub in position, taking care not to bump the DWO assembly. If the DWO assembly does not line up with the drainpipe, remove the tub and adjust the drain location. Many acrylic, fiberglass, and steel tubs will have a much firmer feeling if they are set in a bed of sand-mix concrete. Check manufacturer's instructions and pour concrete or mortar as needed. Set the tub carefully back in the alcove.

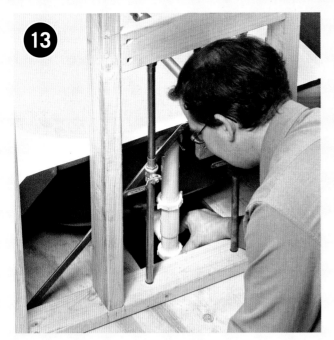

Attach the drain outlet from the DWO assembly to the drain P-trap. This is the part of the job where you will appreciate that you spent the time to create a roomy access panel for the tub plumbing. Test the drain and overflow to make sure they don't leak. Also test the water supply plumbing, temporarily attaching the handles, spout, and shower arm so you can operate the faucet and the diverter.

Drive a 1½" galvanized roofing nail at each stud location, just over the top of the tub's nailing flange. The nail head should pin the flange to the stud. Be careful here—an errant blow or overdriving can cause the enameled finish to crack or craze.

OPTION: You may choose to drill guide holes and nail through the flange instead.

Install the wallcoverings and tub surround. You can also make a custom surround from tileboard or cementboard and tile. Many codes no longer allow the use of moisture-resistant drywall (greenboard) in tub and shower enclosures; choose cementboard instead.

Install fittings. First, thread the shower arm into the shower elbow and attach the spout nipple to the valve assembly. Also attach the shower head and escutcheon, the faucet handle/diverter with escutcheon, and the tub spout. Use Teflon tape on all threads.

Sliding Tub Doors

Curtains on your bathtub shower are a hassle. If you forget to slide them closed, mildew sets up shop in the folds. And every time you brush against them, they stick to your skin. Shower curtains certainly don't add much elegance or charm to a dream bath. Neither does a deteriorated door. Clean up the look of your bathroom, and give it an extra touch of elegance, with a new sliding tub door.

When shopping for a sliding tub door, you have a choice of framed or frameless. A framed door is edged in metal. The metal framing is typically aluminum but is available in many finishes, including those that resemble gold, brass, or chrome. Glass options are also plentiful. You can choose between frosted or pebbled glass, clear, mirrored, tinted, or patterned glass. Doors can be installed on ceramic tile walls or onto a fiberglass tub surround.

A sliding tub door framed in aluminum gives the room a sleek, clean look and is just one of the available options.

How to Install a Sliding Tub Door

Remove the old door if there is one, then inspect the walls and tub ledge for plumb and level. Also remove any remaining old caulk or residue.

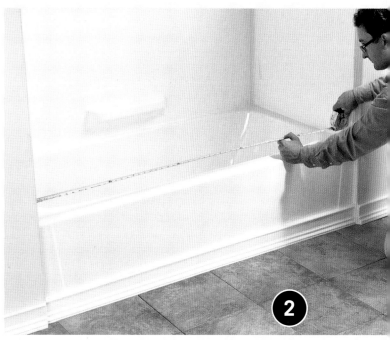

Measure the distance between the finished walls along the top of the tub ledge. Refer to the manufacturer's instructions for figuring the track dimensions. For the product seen here, ³⁄₁₆" is subtracted from the measurement to calculate the track dimensions.

Using a hacksaw and a miter box, carefully cut the track to the proper dimension. Center the track on the bathtub ledge with the taller side out and so the gaps are even at each end. Tape into position with masking tape.

Place a wall channel against the wall with the longer side out, and slide it into place over the track so they overlap. Use a level to check the channel for plumb, and then mark the locations of the mounting holes on the wall with a marker. Repeat for the other wall channel. Remove the track.

(continued)

5

Drill mounting holes for the wall channel at the marked locations. In ceramic tile, mark the surface of the tile with a center punch, use a ¼" masonry bit to drill the hole, and then insert the included wall anchors. For fiberglass surrounds, use a ⅛" drill bit; wall anchors are not necessary.

6

Apply a bead of silicone sealant along the joint between the tub and the wall at the ends of the track. Apply a minimum ¼" bead of sealant along the outside leg of the track underside.

Position the track on the tub ledge and against the wall. Attach the wall channels using the provided screws. Do not use caulk on the wall channels at this time.

7

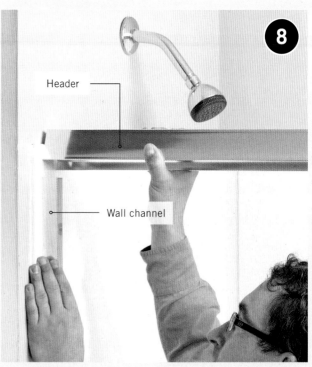

8

Header

Wall channel

Cut and install the header. At a location above the tops of the wall channels, measure the distance between the walls. Refer to the manufacturer's instructions for calculating the header length. For the door seen here, the length is the distance between the walls minus ¹⁄₁₆". Measure the header and carefully cut it to length using a hacksaw and a miter box. Slide the header down on top of the wall channels until seated.

9

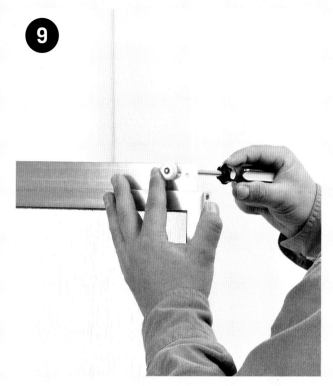

Mount the rollers in the roller mounting holes. To begin, use the second-from-the-top roller mounting holes. Follow the manufacturer's instructions for spacer or washer placement and orientation.

Roller

Carefully lift the inner panel by the sides and place the rollers on the inner roller track. Roll the door toward the shower end of the tub. The edge of the panel should touch both rubber bumpers. If it doesn't, remove the door and move the rollers to different holes. Drive the screws by hand to prevent overtightening.

10

11

Lift the outer panel by the sides with the towel bar facing out from the tub. Place the outer rollers over the outer roller track. Slide the door to the end opposite the shower end of the tub. If the door does not contact both bumpers, remove the door and move the rollers to different mounting holes.

12

Apply a bead of clear silicone sealant to the inside seam of the wall and wall channel at both ends and to the U-shaped joint of the track and wall channels. Smooth the sealant with a fingertip dipped in water.

Jetted Tub

Historically called "whirlpool" tubs—or lumped under the brand name Jacuzzi—jetted tubs are not a single type of bathroom fixture. Technologies vary, and jetted tubs come in diverse sizes and shapes to suit bathrooms from modest to grand. In fact, the only thing they all share is that any jetted tub adds undeniable luxury and comfort to the home.

The big difference lies in the jets. Tubs are equipped with either air jets that blow warmed air into the tub water or water jets that recirculate heated tub water under pressure. Both include a heater, pump, and integral plumbing, that is installed on the tub when it's manufactured. Most require a 220-volt outlet or a direct connection to a 220-volt circuit. A few rare models—and a larger number of older units—do not include a heater (which means they can be plugged into an ordinary 110-volt GFCI outlet). Older unheated tubs can be upgraded, although it is usually worth the additional expense to just buy a new unit complete with integral heater.

Jetted tubs come in the same range of installation styles as standard tubs. Most require more space, however, to allow for the internal plumbing and mechanicals. Apron models can be installed in alcoves, while drop-in styles require the construction

of a custom deck around the tub. That is not only a chance to add style and extra space for drinks, towels, and candles, it also allows you to build in access to plumbing and mechanicals for future maintenance and repairs.

TOOLS + MATERIALS

Jetted tub	PVC primer + cement
Tub faucet	Claw hammer
Thin set mortar	8d nails
Circular saw	Circuit boxes
4' level	Wire strippers
Carpenter's pencil	
Tape measure	Wire nuts
2 × 4, 2 × 6, + plywood sheet lumber	Sponge
	Shovel
Safety glasses	6-mil plastic sheeting
Cement board	Staple gun and staples
Tile	
Keyhole saw	Drill + bits
Jigsaw	Adjustable wrenches
PVC pipe	Heavy-duty work gloves

The simple apron tub here is not typical of most jetted tubs, but is a great way to have the luxury of massaging jets in the confines of a smaller bathroom (this unit is only 30" wide by 60" long). Custom tile adds to the special nature of the tub, and helps blend the tub's knee wall and faucet into the look of the room.

Jetted Tub Options

Jetted tub technologies have evolved to accommodate many different bathing preferences and installation situations. Although this type of tub is more expensive than any other, they also offer an unprecedented level of comfort and luxury, and even a therapeutic value. If you suffer from chronic joint issues such as arthritis, fibromyalgia, or other conditions, a jetted tub can offer tremendous relief.

• **Air jets.** Air is drawn in from the room, heated, and then blown into the tub water. This creates a gentler massage effect than water jets do. Depending on the location and power, the jets produce different types of bubbles for different effects—such as bubbles rising up around the bather or blowing directly onto the body. Air jets require simpler mechanicals, which translates to a slightly lower cost than water jet tubs. However, the jets cannot be adjusted—they just force air straight out at a constant pressure. Even though the air is heated, this type of tub loses heat more quickly than a water-jet unit. The trade-off is that air jets are easier to keep clean and maintain. Air-jet tubs are also much better for bathers who regularly use lotions, bath gels, salts, or other bath additions. Those water-borne chemicals can gum up water jets and the plumbing, because it recirculates the water from the tub. An air jet tub is a good option for anyone looking for a low-maintenance, relaxing experience.

• **Water jet.** This is usually what people think of when they envision a "whirlpool" tub. Water is circulated from the tub, through a heater, and then forced back into the tub through jets. The stream from the jets is more powerful than from air jets, and the massaging action is more vigorous. The direction and force of the jets can often be adjusted. The downside to that power is that the lines should be cleared after each use to avoid mildew and soap scum buildup. Keeping the tub clean is more of a challenge than with air-jet models, and water-jet tubs are usually best for someone who can make therapeutic use of the strong massaging action, such as people who suffer from arthritis or chronic joint or back pain, and active athletes.

Other variables affect both comfort and price. The more jets the bathtub has—and the more adjustable they are—the more expensive the tub will be. Of course, more jets and adjustability give the bather greater control over the experience. The same is true of settings; a range of power settings for jets means a bigger price tag. But it also means that you can dial back the massage when you want a low-key bath, and

A round jetted tub takes up more space than a rectangular version, but allows more flexible positioning for the bather to ensure that jets massage sore spots in just the right way.

Where the budget allows, make a drop-in jetted tub the star of the show, with its own custom deck and lighting. This one features a comfy headrest and multiple controls for an ultimate bathing experience. The deck is big enough to allow easy access to plumbing and heater if repairs are ever needed.

kick it up for the occasions where you're sore from a hard day of weeding the garden and working around the house.

Size and shape will also radically affect the price of any bathtub. Fortunately, you'll find jetted tubs in every style and configuration, from apron versions that fit snugly into an existing alcove, to spacious yet space-conserving corner tubs, to deep standalone versions with their own flair.

Lastly, some high-end tubs come with deluxe options such as adjustable and changeable tub lighting, and integral speakers for bathers who like to play tunes when enjoying a long soak.

Jetted Tub Installation

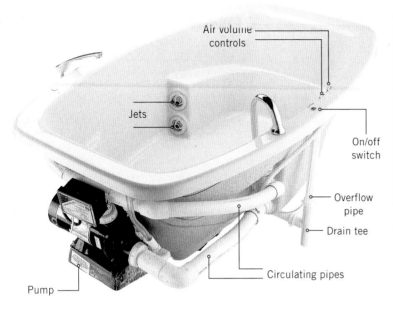

A whirlpool circulates aerated water through jets mounted in the body of the tub. Whirlpool pumps move as much as 50 gallons of water per minute to create a relaxing hydromassage effect. The pump, pipes, jets, and most of the controls are installed at the factory, making the actual hookup in your home quite simple.

Ledger boards may be tacked to the stud walls in the tub installation area. These are for leveling purposes only and are not intended to support the weight of the tub and its contents. Support should be left to the subfloor and joists. If you are installing a tub where there previously was none, check with a building inspector to confirm that the structural members in the installation area are adequate.

A drop-in tub has no apron and is designed to be installed in a framed deck. These decks, typically finished with cementboard and tile, are largely cosmetic and should contain access panels as required by the tub manufacturer. Often, they house a deck-mounted faucet. The deck is not intended to support the tub rim, so leave a small gap between the finished deck and the tub.

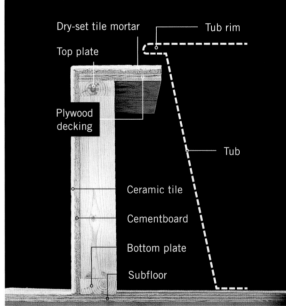

A stub wall may be required at one or both ends of the tub so you can create an access panel to the pump. Stub walls also may be used to install supply and drain plumbing and to mount an electrical box to supply power to the pump motor or heater. The stub wall should not be used to support the tub rim.

How to Install a Jetted Tub

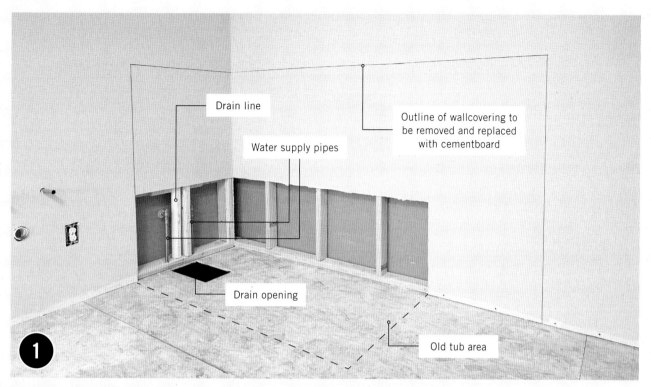

Drain line

Water supply pipes

Outline of wallcovering to be removed and replaced with cementboard

Drain opening

Old tub area

①

Remove the old tub. It is always easiest to replace a tub with one of the same size and orientation. However, if you are upgrading to a jetted tub consider choosing one that is larger than the standard tub you are replacing. In many cases, a wider tub may be installed with very minimal adjustment to the plumbing. The 32"-wide by 60"-long whirlpool tub that is being installed in this project is the same size as the old tub, but in order to accommodate a small deck at the head of the tub (for mounting the faucet set) the drain pipe needed to be extended outward 12". Also, a dedicated 20-amp GFCI electrical circuit needed to be installed for the pump.

NOTE: The model of tub you select, as well as the overall installation method, will determine the exact sequence of steps necessary to install, plumb, and wire your tub. Always read the manufacturer's instructions closely and make certain to follow them.

Remove the tub apron (if it has a removable apron) and set the tub so it fits against the stud walls in the installation area. Shim underneath the tub so it is perfectly level (some models have adjustable feet).

Mark the height of the tub rim or flange onto the wall studs and then remove the tub. If you are using leveling ledgers, you can attach them to the studs directly below the lines. In the installation seen here, a small stub wall will be made for the head and the foot of the tub. If this is your plan, measure from the floor to your reference lines to determine how tall you should build your stub wall or walls.

③

(continued)

Build a small wall frame for the head and the foot using ¾" plywood and 2 × 4s or 2 × 6s. Size the walls so they will be a fraction of an inch shorter than the reference lines near the head and foot locations; include the thickness of the tile backer you are using in the height. The tub seen here has a vertical flange all the way around the rim, so the tile on the tops of the finished walls should just overlap the flange. Secure the wall frames by toe-nailing at floor joist locations.

Tub flange reference line

Extend the old drain hole in the subfloor if necessary. Because of the 12"-wide stub wall at the tub head, the new tub is a foot further away from the wall than the old tub.

Make plumbing connections for the new drain line and P-trap, making sure that the new drain pipe has the correct minimum slope and that the trap is positioned so it will align precisely with the tailpiece on the tub drain kit.

Install electrical boxes and run new circuits if needed to supply power to the tub. If you are not comfortable doing your own wiring or local codes don't allow it, hire a professional electrician. The tub seen here does not have an in-line water heater, so it requires electrical service for the pump motor only—a dedicated 20-amp circuit with GFCI protection. Orient the electrical boxes so the receptacle they contain will be easily accessible from the access panel opening in the walls or tub skirt.

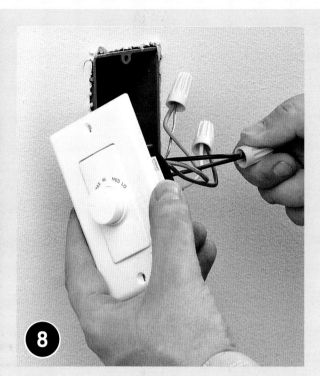

8

OPTION: Install wall-mounted controls for turning the pump on and off and for setting the temperature controls if your tub has a heater. You will need to have all new wiring inspected and approved by your local electrical inspector.

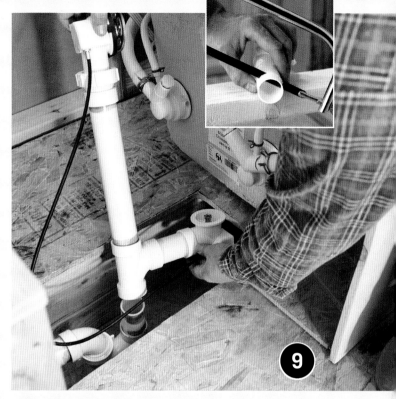

9

Attach the drain/overflow pipe assembly to the tub prior to installation using rubber gaskets and pipe joint compound. Measure the distance the drain tailpiece will need to drop to connect with the drain trap, and trim the tailpiece to fit (inset).

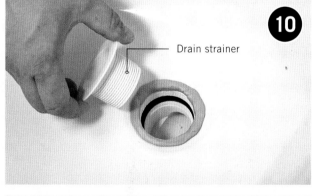

10

Drain strainer

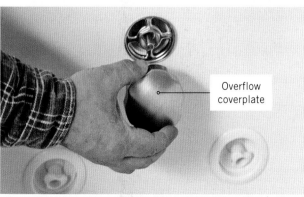

Overflow coverplate

Secure the drain/overflow assembly by tightening the overflow coverplate and the drain strainer onto the assembly from inside the tub.

Mix a batch of thinset mortar and shovel it in a 1"-thick layer in the tub installation area, limiting the material to just those areas that will contact the tub bottom. In many cases, the tub has several pads adhered to the underside that function as feet.

TIP: Moisten the subfloor so it does not draw water out of the thinset too quickly.

11

(continued)

Slide or lower the tub into the installation area, taking care not to disturb the drain/overflow assembly. Make sure the drain tailpiece aligns exactly over the P-trap opening. Seat the tub or tub feet into the mortar bed—apply pressure as needed until the tub aligns with your leveling reference marks or ledgers.

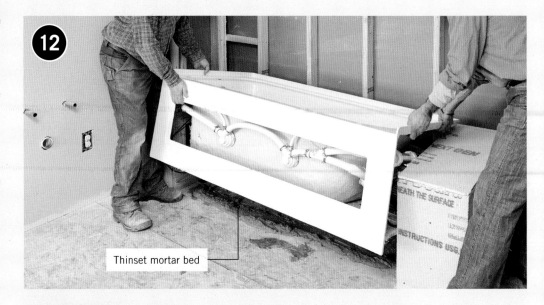

Thinset mortar bed

Double check to make sure the tub is level. If it is too low in any spot, add thinset mortar underneath the tub or foot at that spot. Let the mortar dry overnight.

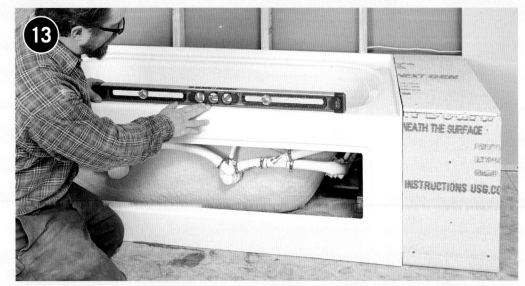

Connect the drain tailpiece from the DWO kit mounted on the tub to the trap in the drain opening. You should be able to access this connection if you reach through the apron area in the front of the tub skirt. Plug the pump motor into the dedicated GFCI circuit. Reattach the tub apron.

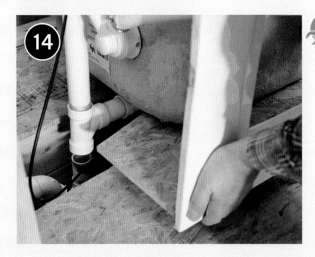

 TIP

Test the drain system to make sure it does not leak. Using a hose, first add a small amount of water and visually inspect the slip fittings and the area around the drain body. If it looks good, fill the tub up past the overflow line to make sure the overflow pipe seal does not leak. Drain the tub.

How to Finish a Jetted Tub

Install a vapor barrier around the tub area by stapling 6-mil plastic sheeting to the wall studs. This is not intended as a waterproofing measure and is not a substitute for a waterproof membrane if you are creating a shower surround.

Install wall surface in the tub area. Use cementboard. Once all the surfaces, both horizontal and vertical, are covered, begin marking layout lines for the tile you're using. Install your finished wall coverings (tile in most cases).

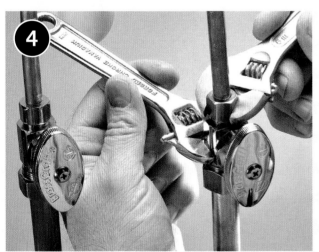

Install the spout supply valves and hook them up to the supply risers. Tubs are not predrilled for faucets as sinks are, so you'll need to decide whether to drill holes for the valves in the tub rim using a step bit or to mount the faucet in the platform or the rim of the support wall.

Attach the spout and the valve handles, and test the supply system. To clear any debris from the lines, remove the spout aerator and run both hot and cold water for a minute or so.

Water Softeners

If your house has hard water coursing through its pipes, then you've got a couple of problems. Not only does your water do a poor job of dissolving soap, but you also have plenty of scale deposits on dishes, plumbing fixtures, and the inside of your water heater.

Softeners fix these problems by chemically removing the calcium and magnesium that are responsible for the hard water (usually described as over 17 grains of minerals per gallon). These units are installed after the water meter but before the water line branches off to appliances or fixtures, with one exception: Piping to outside faucets should branch off the main line before the softener, because treating outside water is a waste of money.

Softeners come with an overflow tube and a purge tube to rinse out the minerals that are extracted from the water. These tubes should drain to a floor drain or to a laundry sink basin, which is the better approach if the sink is close by. Remember to leave an air gap between the tube and the sink or floor drain. Do not connect the tube directly to a drain or vent pipe.

KNOW YOUR TYPES OF SALT

Salt for water softeners comes in three basic types: rock salt, solar salt (crystals), and evaporated salt (pellets). Rock salt is a mineral that's mined from salt deposits. Solar salt is a crystalline residue left behind when seawater is evaporated naturally. It sometimes is sold as pellets or blocks. Evaporated salt is similar to solar salt, but the liquid in the brine is evaporated using mechanical methods. Rock salt is cheapest but leaves behind the most residue and therefore requires more frequent brine tank cleaning. Evaporated salt pellets are the cleanest and require the least maintenance.

TOOLS + MATERIALS

Tape measure	Steel wool
Tubing cutter	Soldering flux
Propane torch	Solder
Slip-joint pliers	4"-thick concrete blocks

A modern water softener is a single appliance, with the softener resting on top of the salt storage tank.

3-VALVE BYPASS

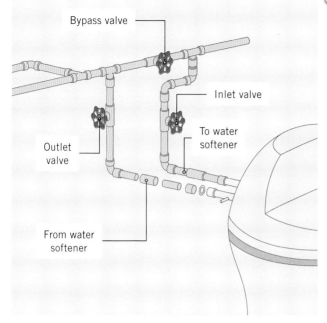

Bypass valve

Inlet valve

To water softener

Outlet valve

From water softener

In some areas you are required to install a water softener with three valves, as shown. This arrangement allows you to bypass the water softener so water can run to the house when and if the softener is disconnected.

SOFTENED WATER

From your plumbing's point of view, the best water softening strategy is to position the softener close to the main, cold-only supply line (as seen here). Doing this results in both hot and cold water being softened. But because some homeowners object to the altered taste and increased salinity of softened water, the softener may be installed after the hot and cold lines have split from the main supply line. This way, the water may be softened immediately before it enters the heater, and the cold water remains unsoftened.

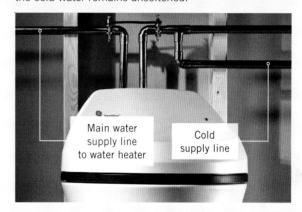

Main water supply line to water heater

Cold supply line

How to Install a Water Softener

Install the bypass valve in the softener's head. One side of the valve goes in the inlet port and the other fits into the outlet port. This valve is held in place with simple plastic clips or threaded couplings.

NOTE: Check local codes for bypass requirements.

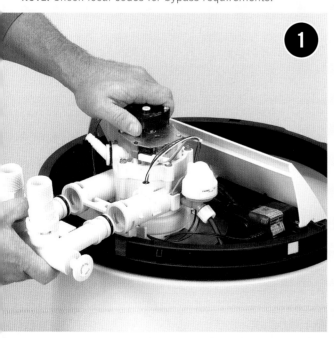

①

②

The overflow tube is usually connected to the side of the softener's tank. Run this tube, along with the discharge tube, to a floor drain or a laundry sink.

(continued)

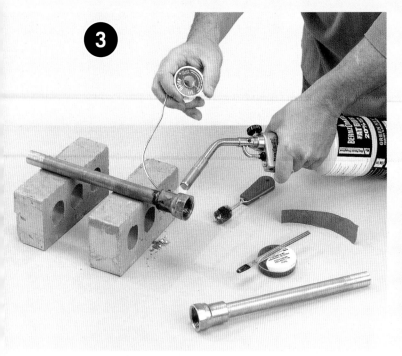

3

Measure the distance between the bypass ports on the tank to the cold water supply line. Cut copper tubing to fit this space, and solder appropriate fittings onto both ends. *NOTE: Plumbing a softener will be even easier using PEX instead of copper, but check local codes to ensure they allow PEX for softeners.*

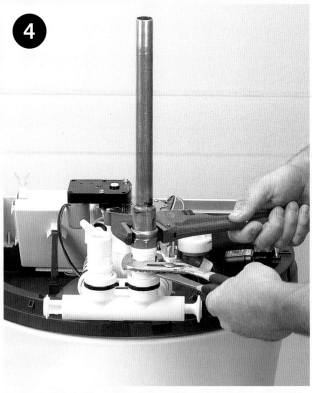

4

Use two wrenches to tighten the tube nuts, one holding the valve stable. Don't overtighten or you may break plastic parts in the valve.

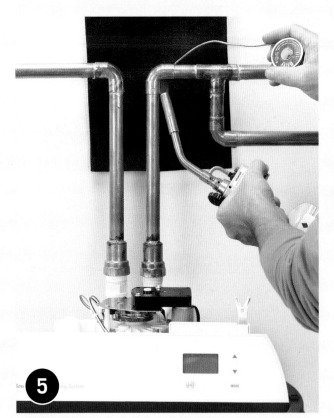

5

Connect the copper tubing from the softener to the water supply lines. Clean all fittings and pipes with steel wool. Then, apply soldering flux to the parts and solder them together with a propane torch.

6

To maintain electrical bonding in a metal supply tube system, connect the copper lines with a bonding clamp.

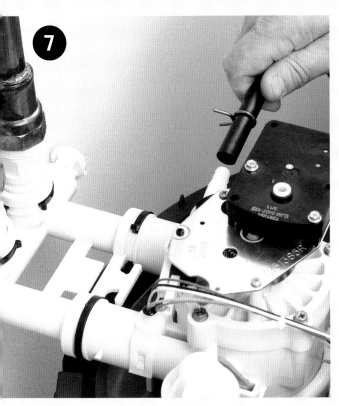

Install the plastic tubing discharge tube on the head of the water softener following the manufacturer's directions.

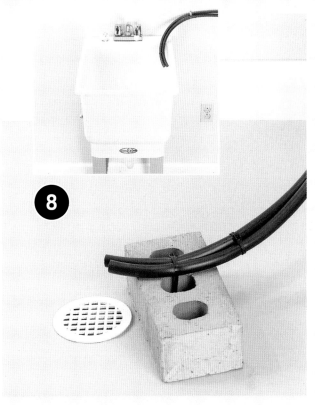

Run the tank overflow hose and the drain tube to a nearby floor drain or utility sink (inset), not into a drain or vent pipe. The hoses should be secured so they don't flop around, and their ends must be at least 1½" above a drain.

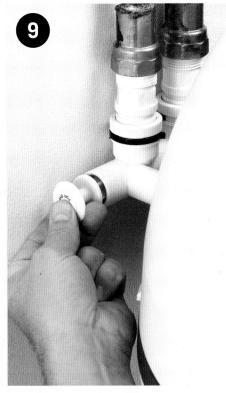

Follow manufacturer's instructions to purge the air from the water softener. First run water with the valve in the bypass position, then pull the valve out so it is in the service position.

Turn on the water supply and make sure the installation works properly. If you see any leaks, fix them. Then add the water softening pellets to the top of the unit in the ratios explained on the package.

Pedestal + Console Sinks

Pedestal sinks remain a popular option for homeowners outfitting space-challenged bathrooms, or just looking for a more streamlined sink option. The tiny footprint allows for easy cleaning and movement around the sinks. This bathroom fixture is available in an amazing array of design styles, and you can be confident that if you opt for a pedestal sink, you can find one to suit exactly your taste or the look of any bathroom.

The primary drawback to pedestal sinks is that they don't offer any storage. Their chief practical benefit is that they usually conceal plumbing some homeowners would prefer to keep out of sight. Console sinks, with their two front legs, offer some space underneath for rolling shelf units or a towel basket.

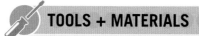

TOOLS + MATERIALS

Pedestal sink	2 × 4 lumber
Caulk gun + silicone caulk	Cement board
	Pencil
Stud finder	Drill + bits
Ratchet wrench	Eye protection
Basin wrench	Work gloves
Lag screws	

Pedestal sinks are mounted in one of two ways. Most inexpensive models are hung in much the same way as wall-mounted sinks are. The pedestal is actually installed after the sink is hung, and its purpose is purely decorative. But other, higher-end pedestal sinks have structural pedestals that bear the weight of the sink. All console sinks are mounted to the wall, although the front legs offer additional support and resistance to users leaning on the front of the sink.

A console bathroom sink is a wall-mounted fixture with two front legs that provide backup support. Many have a narrow apron to conceal the drain trap.

A pedestal sink typically is hung on the wall. The primary function of the pedestal is to conceal plumbing and provide visual appeal.

How to Install a Pedestal Sink

Install 2 × 4 blocking between the wall studs behind the planned sink location. Cover the wall with water-resistant drywall.

Wall surface shown cut away for clarity

Set the basin and pedestal in position and brace them with 2 × 4s. Outline the top of the basin on the wall, and mark the base of the pedestal on the floor. Mark reference points on the wall and floor through the mounting holes found on the back of the sink and the bottom of the pedestal.

Set aside the basin and pedestal. Drill pilot holes in the wall and floor at the reference points, then reposition the pedestal. Anchor the pedestal to the floor with lag screws.

Attach the faucet set to the sink, then set the sink onto the pedestal. Align the holes on the back flange of the sink with the pilot holes drilled in the wall, then drive lag screws with washers into the wall brace using a ratchet wrench. Attach the sink-stopper mechanism to the sink drain.

Hook up the drain and supply fittings. Caulk between the back of the sink and the wall when installation is finished.

Wall-Mounted Sinks

There are many benefits to a wall-mounted sink that, depending on your situation and needs, will offset the inherent lack of storage space. In contrast to the footprint of a traditional vanity-mounted sink, wall-mounted units can save space on the sides and in front of the fixture. More importantly, they are an essential addition to a Universal Design bathroom where wheelchair accessibility is a key consideration. It's why these particular fixtures are sometimes called "roll-under" sinks.

All that practicality aside, early models at the lower end of the price spectrum were somewhat unattractive because their designs simply left the drain tailpiece, trap, and supply shut-off valves in plain sight. But there's no need for you to settle for a less-than-handsome wall-mounted sink. Manufacturers have developed two solutions to the problem of exposed plumbing. Some are designed with a bowl that conceals supply line shut-offs, replacing the trap with sleekly designed tailpieces and squared off trap bends. The other solution, and one more widely available, is a wall-mounted pedestal that covers the plumbing. Sinks with this feature are sometimes called "semi-pedestal."

We've opted to illustrate the installation of just such a sink in the instructions that follow. Keep in mind that different manufacturers sometimes use very different mounting procedures. In any case, the idea remains the same: strongly secure the sink to studs or blocking, so that it is completely stable and will not fall.

The most involved part of the installation process is usually rerouting water supply and drain lines as necessary. You should hire a licensed plumber for this if you're not comfortable with the work. Once the plumbing is in place, the installation is quick and easy.

TOOLS + MATERIALS

4' level	Standard screwdriver
Adjustable wrenches	Jigsaw
Pipe wrench	Basin wrench
Channel pliers	Tape measure
Power drill + bits	Hacksaw
Tubing cutter	2 × 8 lumber
Phillips screwdriver	

Although a wall-mounted sink offers many benefits—accessibility to wheelchair users among them—there's no need to sacrifice chic style for that functionality.

How to Install a Wall-Mounted Sink

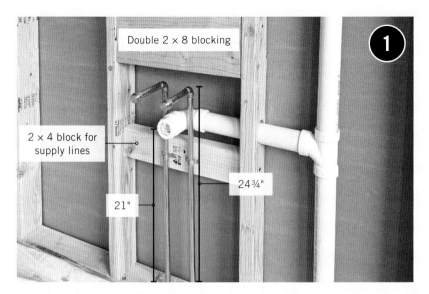

Double 2 × 8 blocking

2 × 4 block for supply lines

24¾"

21"

Remove the existing sink, if any. Remove wall coverings as necessary to install blocking for mounting the sink. Reroute water supply and drain lines as necessary, according to the sink manufacturer's directions. The sink in this project required the centerpoints of the waste pipe be 21" and the supply lines 24¾" up from the finished floor. If unsure of your plumbing skills or code requirements, hire a professional plumber for this part of the project. Install blocking between the studs for attaching the mounting bracket for the sink. A doubled 2 × 8 is installed here. Have your plumbing inspected, if required by your municipality, before you install the drywall and finished wall surface.

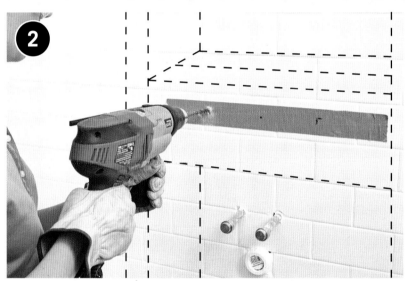

Drill guide holes for the mounting bolts if your sink is a direct-mount model, as this one is. Some wall-hung sinks are hung from a mounting bracket. The bolts used to hang this sink are threaded like lag screws on one end, with a bolt end that projects from the wall. The guide holes should be spaced exactly as the manufacturer specifies so they align with the mounting holes in the back mounting flange on the sink.

TIP: Protect tile surfaces with masking tape in the drilling areas to avoid chip-out.

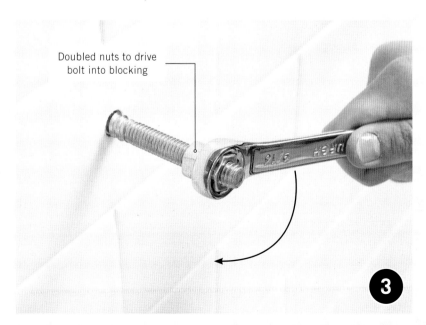

Doubled nuts to drive bolt into blocking

Drive the threaded mounting bolts (screw end first) into the guide holes. There should be pilot holes (smaller than the guide holes) driven into the blocking. To drive this hardware, spin a pair of nuts onto the bolt end and turn the bolt closest to you with a wrench. Drive the mounting bolt until the end is projecting out from the wall by a little more than 1½". Remove the nuts. Install the pop-up drain in the sink, and then slide the sink over the ends of the mounting bolts so the mounting flange is flush against the wall. You'll want help for this. Thread the washers and nuts onto the ends of the mounting bolts, and hand-tighten. Check to make sure the sink is level, and then tighten the nuts with a socket wrench, reaching up into the void between the basin and the flange. Don't overtighten—you could crack the sink flange.

(continued)

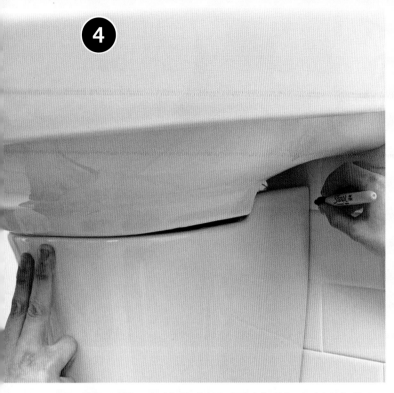

4

Have a helper hold the sink pedestal (in this model, a half-pedestal) in position against the underside of the sink. Mark the edges of the pedestal on the wall covering as reference for installing the pedestal-mounting hardware. Remove the pedestal.

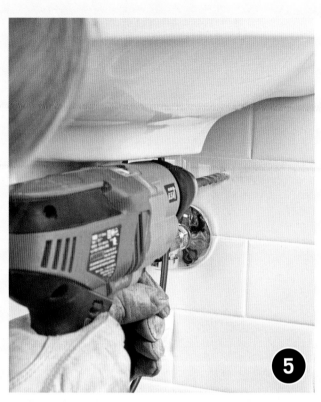

5

Remove the pedestal, and drill the pilot holes for the pedestal-mounting bolts, which work much in the same way as the sink-mounting bolts. Drill guide and pilot holes, then drive the mounting bolts, leaving about 1¼" of the bolt end exposed.

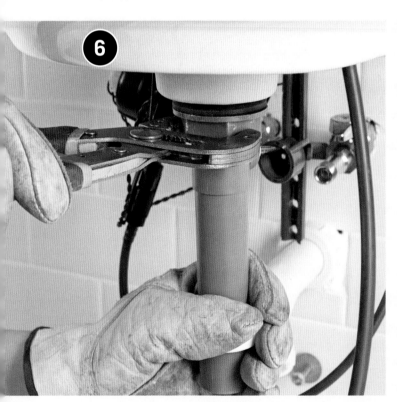

6

Install the drain and drain tailpiece on the sink. Also mount the faucet body to the sink deck if you have not done so already. Attach the drain trap arm to the drain stub out in the wall, and attach shutoff valves to the drain supply lines.

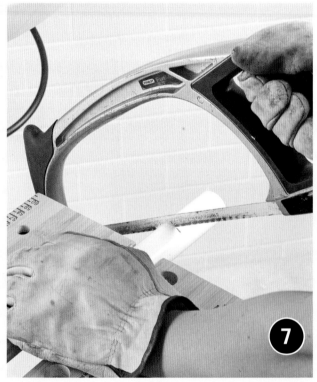

7

Complete the drain connection by installing a P-trap assembly that connects the tailpiece and the trap arm. Also connect the drain pop-up rod that projects out of the tailpiece to the pop-up plunger mechanism you've already installed.

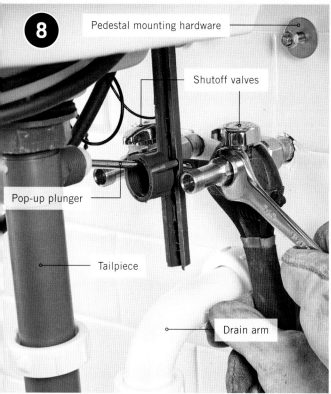

8

Pedestal mounting hardware

Shutoff valves

Pop-up plunger

Tailpiece

Drain arm

Make sure the shutoff valve fittings are tight and oriented correctly, and then hook up the faucet supply risers to the shutoff valves. Turn on the water supply and test.

LEAK FINDER

To quickly and easily find an undersink leak, lay bright white paper or paper towels under the pipes and drain connections. Open the water supply valves and run water in the sinks. It should be clear exactly where the water dripped from by the location of the drip on the paper.

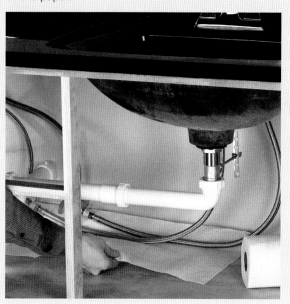

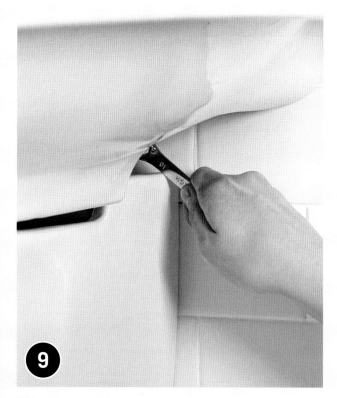

9

Slide the pedestal into place on the mounting studs. Working through the access space under the sink, use a wrench to tighten the mounting nut over the washer on the stud. Carefully tighten the nut until the pedestal is held securely in place. Be careful not to overtighten the nut.

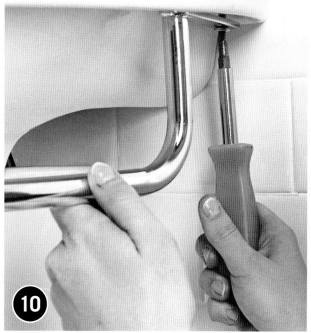

10

Attach the towel bar to the sink by first pushing the well nuts into the holes on the underside of the sink rim. Set the bar in place, and screw in the attachment screws on both sides, just until snug.

Traditional Vanity

Simple vanity bases are stages upon which much of the drama in a bathroom can play out. Because there are now so many sink and counter styles and materials, and ways of incorporating the two, a stable base that can be attractive in its own right is more important than ever.

Although vanity cabinet styles vary, the basic structure—such as incorporating a toe-kick—is common to the majority of them. The process outlined here covers the basic way that most vanities are secured in place to provide ample storage and sturdy foundation for sinks and countertops.

TOOLS + MATERIALS

Pencil	Stud finder
4' level	Tub + tile caulk
Screwdriver	Shims
Basin wrench	3" drywall screws
Cardboard	Drill + bits
Masking tape	Work gloves
Plumber's putty	Eye protection
Lag screws	

A traditional bathroom base cabinet serves to support an integral sink-countertop unit.

How to Install a Vanity Cabinet

Measure and mark the top edge of the vanity cabinet on the wall, then use an electronic level/stud finder to mark the stud locations and a level line.

1

2

Slide the vanity into position so that the back rail of the cabinet can later be fastened to studs at both corners and in the center. The back of the cabinet should also be flush against the wall. (If the wall surface is uneven, position the vanity so it contacts the wall in at least one spot and the back cabinet rail is parallel with the wall.)

Using a level as a guide, shim below the vanity cabinet until the unit is level.

VARIATION: To install two or more cabinets, set the cabinets in position against the wall, and align the cabinet fronts. If one cabinet is higher than the other, shim under the lower cabinet until the two are even. Clamp the cabinet faces together, then drill countersunk pilot holes spaced 12" apart through the face frames so they go at least halfway into the face frame of the second cabinet. Drive wood screws through the pilot holes to join the cabinets together.

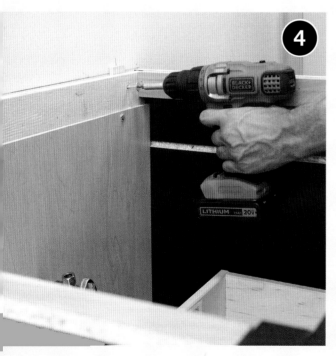

At the stud locations marked on the wall, drive 3" drywall screws through the rail on the cabinet back and into the framing members. The screws should be driven at both corners and in the center of the back rail.

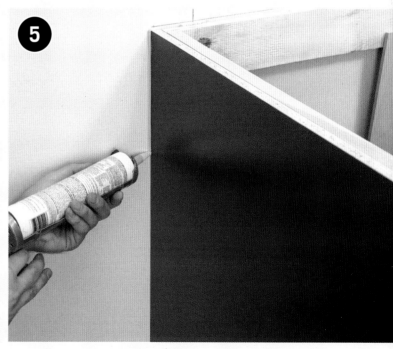

Run a bead of caulk along small gaps between the vanity and wall and between the vanity and floor. For larger gaps, use ¼-round molding between the vanity and wall. Between the vanity and floor, install the same baseboard material used to cover the gap between the wall and floor.

Plumbing a Double-Bowl Vanity

Side-by-side sinks are a bathroom luxury, especially for busy couples (which accounts for why they are called "his-and-her" sinks) or busy bathrooms. Although the basics of installing a vanity for a double sink are structurally the same as a single-bowl vanity, the plumbing requires modification to accommodate the extra fixture.

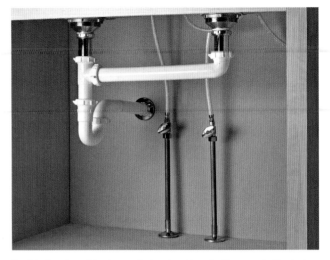

TOOLS + MATERIALS

4' level	Silicone caulk
Screwdrivers	Dual outlet valves
Drill + bits	Braided steel supply lines
Basin wrench	P-trap
Stud finder	PVC connections
Adjustable wrench	Plumber's putty
Hacksaw	Caulk gun

Double-bowl vanities have drain plumbing that's very similar to double-bowl kitchen sinks. In most cases, the drain tailpieces are connected beneath one of the tailpieces at a continuous waste tee. The drainline from the second bowl must slope downward toward the tee. From the tee, the drain should have a trap (usually a P-Trap) that connects to the trap arm coming out of the wall.

 How to Plumb a Double Sink

Shut off the supply valves located under the sink. Disconnect and remove the supply lines connecting the faucet to the valves. Loosen the P-trap nuts at both ends and remove the P-trap.

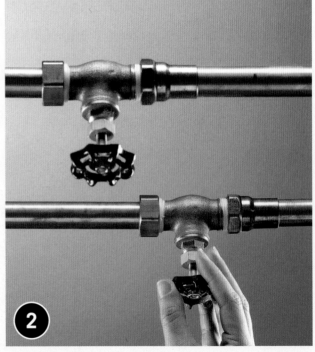

Remove the existing countertop and vanity. Turn off the house water supply at the main shut-off valve. Drain the remaining water by opening the faucet at the lowest point in the house. Use a hacksaw to remove existing undersink shutoff valves.

3

Slide the new dual-outlet valve onto the hot water supply line, pass the nut and compression washer over the pipe, and tighten with a wrench. Install the dual-outlet valve on the cold supply line in the same way.

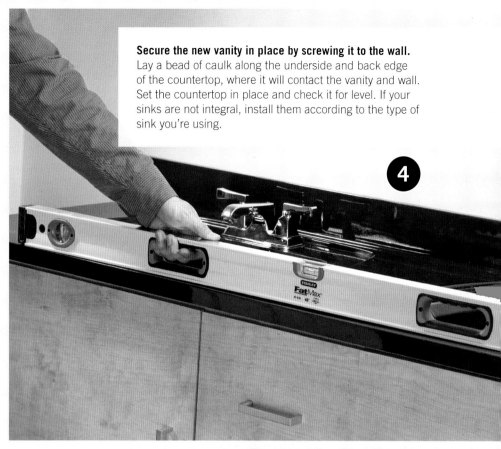

4

Secure the new vanity in place by screwing it to the wall. Lay a bead of caulk along the underside and back edge of the countertop, where it will contact the vanity and wall. Set the countertop in place and check it for level. If your sinks are not integral, install them according to the type of sink you're using.

5

Seat the faucets for the double sinks as you would for a single sink, by applying a bead of putty on the underside of the bases (unless they are to be used with gaskets instead of putty). Secure them in place by tightening the locking nuts on the underside of the faucets.

Connect a new PVC P-trap to the undersink drain pipe, and attach a tee connector to the trap. Extend PVC connections to the drain assemblies of both sinks.

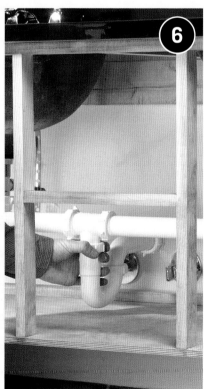

6

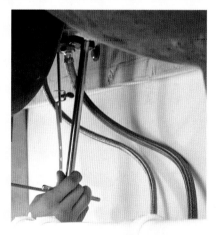

7

Connect the pop-up stopper linkage. Connect the cold water supply lines to the appropriate faucet tailpieces and repeat with the hot water supply lines. Turn on the main water supply, remove the faucet aerator, and run the water in the sinks. Check for leaks, and then replace the aerator.

Kitchen Sinks

Most drop-in, self-rimming kitchen sinks are easily installed. Drop-in sinks for do-it-yourself installation are made from cast iron coated with enamel, stainless steel, enameled steel, acrylic, fiberglass, or resin composites. Because cast-iron sinks are heavy, their weight holds them in place and they require no mounting hardware. Except for the heavy lifting, they are easy to install. Stainless steel and enameled-steel sinks weigh less than cast-iron, and most require mounting brackets on the underside of the countertop. Some acrylic and resin sinks rely on silicone caulk to hold them in place.

If you are replacing a sink, but not the countertop, make sure the new sink is the same size or larger. All old silicone caulk residue must be removed with acetone or denatured alcohol, or else the new caulk will not stick.

SHOPPING TIPS

- When purchasing a sink, you also need to buy strainer bodies and baskets, sink clips, and a drain trap kit.

- Look for basin dividers that are lower than the sink rim—this reduces splashing.

- Drain holes in the back or to the side make for more usable space under the sink.

- When choosing a sink, make sure the predrilled openings will fit your faucet.

Drop-in sinks, also known as self-rimming sinks, have a wide sink flange that extends beyond the edges of the sink cutout. They also have a wide back flange to which the faucet is mounted directly.

How to Install a Self-Rimming Sink

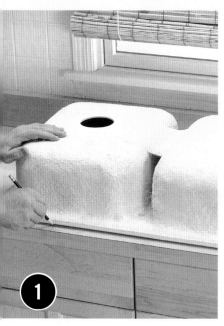

1

Invert the sink and trace around the edges as a reference for making the sink cutout cutting lines, which should be parallel to the outlines, but about 1" inside of them to create a 1" ledge. If your sink comes with a template for the cutout, use it.

2

Drill a starter hole and cut out the sink opening with a jigsaw. Cut right up to the line. Because the sink flange fits over the edges of the cutout, the opening doesn't need to be perfect, but as always you should try to do a nice, neat job.

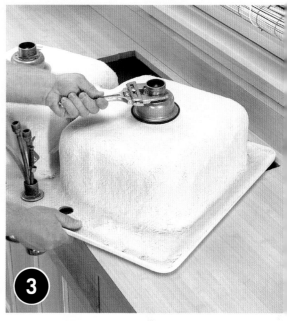

3

Attach as much of the plumbing as makes sense to install prior to setting the sink into the opening. Having access to the underside of the flange is a great help when it comes to attaching the faucet body, sprayer, and strainer, in particular.

4

Apply a bead of silicone caulk around the edges of the sink opening. The sink flange most likely is not flat, so try and apply the caulk in the area that will make contact with the flange.

5

Place the sink in the opening. Try to get the sink centered right away so you don't need to move it around and disturb the caulk, which can break the seal. If you are installing a heavy cast-iron sink, it's best to leave the strainers off so you can grab onto the sink at the drain openings.

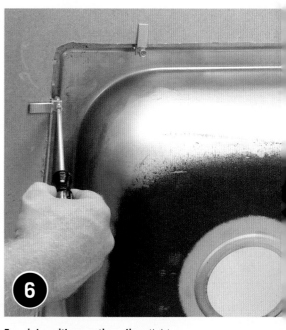

6

For sinks with mounting clips, tighten the clips from below using a screwdriver or wrench (depending on the type of clip your sink has). There should be at least three clips on every side. Don't overtighten the clips—this can cause the sink flange to flatten or become warped.

FIXTURES, FAUCETS, DRAINS + APPLIANCES ● 211

Standpipe Drains

A standpipe drain allows you to drain a water-consuming appliance (usually a washing machine) directly into the waste system, instead of into a utility tub (also called a laundry tray). This eliminates the possibility of the sink drain plugging and causing the sink basin to overflow (most utility sinks do not have an overflow hole).

Some standpipes come with attached P-traps and can be purchased at many home centers.

A 2-inch pipe is required by most building codes. The top of the standpipe should be at least 18 inches high but no more than 42 inches above the floor. Hose bibs are installed in the hot and cold supply lines at the utility sink to provide the water supply to the washing machine.

A washing machine with standpipe drain: washing machine drain hose (A), 2" standpipe drain with trap (B), waste line (C), utility sink drain pipe (D), hot and cold supply lines with hose bibs (E), rubber supply hoses to washing machine (F), and utility sink (G).

TOOLS + MATERIALS

Reciprocating saw	2 × 4 backer	Teflon tape
Utility knife	2½" deck screws	Rubber supply hose
Waste wye fitting	½" screws	Eye protection
PVC primer + cement	Pipe strap	Work gloves
90° elbow	Hose bibs	
2" standpipe with trap	Solder	

How to Install a Washing Machine Standpipe Drain

Provide venting for the standpipe and/or the utility sink. Some locales allow you to install an unvented standpipe, but most building departments now require some sort of venting. In an extreme case, you may need to run a new vent up through the roof.

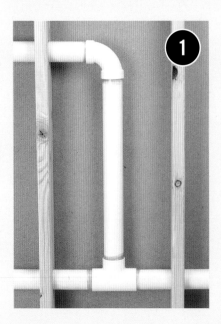

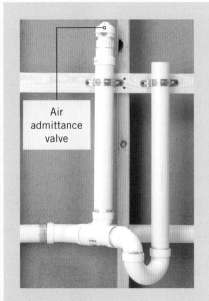

Air admittance valve

OPTION: Your building department may allow you to vent the standpipe by installing an air admittance valve (AAV). Consult with your inspector to be sure you locate the AAV in a code-approved manner. If you are installing a utility sink instead of a standpipe, you may be able to install an AAV onto the drain trap under the sink.

Utility sink drain pipe

2

Measure and mark the size and location of a waste wye fitting in the drain line. Remove the marked section using a reciprocating saw. Make cuts as straight as possible.

3

Use a utility knife to remove rough burrs on the cut ends of the pipe. Dry-fit the waste wye fitting into the drain line to make sure it fits properly, then attach the wye fitting using primer and solvent cement.

4

Dry-fit a 90° elbow and a 2" standpipe with trap to the waste wye fitting. Make sure the top of the standpipe is between 18" and 42" above the floor. Cement all the pipes in place.

5

Attach a 2 × 4 backer behind the top of the standpipe for support using 2½" deck screws. Fasten the standpipe to the wood support using a length of pipe strap and ½" screws. Insert the washing machine's rubber drain hose into the standpipe.

Freestanding Bathtubs

A large bathroom offers all kinds of design and comfort possibilities to the homeowner willing to exploit the space. One of the best uses for ample floor space is a freestanding tub. Although more expensive than many other versions, freestanding units offer flexibility in placement and most are deeper and more spacious than alcove or even drop-in tubs. They also come in impressive selection of styles, from updated classic clawfoot versions, to body-cradling egg shapes and beyond. There are even jetted freestanding models.

These tubs are usually no more difficult to install than other types, although you must make sure there is adequate support for the tub full of water (if the location could support another type of tub, it will support a freestanding version). They should not be positioned where there is no joist under the floor. However, if you've gone to the expense of a buying a stunning freestanding tub, give it as much exposure as you can.

Once you've determined the location, installation may require running a drain line to where the tub drain will be placed, but that is fairly fundamental plumbing requiring only the basic skills you'd need for any project in this book. You'll also need to plumb in a faucet, so we've included instructions that will work for adding most freestanding faucets, including those with both a fixed and a handheld head.

The contemporary "eggshell" style of the tub shown here is similar to the look of most contemporary freestanding tubs. You can, however, find versions with more dramatic designs, or period styles such as Victorian clawfoot tubs. Connecting them to drain and water supplies involves a similar process no matter what the style.

How to Install a Freestanding Bathtub

1

Use a helper to remove the tub from its box and inspect for damage. Check that all necessary hardware has been supplied. Set the tub on two 2 × 4 bolsters. Slide a large, deep roasting pan or tray beneath the tub, under the drain. Check that the pop-up drain and overflow are properly sealed. Close the drain and fill the tub with water to above the overflow. Check the drain and overflow for leaks. Empty the tub. Remove and reassemble drain and overflow as necessary, waterproofing the connections with silicone caulk.

2

Clean and level the floor as necessary. Mark the center of the existing drain, or where you will plumb the floor drain Set the tub in place with the drain centered over the floor drain. Adjust the tub position until you're happy with it. Trace around the base of the tub with a carpenter's pencil. Mark the drain hole location.

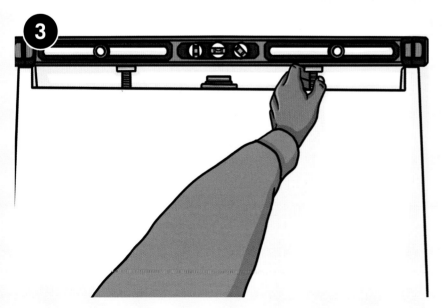

3

Move the tub out of the way, placing it upside down on a soft blanket or beach towel. Rest a level across the tub walls and leveling feet. Raise the feet until they touch the level, and then ⅛" more, so that the tub full of water will not rest on the walls.

(continued)

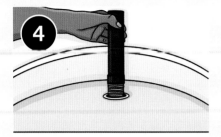

If not already installed, install a 1½"
underfloor P trap and drain pipe to
floor level. Slide a flanged washer
onto the tub's drain body and fasten a
1½" tailpiece to the drain body (some
manufacturers supply this, while others
require the homeowner to supply it—
check before installation).

*NOTE: This tub is meant to be installed
directly over the drain; many use
an integral P trap and flexible hose
that allows for some flexibility in tub
placement. Use the system intended
by the manufacturer.*

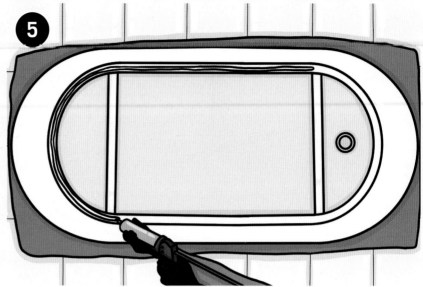

Slip the drain trap adapter into the floor drain. Lay a bead of silicone adhesive along
the bottom edge of the tub.

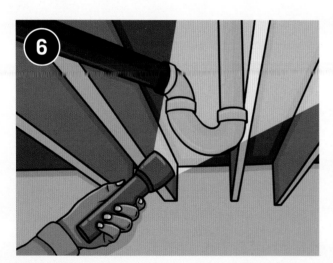

Use a helper to gently flip the tub over and carefully place
it into position, sliding the drain tailpiece in the floor drain,
and aligning the tub with the marked outline. Fill the tub to
overflow and check for leaks.

Drain the tub. If recommended by the manufacturer, lay a
bead of tub-and-tile caulk along the bottom seam of the tub,
between the tub edge and bathroom floor.

How to Install a Freestanding Tub Faucet

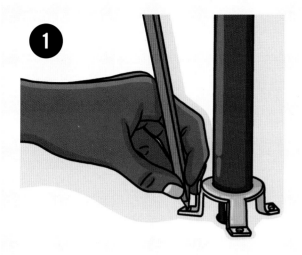

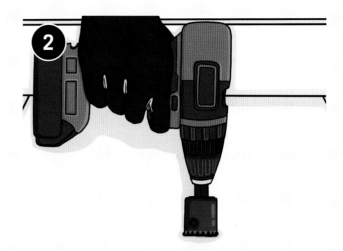

Turn off the water supply. Remove and stage all the faucet pieces on a clean towel or blanket. Check that all the pieces you will need have been supplied (you may need to purchase additional hardware for supply connections). Assemble and position the faucet body without the mounting escutcheon. Place it in position so that the faucet correctly extends over the lip the tub. Mark the mounting flange holes and access hole.

Drill the access hole for the supply lines and the mount screw holes. Install the required mating connectors onto the end of the hot and cold water supplies under the floor.

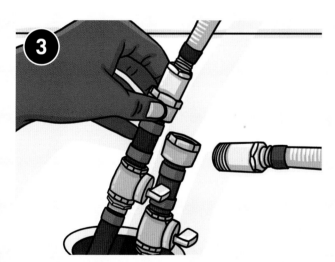

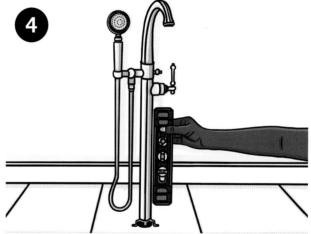

Connect the faucet hoses to the water supply lines.

NOTE: Make sure the hot water supply is on the left as someone faces the faucet from the tub. Turn on the water, open the faucet, and check the connections and faucet for leaks.

Disassemble the faucet and connect the supplied water hoses up through the body to the faucet head. Reassemble the faucet body, sliding the escutcheon onto the post. Set the faucet in place, guiding the hoses down through the access hole. Screw the base to the floor and check the body for plumb with a torpedo level (adjust as necessary by adding washers under one or more of the base screws).

Whole-House Water Filters

It's easy to take tap water for granted, but municipal water is increasingly contaminated with excessive amounts of chlorine, heavy metals, and other impurities. Those unseen elements can affect everything from the taste of tap water to the health of family members who drink it.

As municipal water systems age, and private wells need to be dug deeper and deeper to find a consistent supply of water, contaminants in home water supplies become more common. These range from the annoying, like the chlorine used to treat city water, to the more worrying, like arsenic and lead. The question for many homeowners has become how to ensure that the water they drink (and bathe in, use for cooking, and brush their teeth with) is safe to consume?

The answer is a whole-house water filter, sometimes called a point-of-entry system.

If you've dealt with tub rust stains, a chlorine or rotten-eggs taste in your tap water, premature corrosion in pipes, clothes that don't seem to get clean, or streaking on glassware, you water may have impurities. However, the greater concern are contaminants that you can't see, smell, or taste, such as nitrates, arsenic, and pesticides.

TOOLS + MATERIALS

Whole-house water filter	¾" push-fit tees
Plywood scrap or 2 × 4 or 2 × 6 brace	¾" push-fit shutoff valves
Blue PEX pipe	Step-down 1" to ¾" threaded adapter
PEX cutter	Teflon tape
Sharpie	Drill + bits
Tape measure	4' Level
Stainless steel crimp fittings + crimping tool	Emery cloth
¾" × 90° crimp fixture	Copper pipe cutter

Unlike a point-of-use filter that removes a limited number of contaminants (some do little more than make tap water taste better), a whole-house system runs water supply through three or more filters, to remove increasingly smaller contaminants. These filters are installed right where the water supply enters the house and before it is routed to the water heater. The filter can stop larger particulates from damaging the water heater itself, and prevent them from fouling showers and baths.

The place to start is with a water test. This is especially essential if you draw your water from a well, rather than a municipal water supply. Local governments test city water sources regularly and municipal supplies are well protected from chemical spills and pesticide runoff from agricultural operations. But only you are responsible for your well water.

You can buy home test kits that will provide immediate results for a limited number of contaminants. For a more complete picture of what might be in your water, however, you'll need to spend a bit more and buy a send-away kit. These involve taking samples from multiple points of use around the house, and then sending them to an EPA-approved lab. The lab usually sends back the results within a few weeks. Send-away tests are the only way to check if your water contains potentially harmful contaminants such as volatile organic compounds (VOCs) that can infiltrate well water from nearby industrial operations.

Although they may look complex, a whole-house filter is not difficult to install. Keep in mind, though, the filter is only good as the maintenance and upkeep—you need to regularly clean or replace the filters (depending on the type) to keep the unit doing working at peak efficiency.

How to Install a Whole-House Filter

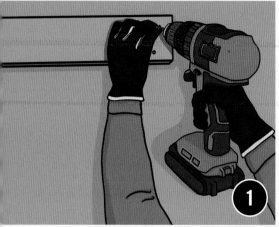

Turn off the main water supply valve and open all the faucets in the house. Choose a location for the filtration system. It needs to be securely mounted on a backing (into studs or on a backer board) and should be as close as possible to the main water supply coming into the house. Fasten a plywood backer board to an unfinished basement wall (using masonry screws) or add blocking between studs, as necessary.

Hold the filter bracket in place and check for level. Mark the screw holes and then screw the bracket to the backer board or support. If there are pressure gauges included with your unit, wrap the threads with Teflon tape and install the pressure gauges.

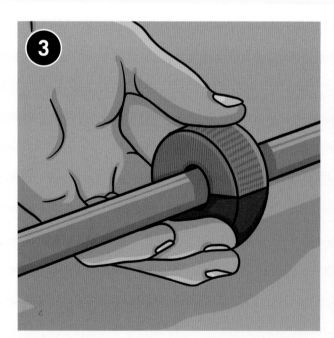

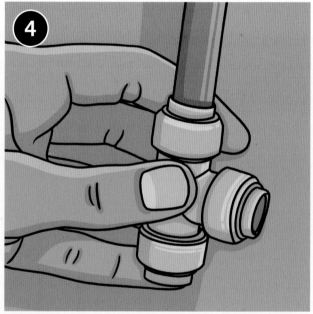

Clean the copper water supply line if necessary, prior to cutting. Have a bucket handy to drain any remaining water in the line. You will most likely need to install a shut-off valve in the line, as well as tee fittings for the filter water line before and after the valve. First, cut the copper pipe where the tees will be spliced in.

Smooth and deburr the ends of the copper supply pipe, and mark both ends with the depth gauge for the push-fit tees. Push the tees onto both ends of the cut water pipe. Measure and cut the middle section of copper pipe that you removed for the push-fit shut-off valve. Mark the depth using the depth gauge and install the push-fit shut-off valve.

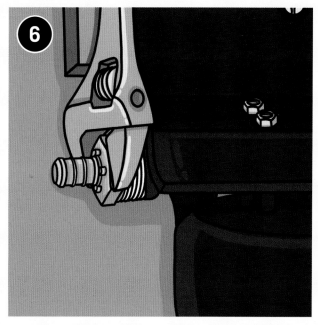

Mark each end of the center section of copper pipe with the depth gauge, and push each end into the respective-tee openings, to complete the water filter bypass. Measure for the PEX lines from the tees to the filters, allowing for the in-line push-fit shut off valves on both the inlet and outlet PEX lines. Routing the PEX lines from the water supply to the filter will usually involve adding 90° crimp fittings). Cut the PEX sections, push them into the shutoff valves, and crimp the 90° fittings in place.

Wrap the water filter's inlet and outlet fittings with Teflon tape and install the fittings. Crimp step-up adapters to the ends of the inlet and outlet PEX pipe (most whole-house inlet and outlets are 1", so ¾" PEX will need to be stepped up to fit the filter's fittings). Fasten the PEX inlet and outlet lines to each side of the filter.

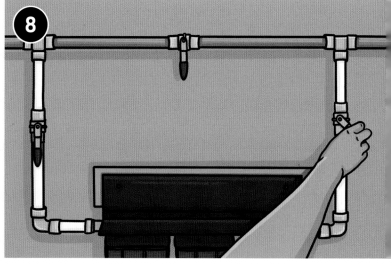

Fasten the inlet and outlet PEX lines to the push-fit shut-off valve in the water supply line. Remove the filter cannisters and remove the filters from their plastic wrapping. Place the filters in the cannisters and, making sure they are in the correct order, use the supplied wrench to tighten the cannisters into the filter housing. Be careful not to overtighten.

Turn the shutoff valves to the proper positions—water supply closed, and both the inlet and outlet PEX lines to and from the filter, open. Make sure all the faucets in the house are closed, and open the main water valve. Check for leaks, and tighten connections as necessary.

Common Plumbing Repairs

Modern technology has made many key parts of residential plumbing systems much more reliable. Faucets are easier to install and repair, toilets clog and leak less often, and supply pipes have become ever easier to replace or modify with the proliferation of PEX pipe and fasteners.

Still, it pays to understand how plumbing fixtures and structures work, and how to repair them when they don't. Fortunately, the same technology that has improved reliability and longevity, has made fixing things a whole lot easier. When you jump in and take care of small repairs right away, you stop them from becoming larger problems. You can also save a bundle on plumber house calls.

This is simply a matter of taking control and part of being the master of your own castle. Understand how to clear a drain, or replace a faucet cartridge, and you never have to tolerate an ongoing leak, or the irritation of a daily-use fixture that doesn't work as it should. You likely have most of the tools you'll need in your toolbox right now; the information that will teach you how to use those tools is laid out in this chapter.

In this chapter:
- Common Toilet Problems
- Clogged Toilets
- Toilet Flanges
- Sink Faucets
- Kitchen Sprayers
- Fixing Leaky Tubs + Shower Faucets
- Single-Handle Tub + Shower Faucet with Scald Control
- Tubs + Showers
- Sink Drains
- Branch + Main Drains
- Noisy Pipes

Common Toilet Problems

A clogged toilet is one of the most common plumbing problems. If a toilet overflows or flushes sluggishly, clear the clog with a plunger or closet auger. If the problem persists, the clog may be in a branch drain or a drainage stack.

Most other toilet problems are fixed easily with minor adjustments that require no disassembly or replacement parts. You can make these adjustments in a few minutes, using simple tools.

If minor adjustments do not fix the problem, further repairs will be needed. The parts of a standard toilet are not difficult to take apart, and most repair projects can be completed in less than an hour.

A recurring puddle of water on the floor around a toilet may be caused by a crack in the toilet base or in the tank. A damaged toilet should be replaced. Installing a new toilet is an easy project that can be finished in three or four hours.

An older toilet may have a tank ball that settles onto the flush valve to stop the flow of water into the bowl. The ball is attached to a lift wire, which is in turn attached to the lift rod. A ballcock valve is usually made of brass, with rubber washers that can wear out. If the ballcock valve malfunctions, you might be able to find old washers to repair it, but replacing both the ballcock and the tank ball with a float-cup assembly and flapper is easier and makes for a more durable repair.

A modern float-cup valve with flapper is inexpensive and made of plastic, but it is more reliable than an old ballcock valve and ball.

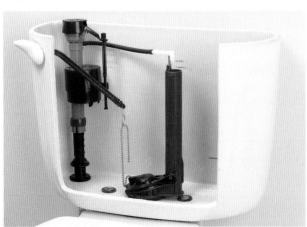

A pressure-assist toilet has a large vessel that nearly fills the tank. As water enters the vessel, pressure builds up. When the toilet is flushed, this pressure helps push water forcefully down into the bowl. As a result, a pressure-assist toilet provides strong flushing power with minimal water consumption.

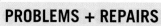

PROBLEMS	REPAIRS
Toilet handle sticks or is hard to push.	1. Adjust lift wires (see page 228). 2. Clean and adjust handle (see page 226).
Handle must be held down for entire flush.	1. Adjust handle (see page 226). 2. Shorten lift chain or wires (see page 226). 3. Replace waterlogged flapper.
Handle is loose.	1. Adjust handle (see page 226). 2. Reattach lift chain or lift wires to lever (see page 226).
Toilet will not flush at all.	1. Make sure water is turned on. 2. Adjust lift chain or lift wires (see page 226).
Toilet does not flush completely.	1. Adjust lift chain (see page 226). 2. Adjust water level in tank (see page 228). 3. Increase pressure on pressure-assisted toilet.
Toilet overflows or flushes sluggishly.	1. Clear clogged toilet (see page 239). 2. Clear clogged branch drain or drainage stack (see page 241).
Toilet runs continuously or there are phantom flushes.	1. Adjust lift wires or lift chain (see page 236). 2. Replace leaky float ball (see page 230). 3. Adjust water level in tank (see page 228). 4. Adjust and clean flush valve (see page 229). 5. Replace flush valve (see page 232). 6. Replace flapper. 7. Service pressure-assist valve.
Water on floor around toilet.	1. Tighten tank bolts and water connections. 2. Insulate tank to prevent condensation. 3. Replace wax ring (see page 94). 4. Replace cracked tank or bowl.
Toilet noisy when filling.	1. Open shutoff valve completely. 2. Replace ballcock and float valve. 3. Refill tube is disconnected. Reconnect refill tube.
Weak flush.	1. Clean clogged rim openings. 2. Replace old low-flow toilet.
Toilet rocks.	1. Replace wax ring and bolts. 2. Replace toilet flange (see page 243).

Making Minor Adjustments

Many common toilet problems can be fixed by making minor adjustments to the handle and the attached lift chain (or lift wires).

If the handle sticks or is hard to push, remove the tank cover and clean the handle-mounting nut. Make sure the lift wires are straight.

If the toilet will not flush completely unless the handle is held down, you may have to remove excess slack in the lift chain.

If the toilet will not flush at all, the lift chain may be broken or may have to be reattached to the handle lever.

A continuously running toilet can be caused by bent lift wires, kinks in a lift chain, or lime buildup on the handle mounting nut. Clean and adjust the handle and the lift wires or chain to fix the problem.

How to Adjust a Toilet Handle + Lift Chain (or Lift Wires)

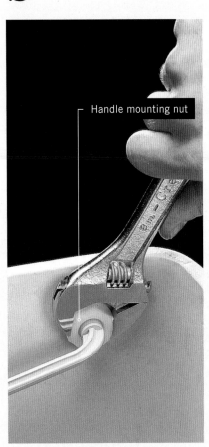

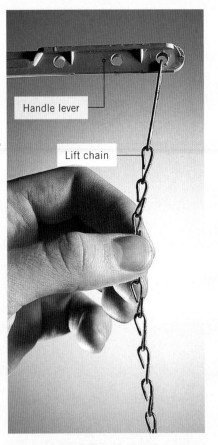

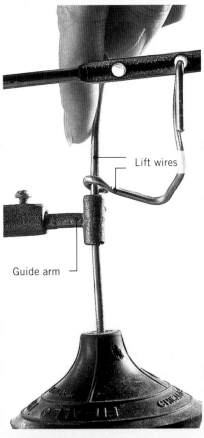

Clean and adjust the handle-mounting nut so the handle operates smoothly. A mounting nut has reversed threads. Loosen the nut by turning it clockwise; tighten by turning it counterclockwise. Remove lime buildup with a brush dipped in vinegar.

Adjust the lift chain so it hangs straight from the handle lever, with about ½" of slack. Remove excess slack in the chain by hooking the chain in a different hole in the handle lever or by removing links with needlenose pliers. A broken lift chain must be replaced.

Adjust the lift wires (found on older toilets without lift chains) so that the wires are straight and operate smoothly when the handle is pushed. A sticky handle often can be fixed by straightening bent lift wires. You can also buy replacement wires or replace the whole assembly with a float cup.

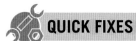

Phantom flushes? Phantom flushes are weak flushes that occur without turning the handle. The flapper may not be completely sealing against the flush valve's seat. Make sure the chain is not tangled and that the flapper can go all the way down. If that does not solve the problem, shut off the water and drain the tank. If the problem persists, the flapper may need to be replaced.

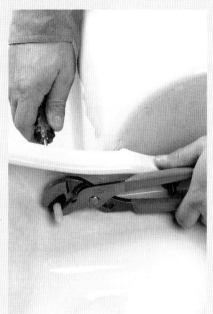

Seat loose? Loose seats are almost always the result of a loose nut on the seat bolts. Tighten the nuts with pliers. If the nut is corroded or stripped, replace the bolts and nuts or replace the whole seat.

Tank fills too slowly? The first place to check is the shutoff valve where the supply tube for the toilet is connected. Make sure it is fully open. If it is, you may need to replace the shutoff—these fittings are fairly cheap and frequently fail to open fully.

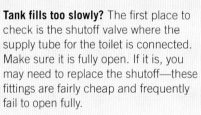

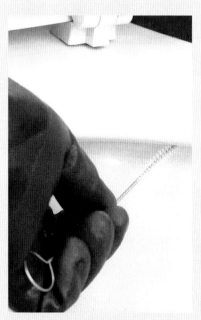

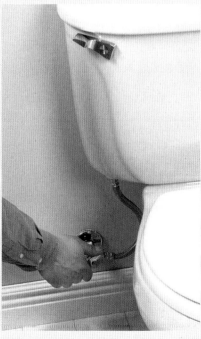

Bowl not refilling well? The rim holes may be clogged; many toilets have small holes on the underside of the bowl rim, through which water squirts during a flush. If you notice that some of these holes are clogged, use a stiff-bristled brush to clear out debris. You may need to first apply toilet bowl cleaner or mineral cleaner.

Seat uncomfortably low? Instead of going to the trouble of raising the toilet or replacing it with a taller model, you can simply replace the seat with a thicker, extended seat.

Toilet running? Running toilets are usually caused by faulty or misadjusted fill valves, but sometimes the toilet runs because the tank is leaking water into the bowl. To determine if this is happening with your toilet, add a few drops of food coloring to the tank water. If, after a while, the water in the bowl becomes colored, then you have a leak and probably need to replace the rubber gasket at the base of your flush valve.

Reset Tank Water Level

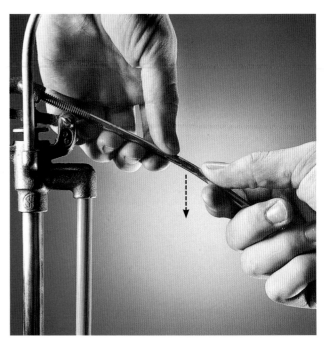

Tank water flowing into the overflow pipe is the sound we hear when a toilet is running. Usually, this is caused by a minor misadjustment that fails to tell the water to shut off when the toilet tank is full. The culprit is a float ball or cup that is adjusted to set a water level in the tank that's higher than the top of the overflow pipe, which serves as a drain for excess tank water. The other photos on this page show how to fix the problem.

A ball float is connected to a float arm that's attached to a plunger on the other end. As the tank fills, the float rises and lifts one end of the float arm. At a certain point, the float arm depresses the plunger and stops the flow of water. By simply bending the float arm downward a bit, you can cause it to depress the plunger at a lower tank water level, solving the problem.

Spring clip

A diaphragm fill valve usually is made of plastic and has a wide bonnet that contains a rubber diaphragm. Turn the adjustment screw clockwise to lower the water level and counterclockwise to raise it.

A float cup fill valve is made of plastic and is easy to adjust. Lower the water level by pinching the spring clip with fingers or pliers and moving the clip and cup down the pull rod and shank. Raise the water level by moving the clip and cup upward.

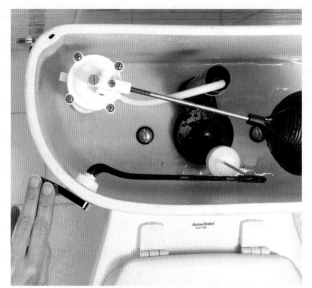

Sometimes there is plenty of water in the tank, but not enough of it makes it to the bowl before the flush valve shuts off the water from the tank. Modern toilets are designed to leave some water in the tank, since the first water that leaves the tank does so with the most force. (It's pressed out by the weight of the water on top.) To increase the duration of the flush, shorten the length of the chain between the flapper and the float (yellow in the model shown).

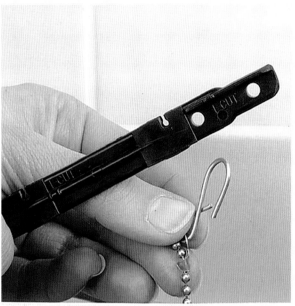

If the toilet is not completing flushes and the lever and chain for the flapper or tank ball are correctly adjusted, the problem could be that the handle mechanism needs cleaning or replacement. Remove the chain/linkage from the handle lever. Remove the nut on the backside of the handle with an adjustable wrench. It unthreads clockwise (the reverse of standard nuts). Remove the handle from the tank.

The handle lever should pull straight up on the flapper. If it doesn't, reposition the chain hook on the handle lever. When the flapper is covering the opening, there should be just a little slack in the chain. If there is too much slack, shorten the chain and cut off excess with the cutters on your pliers.

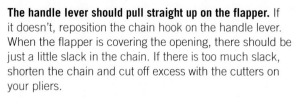

Unless the handle parts are visibly broken, try cleaning them with an old toothbrush dipped in white vinegar. Replace the handle and test the action. If it sticks or is hard to operate, replace it. Most replacement handles come with detailed instructions that tell you how to install and adjust them.

How to Replace a Fill Valve

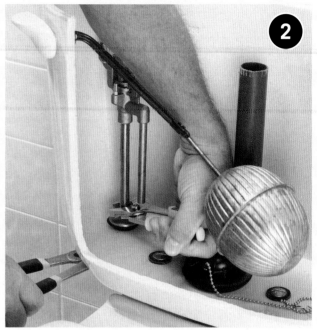

Toilet fill valves wear out eventually. They can be repaired, but it's easier and a better fix to just replace them. Before removing the old fill valve, shut off the water supply at the fixture stop valve located on the tube that supplies water to the tank. Flush the toilet, and sponge out the remaining water. Loosen the nut and disconnect the supply tube, then loosen and remove the mounting nut.

If the fill valve spins while you turn the mounting nut, you may need to hold it still with locking pliers. Lift out the fill valve. In the case of an old ballcock valve, the float ball will likely come out as well. When replacing an old valve like this, you will likely also need to replace the flush valve.

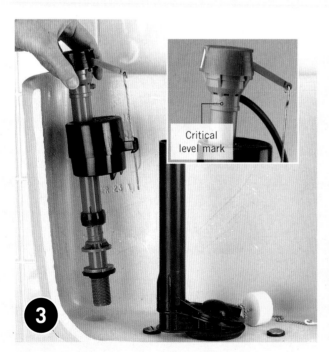

The new fill valve must be installed so the critical level ("CL") mark is at least 1" above the overflow pipe (inset). Slip the shank washer on the threaded shank of the new fill valve, and place the valve in the hole so the washer is flat on the tank bottom. Compare the locations of the "CL" mark and the overflow pipe.

Adjust the height of the fill valve shank so the "CL" line and overflow pipe will be correctly related. Different products are adjusted in different ways—the fill valve shown here telescopes when it's twisted.

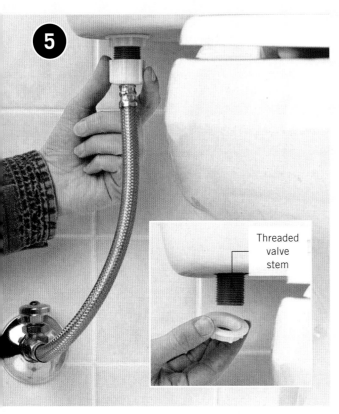

5

Slip the valve's threaded end down through the tank. Push down on its shank (not the top) while tightening the locknut (inset). Hand tighten, then use a wrench to make an extra ¼ turn. Hook up the water supply tube, and tighten in the same way.

Threaded valve stem

If the overflow pipe has a cap, remove it. Attach one end of the refill tube from the new valve to the plastic angle adapter and the other end to the refill nipple near the top of the valve. Attach the angle adapter to the overflow pipe. Cut off excess tubing with scissors to prevent kinking.

WARNING: Don't insert the refill tube into the overflow pipe. The outlet of the refill tube needs to be above the top of the pipe for it to work properly.

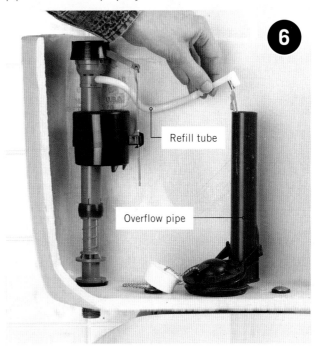

6

Refill tube

Overflow pipe

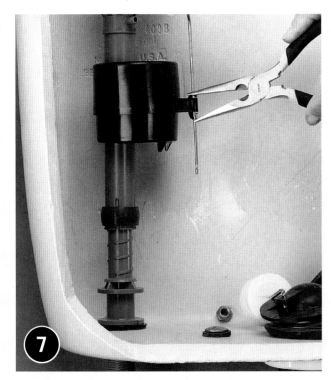

7

Turn the water on fully. Slightly tighten any fitting that drips water. Adjust the water level in the tank by squeezing the spring clip on the float cup with needlenose pliers and moving the cup up or down on the link bar. Test the flush.

OPTION: Newer diaphragm valves cost a bit more than float cups, but they boast quieter water flow. Install one the same way you would a float cup.

How to Replace a Flush Valve

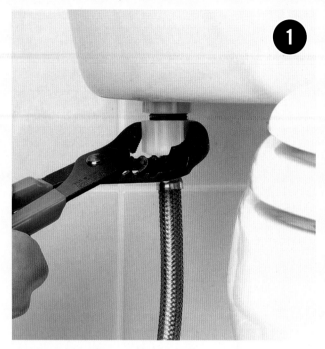

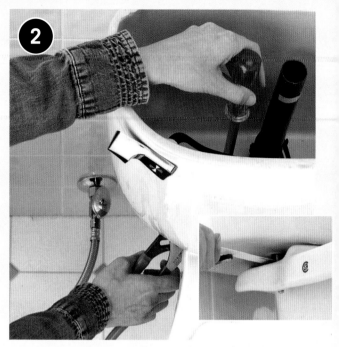

Before removing the old flush valve, shut off the water supply at the fixture stop valve located on the tube that supplies water to the tank. Flush the toilet, and sponge out the remaining water. To make this repair you'll need to remove the tank from the bowl. Start by unscrewing the water supply coupling nut from the bottom of the tank.

Unscrew the bolts holding the toilet tank to the bowl by loosening the nuts from below. If you are having difficulty unscrewing the tank bolts and nuts because they are fused together by rust or corrosion, apply penetrating oil or spray lubricant to the threads, give it a few minutes to penetrate, and then try again. If that fails, slip an open-ended hacksaw (or plain hacksaw blade) between the tank and bowl and saw through the bolt (inset).

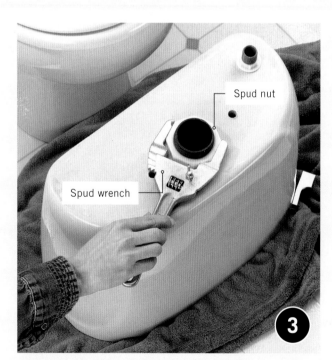

Spud nut

Spud wrench

Unhook the chain from the handle lever arm. Remove the tank and carefully place it upside-down on an old towel. Remove the spud washer and spud nut from the base of the flush valve using a spud wrench or large channel pliers. Remove the old flush valve.

Place the new flush valve in the valve hole and check to see if the top of the overflow pipe is at least 1" below the critical level line and the tank opening where the handle is installed. If the pipe is too tall, cut it to length with a hacksaw.

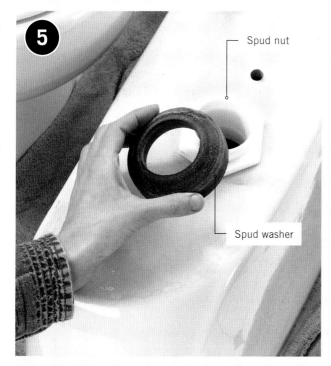

Spud nut

Spud washer

Intermediate nut goes between tank and bowl

Position the flush valve flapper below the handle lever arm, and secure it to the tank from beneath with the spud nut. Tighten the nut one-half turn past hand tight with a spud wrench or large channel pliers. Overtightening may cause the tank to break. Put the new spud washer over the spud nut, small side down.

With the tank lying on its back, thread a rubber washer onto each tank bolt and insert it into the bolt holes from inside the tank. Then, thread a brass washer and hex nut onto the tank bolts from below and tighten them to a quarter turn past hand tight. Do not overtighten.

Intermediate nut

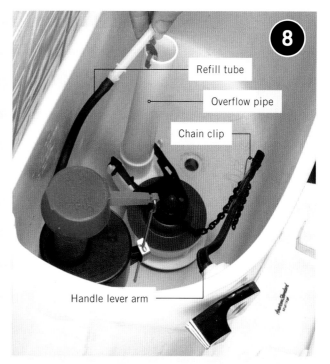

Refill tube

Overflow pipe

Chain clip

Handle lever arm

With the hex nuts tightened against the tank bottom, carefully lower the tank over the bowl and set it down so the spud washer seats neatly over the water inlet in the bowl and the tank bolts fit through the holes in the bowl flange. Secure the tank to the bowl with a rubber washer, brass washer, and nut or wing nut at each bolt end. Press the tank to level as you hand-tighten the nuts. Hook up the water supply at the fill valve inlet.

Connect the chain clip to the handle lever arm and adjust the number of links to allow for a little slack in the chain when the flapper is closed. Leave a little tail on the chain for adjusting, cutting off any excess. Attach the refill tube to the top of the overflow pipe the same way it had been attached to the previous refill pipe. Turn on the water supply at the stop valve, and test the flush. (Some flush valve flappers are adjustable.)

Dual-Flush Toilets + Valves

Dual-flush toilet valves are a fairly recent development dating from the 1980s. They were an early response to the need for water conservation and predate the EPA's adoption of the 1.6-gallon flush limit on new toilet installations after 1994. The theory behind dual-flush toilets is basic and—logically—sound: the toilet's valve offers two levels of flushes, one for solid wastes and one for liquids.

Putting that theory in practice has been a bit of a challenge. The first dual-flush toilets were infamously underpowered, often requiring multiple flushes that defeated the very purpose of the technology. New dual-flush toilets feature more efficient designs. Still, a key problem remains user confusion over what button or handle direction to use for which flush. Most dual-flush toilets use a round, tank-top button divided into two sections respectively featuring a full-circle, and half-circle icon. Dual-flush lever handles are meant to be pushed down for one type of flush and up for the other.

Although most new toilets already improve on the 1.6 gallon-per-flush mandate, many manufacturer's offer new dual-flush models that beat that standard. Easier still, you can retrofit an older 5-gallon flush model with a dual-flush valve, often for less than $30 dollars. These are fairly easy to install and are a quick way to improve your toilet's water usage. There are many different styles, but the valve used in the project shown here is typical. Follow the manufacturer's directions in any case. Because a toilet sees so much use, the savings can be substantial in terms of both water and a smaller water bill.

A typical tank-top dual-flush button used on the majority of dual-flush toilets. Although the icons are simple (full moon for full-force flush; half-moon for liquid-waste flush), confusion over which button to push has often led users to waste water by flushing multiple times after pushing the wrong button. Adapting a flush handle, like the one in the project shown here, is often the better option.

Newer, upscale dual-flush toilets include a wall-mounted control switch that is somewhat more clear—small circle for light flush and large circle for heavier flush.

TOOLS + MATERIALS

Dual-flush valve kit	Screwdriver
Spud gasket	Teflon tape
Spud nut	Channel pliers
Spud wrench	Grease pencil
Tank bolts	Bucket
Rubber tank bolt washers	Sponge
Brass tank bolt washers	Towel

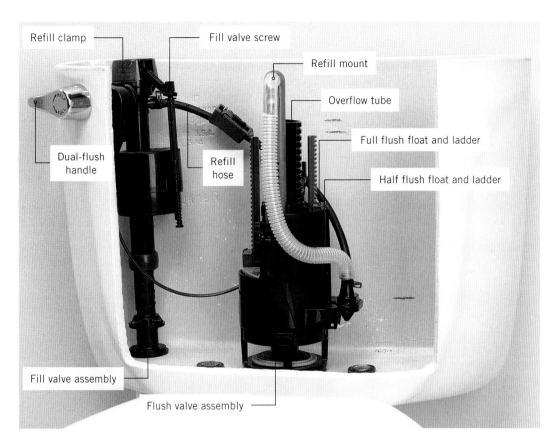

Refill clamp

Fill valve screw

Refill mount

Overflow tube

Dual-flush
handle

Refill
hose

Full flush float and ladder

Half flush float and ladder

Fill valve assembly

Flush valve assembly

A dual-flush valve is easier to install than it looks. All the component pieces are seen on the left.

How to Install a Dual-flush Valve

1

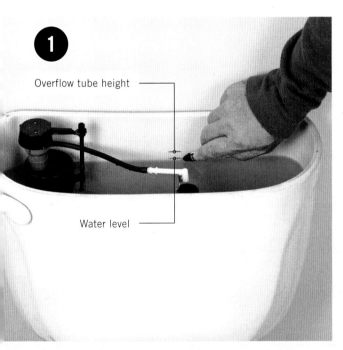

Overflow tube height

Water level

Turn off the water supply. Remove the top of the tank, and mark both the water level and the top of the overflow tube using a grease pencil. Remove the old assemblies, flush a single time, and mark the level of the remaining water in the bottom of the tank. Hold the toilet handle to flush once more, and remove excess water with a sponge.

Disconnect the supply line from behind the tank. Use channel pliers to remove the lock nut from the valve shank, allowing excess water to drip into a bucket. Next, remove the tank after loosening the flush valve nuts. Remove the old gasket from the flush valve shank, but keep all the old parts together—they may still be needed. Remove the spud gasket and spud nut.

2

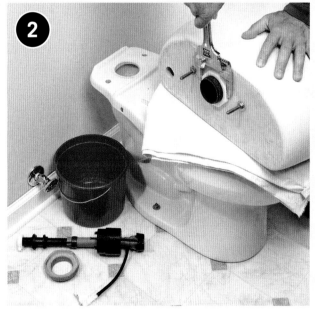

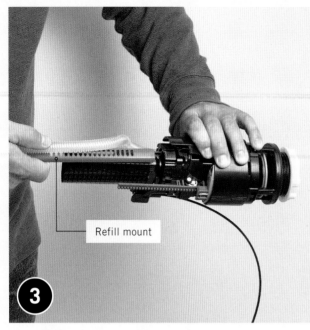

Refill mount

3

After removing the flush valve lock nut from the new flush valve assembly, place the new flush valve assembly into the tank, ensuring it is level and comfortably seated atop the shank. Mark the height of the new overflow tube to match the height of the old tube recorded in step 1; cut the tube to match, removing the assembly from the tank if necessary. Removing the refill mount from the flush valve assembly (above) makes marking and cutting the tube easier.

Re-attach the refill mount, making sure it is low enough to fit inside the tank and high enough to clear the lid. Cut excess refill hose if necessary. To install the entire valve, hand-tighten the lock nut to the threaded shank. Do not over-tighten.

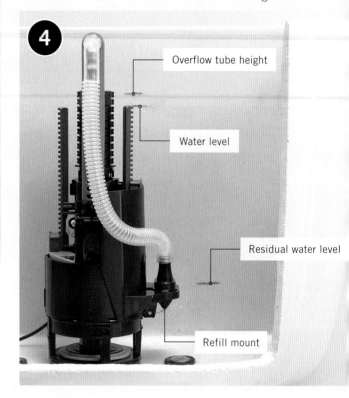

4

Overflow tube height

Water level

Residual water level

Refill mount

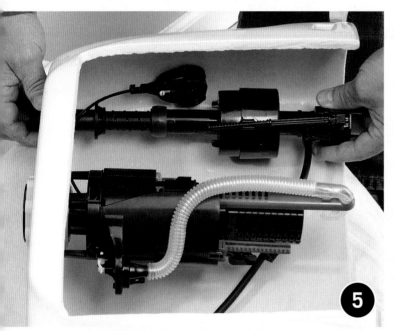

5

Reassemble the tank with bolts, rubber washers, brass washers, and a spud nut. Use the old rubber gasket if necessary and install the fill valve in much the same way as the flush valve; remove the fill valve lock nut and shank washer, and insert the valve onto the fill valve shank adjacent to the flush valve. The height of the fill valve must be approximately 3" greater than the flush valve; adjust as necessary by twisting the threaded shank in and out. When the desired height is reached, hand-tighten the fill valve lock nut to the shank.

The refill hose connects the dual valve assemblies; attach the refill hose from the fill valve to the nipple on the dual flush valve (inset), and ensure both ends are clear of the valve operations. If you need to change the orientation of the flush valve, release the base by turning the assembly counterclockwise until the tabs unlock, lift the valves out, and adjust as needed.

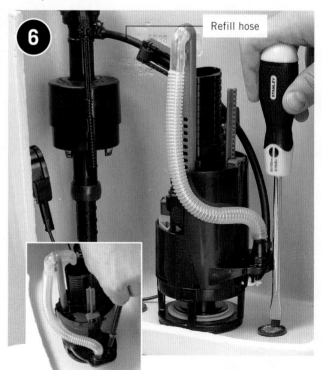

6

Refill hose

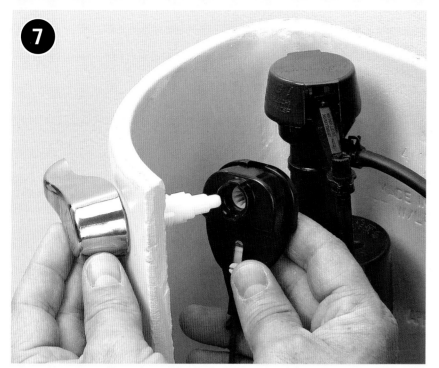

7

Install the dual flush handle to the tank and hand-tighten the lever lock-nut. The nut is reverse-threaded, so be sure the tabs on the collar are oriented vertically and aligned with the handle's tabs. Reconnect and turn on the water supply, checking for leaks. Do not use plumber's putty or thread lubricants to seal the fittings, as they may damage the plastic nut. Teflon tape is a good alternative.

ADJUSTING THE FLUSH AND TANK LEVELS

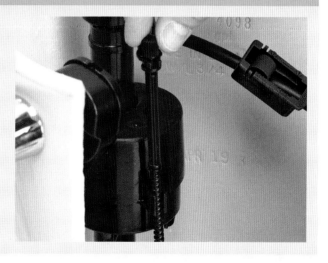

If the water in the tank is uneven with the original high water mark from step 1, turn the screw near the top of the fill valve clockwise to increase the water level or counterclockwise to decrease it.

To adjust the level of half or full flushes, look to the flush valve assembly on the right; the higher float near the refill hose adjusts the half flush, while the opposing lower float on the other side of the assembly adjusts the full. Use a small amount of toilet paper and a test flush to gauge the amount of water used; if unsatisfied, adjust the appropriate flush by pulling out each float's stop and raising or lowering each float to properly adjust the refill level. See the manufacturer's instructions, because the adjustment varies per manufacturer.

ADJUSTING THE REFILL LEVEL IN THE BOWL

The refill tube connects both valve assemblies, and the roller clamp on the tube can be adjusted to monitor the level of water in the bowl. To adjust, add a gallon of water to the bowl and wait 10 minutes, then mark the water level with a grease pencil. Flush the toilet. If the refill valve is still running once the water mark has been reached, decrease the volume of water by moving the roller clamp toward zero. If there's not enough water, do the opposite, moving the clamp toward higher numbers. Continue adjusting until the water reaches the mark in the tank at the same time the valve turns off.

Clogged Toilets

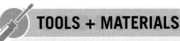

TOOLS + MATERIALS

Towels
Closet auger

Plunger with foldout skirt
(force cup)

The toilet is clogged and has overflowed. Have patience. Now is the time for considered action. A second flush is a tempting but unnecessary gamble. First, do damage control. Mop up the water if there's been a spill. Next, consider the nature of the clog. Is it entirely "natural" or might a foreign object be contributing to the congestion? Push a natural blockage down the drain with a plunger. A foreign object should be removed, if possible, with a closet auger. Pushing anything more durable than toilet paper into the sewer may create a more serious blockage in your drain and waste system.

If the tub, sink, and toilet all back up at once, the branch drainline that serves all the bathroom fixtures is probably blocked and your best recourse is to call a drain clearing service.

A blockage in the toilet bowl leaves flush water from the tank nowhere to go but on the floor.

The trap is the most common catching spot for toilet clogs.
Once the clog forms, flushing the toilet cannot generate enough water power to clear the trap, so flush water backs up. Traps on modern 1.6-gallon toilets have been redesigned to larger diameters and are less prone to clogs than the first generation of 1.6-gallon toilets.

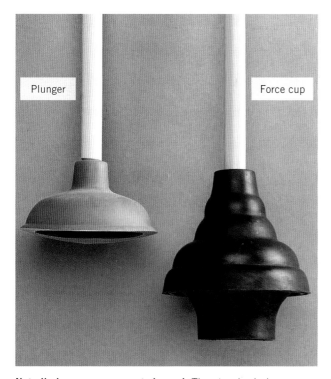

Not all plungers were created equal. The standard plunger (left) is simply an inverted rubber cup and is used to plunge sinks, tubs, and showers. The flanged plunger, also called a force cup, is designed to get down into the trap of a toilet drain. You can fold the flange up into the flanged plunger cup and use it as a standard plunger.

DRAIN CLEARERS

The home repair marketplace is filled with gadgets and gimmicks, as well as well-established products, that are intended to clear drains of all types. Some are caustic chemicals, some are natural enzymes, others are more mechanical in nature. Some help, some are worthless, some can even make the problem worse. Nevertheless, if you are the type of homeowner who is enamored with new products and the latest solutions, you may enjoy testing out new drain cleaners as they become available. In this photo, for example, you'll see a relatively new product that injects blasts of compressed CO_2 directly into your toilet, sink, or tub drain to dislodge clogs. It does not cause any chemicals to enter the waste stream, and the manufacturers claim the CO_2 blast is very gentle and won't damage pipes. As with any new product, use it with caution. But if a plunger or a snake isn't working, it could save you the cost of a house call.

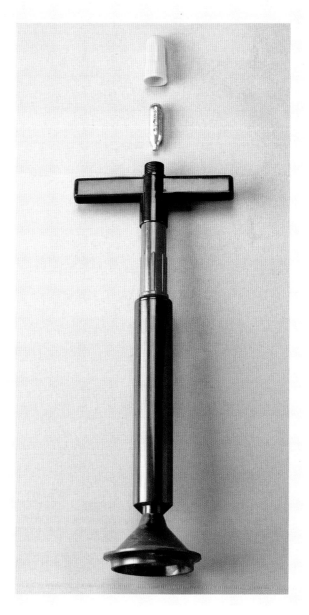

How to Plunge a Clogged Toilet

Plunging is the easiest way to remove "natural" blockages. Take time to lay towels around the base of the toilet and remove other objects to a safe, dry location, since plunging may result in splashing. Often, allowing a very full toilet to sit for twenty or thirty minutes will permit some of the water to drain to a less precarious level.

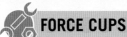 **FORCE CUPS**

A flanged plunger (force cup) fits into the mouth of the toilet trap and creates a tight seal so you can build up enough pressure in front of the plunger to dislodge the blockage and send it on its way.

There should be enough water in the bowl to completely cover the plunger. Fold out the skirt from inside the plunger to form a better seal with the opening at the base of the bowl. Pump the plunger vigorously half a dozen times, take a rest, and then repeat. Try this for four to five cycles.

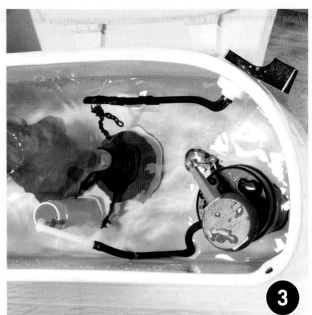

If you force enough water out of the bowl that you are unable to create suction with the plunger, put a controlled amount of water in the bowl by lifting up on the flush valve in the tank. Resume plunging. When you think the drain is clear, you can try a controlled flush, with your hand ready to close the flush valve should the water threaten to spill out of the bowl. Once the blockage has cleared, dump a five-gallon pail of water into the toilet to blast away any residual debris.

How to Clear Clogs with a Closet Auger

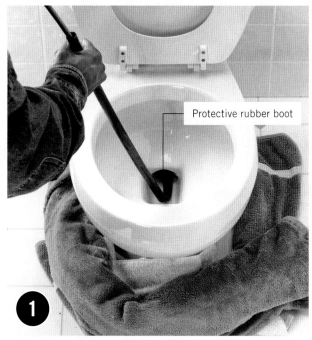

Protective rubber boot

1

Place the business end of the auger firmly in the bottom of the toilet bowl with the auger tip fully withdrawn. A rubber sleeve will protect the porcelain at the bottom bend of the auger. The tip will be facing back and up, which is the direction the toilet trap takes.

 ## CLOSET AUGERS

A closet auger is a semirigid cable housed in a tube. The tube has a bend at the end so it can be snaked through a toilet trap (without scratching it) to snag blockages.

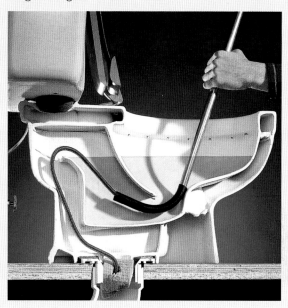

2

Fully retract the auger until you have recovered the object. This can be frustrating at times, but it is still a much easier task than the alternative—to remove the toilet and go fishing.

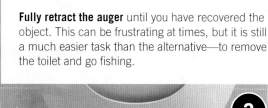

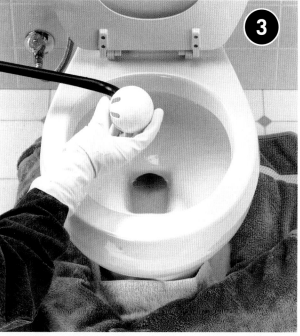

3

Rotate the handle on the auger housing clockwise as you push down on the rod, advancing the rotating auger tip up into the back part of the trap. You may work the cable backward and forward as needed, but keep the rubber boot of the auger firmly in place in the bowl. When you feel resistance, indicating you've snagged the object, continue rotating the auger counterclockwise as you withdraw the cable and the object.

Toilet Flanges

If your toilet rocks, it will eventually leak. The rocking means that the bolts are no longer holding the toilet securely to the floor. If you have tightened the bolts and it still rocks, it is possible that a bolt has broken a piece of the flange off and is no longer able to hold. Rocking might also be because an ongoing leak has weakened the floor and it is now uneven. Whatever the reason, a rocking toilet needs to be fixed.

If your flange is connected to cast-iron piping, use a repair flange. This has a rubber compression ring that will seal the new flange to the cast-iron pipe. If the old flange is too close to a wall or cabinet to fit your new toilet, you can "relocate" the flange by as much as 2 inches by replacing it with an offset toilet flange.

Toilets that rock often only need to have the nuts on the closet bolts tightened. But if you need to tighten the bolts on an ongoing basis, you very likely have a problem with the closet flange.

TOOLS + MATERIALS

New toilet flange or offset flange

Drill

Tape measure

Wrench

Internal pipe cutter

#10 stainless-steel flathead wood screws

Jigsaw (optional)

PVC primer + cement

Marker

Rubber gloves

Safety glasses

Spray expanding foam

TOILET SHIMS

If the toilet is wobbly because of an uneven floor, shims may solve the problem. (Do not install shims if the toilet leaks at the base; they will not solve that problem.) Slip two or more plastic toilet shims under the toilet until it is stabilized. Press the shims with only medium pressure; don't force them too hard. Cut the exposed portions of the shims with a utility knife.

How to Replace a PVC Closet Flange

1

Begin by removing the toilet and wax ring. Cut the pipe just below the bottom of the flange using an internal pipe cutter (inset, available at plumbing supply stores). Remove the flange.

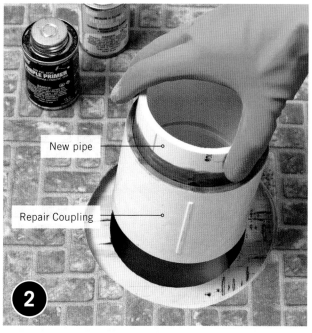

New pipe

Repair Coupling

2

If your flange is attached to a closet bend, you will need to open up the floor around the toilet to get at the horizontal pipe connecting the bend to the stack to make the repair. If it is connected to a length of vertical plastic pipe, use a repair coupling and a short length of pipe to bring the pipe back up to floor level. Cement the new pipe into the repair coupling first and allow it to set. Clean the old pipe thoroughly before cementing.

3

Cut the replacement pipe flush with the floor. Dry-fit the new flange into the pipe. Turn the flange until the side cut-out screw slots are parallel to the wall. (Do not use the curved keyhole slots, as they are not as strong.) Draw lines to mark the location of the slots on the floor.

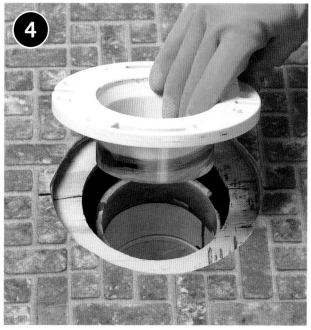

4

Prime and cement the pipe and flange, inserting the flange slightly off the marks and twisting it to proper alignment. Secure the flange to the floor with #10 stainless-steel flathead wood screws.

How to Install an Offset Toilet Flange

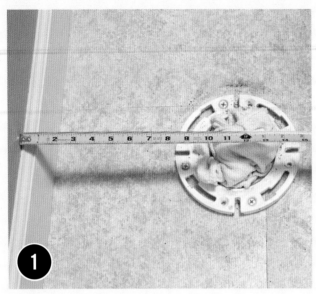

You can adjust the flange location by as much as 2" if you replace the old flange with an offset flange (a much easier job than moving the drain line). To remove the old flange, cut the pipe directly beneath the flange from the inside out using an internal pipe cutter chucked into your drill. Cut all the way around the pipe, and then remove the old flange.

Most toilets sold today are 12" models, which means the distance from the wall at the tank side to the center of the drain outlet is 12". If you are replacing a toilet, the existing toilet (closet) flange might be either so close to the wall that the new model will not fit or far enough out (many older toilets are 14" fixtures) that there would be a 2" gap between the tank and wall if you installed the new model on the old flange. If your current toilet is still in place, you can determine the distance by measuring from the center of the floor bolts to the wall. Or remove the old toilet and measure from the wall to the center point of the toilet flange opening.

Solvent-glue a section of new drain pipe of the correct diameter into a repair coupling, and then glue the coupling to the cut pipe in the floor repair coupling. The goal is to have fresh drain pipe of the correct height so the ring of the new flange will rest directly on the floor surface. It's not a bad idea to cut the new pipe so it is slightly overlong and then trim it to the correct height once it is installed and you can test-fit the new flange.

Position the offset flange into the drain opening and spin it until the center of the flange is in the desired position. You will most likely need to remove some flooring and subfloor to create access for the new flange. Trace around the rim of the flange.

Cut along the marked line for the new opening with a jigsaw and remove the waste. Try to avoid getting debris in the pipe opening.

Solvent glue the new offset flange into the drain pipe, making sure it is oriented in the correct position and that the flange ring rests on the floor.

TIP: When choosing an offset flange, select a model that has a metal, not plastic, flange ring, because metal is much less likely crack or fail.

Attach the new flange to the floor by driving corrosion-resistant screws through the pre-drilled holes in the flange and into the subfloor. It is okay to skip one or two holes if there is no attaching surface below them.

OPTION: To reduce noise and air transfer, fill in the empty space around the drain pipe with minimal expanding spray foam, but if there are any more, then you should patch the subfloor beneath the flange. Install your new toilet.

Sink Faucets

It's not surprising that sink faucets leak and drip. Any fitting that contains moving mechanical parts is susceptible to failure. But add to the equation the persistent force of water pressure working against the parts, and the real surprise is that faucets don't fail more quickly or often. It would be a bit unfair to say that the inner workings of a faucet are regarded as disposable by manufacturers, but it is safe to say that these parts have become easier to remove and replace.

The older your faucet, the more likely you can repair it by replacing small parts such as washers and O-rings. Many newer faucets can be repaired only by replacing the major inner components, such as a ceramic disk or a cartridge that encapsulates all the washers and O-rings that could possibly wear out.

The most important aspect of sink faucet repair is identifying which type of faucet you own. In this chapter we show all of the common types and provide instructions on repairing them. In every case, the easiest and most reliable repair method is to purchase a replacement kit with brand-new internal working parts for the model and brand of faucet you own.

TOOLS + MATERIALS

Pliers
Needlenose pliers
Channel pliers
Utility knife
White vinegar
Old toothbrush
Tape measure
Repair kit (exact type varies)
Teflon tape
Screwdrivers
Plumber's putty
Rag
Plumber's grease
Adjustable wrench
Handle puller (optional)
Seat wrench (optional)

Eventually, just about every faucet develops leaks and drips.
Repairs can usually be accomplished simply by replacing the mechanical parts inside the faucet body (the main trick is figuring out which kind of parts your faucet has).

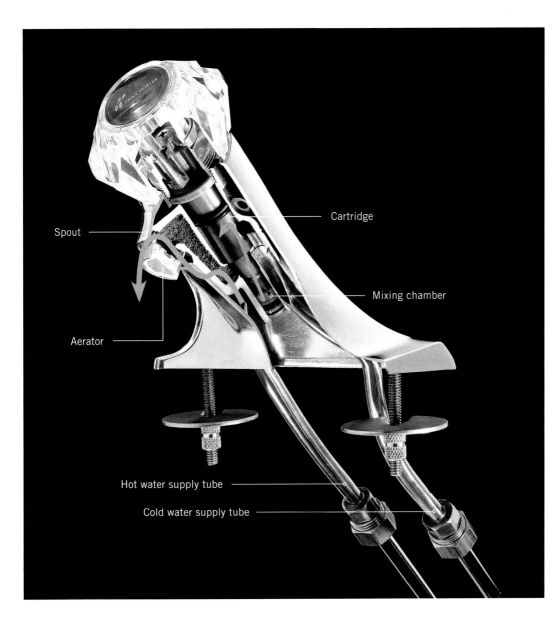

Spout

Cartridge

Mixing chamber

Aerator

Hot water supply tube

Cold water supply tube

All faucets, no matter the type, have valves that move many thousands of times to open and close hot- and cold-water ports. These valves—or the rubber or plastic parts that rub against other parts when the faucet is being adjusted—wear out in time. Depending on the faucet, you may be able to fix the leak by cleaning or replacing small parts, such as washers or O-rings; or you may need to buy a repair kit and replace a number of parts; or the only solution may be to replace a self-enclosed "cartridge" that contains all the moving parts.

COMMON PROBLEMS AND REPAIRS

PROBLEMS	REPAIRS
Faucet drips from the end of the spout or leaks around the base.	1. Identify the faucet design, then install appropriate replacement parts using directions on the following pages.
Old worn-out faucet continues to leak after repairs are made.	1. Replace the old faucet.
Water pressure at spout seems low, or water flow is partially blocked.	1. Clean faucet aerator. 2. Replace corroded galvanized pipes with copper or PEX.
Water pressure from sprayer seems low, or sprayer leaks from handle.	1. Clean sprayer head. 2. Fix diverter valve.
Water leaks onto floor underneath faucet.	1. Replace cracked sprayer hose. 2. Tighten water connections, or replace supply tubes and shutoff valves. 3. Fix leaky sink strainer.
Hose bib or valve drips from spout or leaks around handle.	1. Take valve apart and replace washers and O-rings.

Identifying Your Faucet and the Parts You Need

A leaky faucet is the most common home plumbing problem. Fortunately, repair parts are available for almost every type of faucet, from the oldest to the newest, and installing these parts is usually easy. But if you don't know your make and model, the hardest part of fixing a leak may be identifying your faucet and finding the right parts. Don't make the common mistake of thinking that any similar-looking parts will do the job; you've got to get exact replacements.

There are so many faucet types that even experts have trouble classifying them into neat categories. Two-handle faucets are either compression (stem) or washerless two-handle. Single-handle faucets are classified as mixing cartridge; ball; disc; or disc/cartridge.

A single-handle faucet with a rounded, dome-shaped cap is often a ball type. If a single-handle faucet has a flat top, it is likely a cartridge or a ceramic disc type. An older two-handle faucet is likely of the compression type; newer two-handle models use washerless cartridges.

Shut off the water supply. Dismantle the faucet carefully. Look for a brand name: it may be clearly visible on the baseplate or printed on an inner part, or it may not be printed anywhere. Put all the parts into a plastic bag and take them to your home

center or plumbing supply store. A knowledgeable salesperson can help you identify the parts you need.

If you cannot find what you are looking for at a local store, check online sites or the manufacturers' sites; they often have step-by-step instruction for identifying what you need. Note that manufacturers' terminology may not match the terms we use here. For example, the word "cartridge" may refer to a ceramic-disc unit.

Most faucets have repair kits, which include all the parts you need, and sometimes a small tool as well. Even if some of the parts in your faucet look fine, it's a good idea to install the parts provided in the kit to ensure against future wear.

REPAIR TIPS

If water flow is weak, unscrew the aerator at the tip of the spout. If there is sediment, then dirty water is entering the faucet, which could damage the faucet's inner workings.

To remove handles and spouts, work carefully and look for small screw heads. You often need to first pry off a cap on top, but not always. Parts may be held in place with small setscrews.

Cleaning and removing debris can sometimes solve the problem of low water flow and occasionally can solve a leak as well.

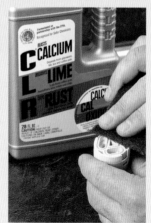

Some manufacturers may specify that you coat replacement parts with valve grease before installing. Follow the instructions for your particular model.

Compression Faucets

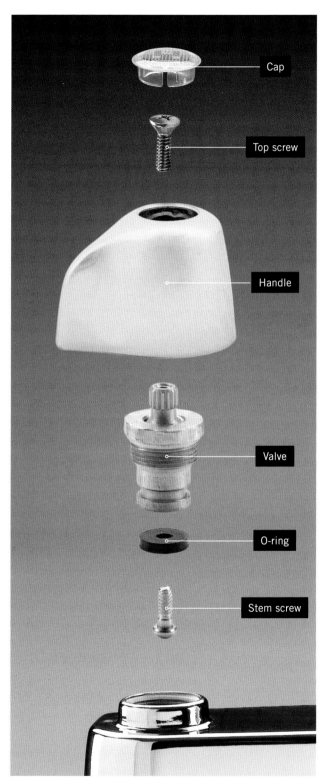

Cap

Top screw

Handle

Valve

O-ring

Stem screw

Pry off the cap on top of the handle and remove the screw that holds the cap onto the stem. Pull the handle up and out. Use an adjustable wrench or pliers to unscrew the stem and pull it out.

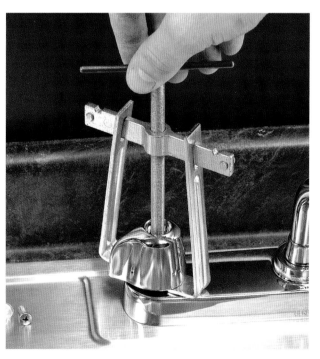

A compression faucet has a stem assembly that includes a retaining nut, threaded spindle, O-ring, stem washer, and stem screw. Dripping at the spout occurs when the washer becomes worn. Leaks around the handle are caused by a worn O-ring.

If the handle is stuck, try applying mineral cleaner from above. If that doesn't work, you may need to buy a handle puller. With the cap and the hold-down screw removed, position the wings of the puller under the handle and tighten the puller to slowly pull the handle up.

Remove the screw that holds the rubber washer in place, and pry out the washer. Replace a worn washer with an exact replacement—one that is the same diameter, thickness, and shape.

Replace any O-rings. A worn O-ring can cause water to leak out the handle. Gently pry out the old O-ring and reinstall an exact replacement. Apply plumber's grease to the rubber parts before reinstalling the stem.

If washers wear out quickly, the seat is likely worn. Use a seat wrench to unscrew the seat from inside the faucet. Replace it with an exact duplicate. If replacing the washer and O-ring doesn't solve the problem, you may need to replace the entire stem.

Washerless Two-Handle Faucet

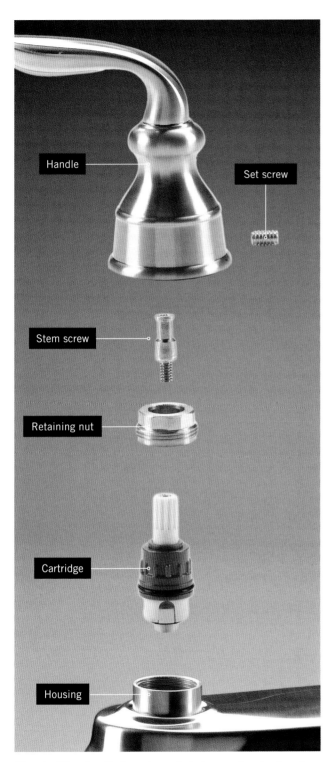

Handle

Set screw

Stem screw

Retaining nut

Cartridge

Housing

Remove the faucet handle, and withdraw the old cartridge. Make a note of how the cartridge is oriented before you remove it. Purchase a replacement cartridge.

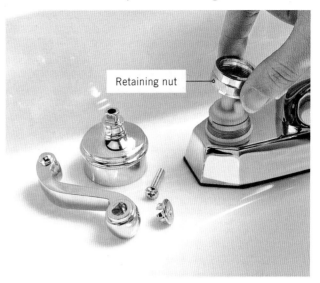

Retaining nut

Install the replacement cartridge. Clean the valve seat first, and coat the valve seat and O-rings with faucet grease. Be sure the new cartridge is in the correct position, with its tabs seated in the slotted body of the faucet. Re-assemble the valve and handles.

Almost all two-handle faucets made today are "washerless." Instead of an older-type compression stem, there is a cartridge, usually with a plastic casing. Many of these cartridges contain ceramic discs, while others have metal or plastic pathways. No matter the type of cartridge, the repair is the same; instead of replacing small parts, you simply replace the entire cartridge.

Single-Handle Cartridge Faucets

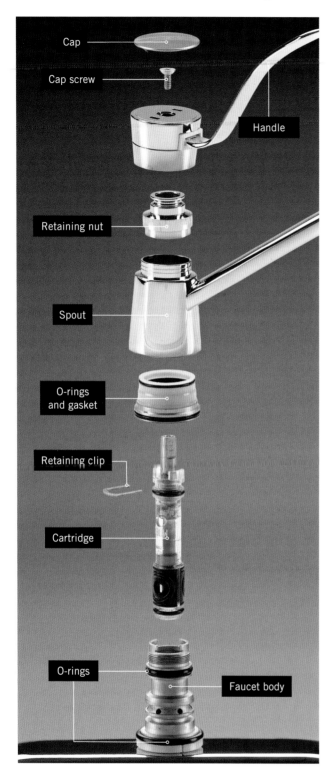

Cap

Cap screw

Handle

Retaining nut

Spout

O-rings and gasket

Retaining clip

Cartridge

O-rings

Faucet body

Single-handle cartridge faucets such as this work by moving the cartridge up and down and side to side, which opens up pathways to direct varying amounts of hot and cold water to the spout. Moen, Price-Pfister, Delta, Peerless, Kohler, and others make many types of cartridges, some of which look very different from this one.

To remove the spout, pry off the handle's cap and remove the screw below it. Pull the handle up and off. Use an adjustable wrench to remove the pivot nut.

Lift out the spout. If the faucet has a diverter valve, remove it as well. Use a screwdriver to pry out the retainer clip, which holds the cartridge in place.

Remove the cartridge. If you simply pull up with pliers, you may leave part of the stem in the faucet body. If that happens, replace the cartridge and buy a stem puller made for your model.

Gently pry out and replace all O-rings on the faucet body. Smear plumber's grease onto the new replacement cartridge and the new O-rings, and reassemble the faucet.

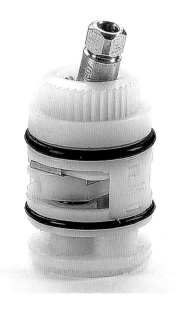

Here is one of many other types of single-handle cartridges. In this model, all the parts are plastic except for the stem, and it's important to note the direction in which the cartridge is aligned. If you test the faucet and the hot and cold are reversed, disassemble and realign the cartridge.

Ball Faucets

Remove the old ball and cam after removing the faucet handle and ball cap. Some faucets may require a ball faucet tool to remove the handle. Otherwise, simply use a pair of channel pliers to twist off the ball cap.

The ball-type faucet is used by Delta, Peerless, and a few others. The ball fits into the faucet body and is constructed with three holes (not visible here)—a hot inlet, a cold inlet, and the outlet, which fills the valve body with water that then flows to the spout or sprayer. Depending on the position of the ball, each inlet hole is open, closed, or somewhere in-between. The inlet holes are sealed to the ball with valve seats, which are pressed tight against the ball with springs. If water drips from the spout, replace the seats and springs or purchase an entire replacement kit and replace all the working parts.

Pry out the neoprene valve seals and springs. Place thick towels around the faucet. Slowly turn on the water to flush out any debris in the faucet body. Replace the seals and springs with new parts. Also replace the O-rings on the valve body. You may want to replace the ball and cam too, especially if you're purchasing a repair kit. Coat all rubber parts in faucet grease, and reassemble the faucet.

Disc Faucets

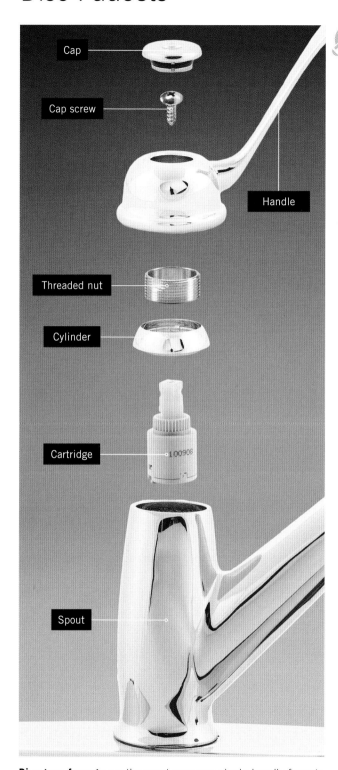

Cap

Cap screw

Handle

Threaded nut

Cylinder

Cartridge

Spout

Disc-type faucets are the most common single-handle faucets currently being made. A pair of ceramic discs encased in a cylinder often referred to as a "cartridge" rub together as they rotate to open ports for hot and cold water. The ceramic discs do wear out in time, causing leaks, and there is only one solution—replace the disc unit/cartridge. This makes for an easy—through comparatively expensive—repair.

OTHER CARTRIDGES

Many modern cartridges do not have seals or O-rings that can be replaced, and some have a ball rather than a ceramic disk inside. For the repair, the cartridge's innards do not matter; just replace the whole cartridge.

Replace the cylinder with a new one, coating the rubber parts with faucet grease before installing the new cylinder. Make sure the rubber seals fit correctly in the cylinder openings before you install the cylinder. Assemble the faucet handle.

Kitchen Sprayers

If water pressure from a sink sprayer seems low, or if water leaks from the handle, it is usually because lime buildup and sediment have blocked small openings inside the sprayer head. To fix the problem, first take the sprayer head apart and clean the parts. If cleaning the sprayer head does not help, the problem may be caused by a faulty diverter valve. The diverter valve inside the faucet body shifts water flow from the faucet spout to the sprayer when the sprayer handle is pressed. Cleaning or replacing the diverter valve may fix water pressure problems.

Whenever making repairs to a sink sprayer, check the sprayer hose for kinks or cracks. A damaged hose should be replaced.

If water pressure from a faucet spout seems low, or if the flow is partially blocked, take the spout aerator apart and clean the parts. The aerator is a screw-on attachment with a small wire screen that mixes tiny air bubbles into the water flow. Make sure the wire screen is not clogged with sediment and lime buildup. If water pressure is low throughout the house, it may be because galvanized steel water pipes are corroded. Corroded pipes should be replaced with copper or PEX pipe.

TOOLS + MATERIALS

Screwdriver	Vinegar
Channel pliers	Universal washer kit
Needlenose pliers	Heatproof grease
Small brush	Replacement sprayer hose

Kitchen sprayers are very convenient and, in theory, quite simple. Yet, they break down with surprising regularity. Fixing or replacing one is an easy job, however.

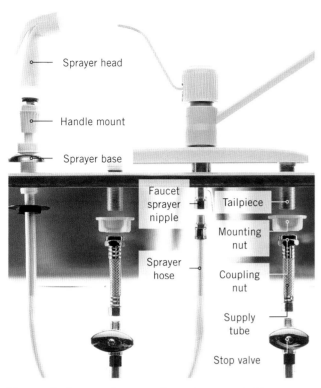

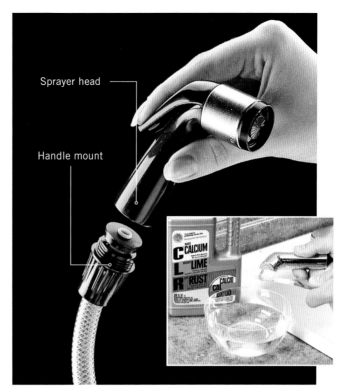

The standard sprayer hose attachment is connected to a nipple at the bottom of the faucet valve. When the lever of the sprayer is depressed, water flows from a diverter valve in the faucet body out to the sprayer. If your sprayer stream is weak or doesn't work at all, the chances are good that the problem lies in the diverter valve.

Sprayer heads can be removed from the sprayer hose, usually by loosening a retaining nut. A sprayer's head can get clogged with minerals. Unscrew the sprayer from the hose and remove any parts at its tip. Soak it in mineral cleaner, and use a small brush to open any clogged orifices.

 How to Repair a Sprayer

Shut off the water at the stop valves, and remove the faucet handle to gain access to the faucet parts. Disassemble the faucet handle and body to expose the diverter valve. Ball-type faucets such as the one shown here require that you also remove the spout to get at the diverter.

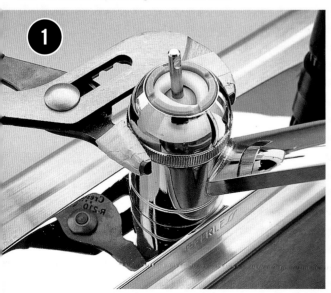

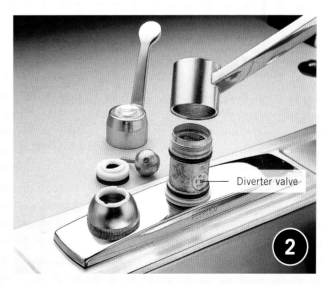

Locate the diverter valve, seen here at the base of the valve body. Because different types and brands of faucets have differently configured diverters, do a little investigating beforehand to try and locate information about your faucet. The above faucet is a ball type.

(continued)

FINDING THE DIVERTER ON A TWO-HANDLE FAUCET

On a two-handle faucet, the diverter is usually located in a vertical position just under the spout. Remove the spout. You may need to use longnose pliers to pull out the diverter. Try cleaning out any debris. If that does not restore operation, replace the valve.

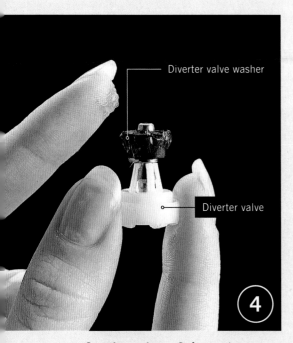

3

Pull the diverter valve from the faucet body with needlenose pliers. Use a toothbrush dipped in white vinegar to clean any lime buildup from the valve. If the valve is in poor condition, bring it to the hardware store and purchase a replacement.

Diverter valve washer

Diverter valve

4

Coat the washer or O-ring on the new or cleaned diverter valve with faucet grease. Insert the diverter valve back into the faucet body. Reassemble the faucet. Turn on the water, and test the sprayer. If it still isn't functioning to your satisfaction, remove the sprayer tip and run the sprayer without the filter and aerator in case any debris has made its way into the sprayer line during repairs.

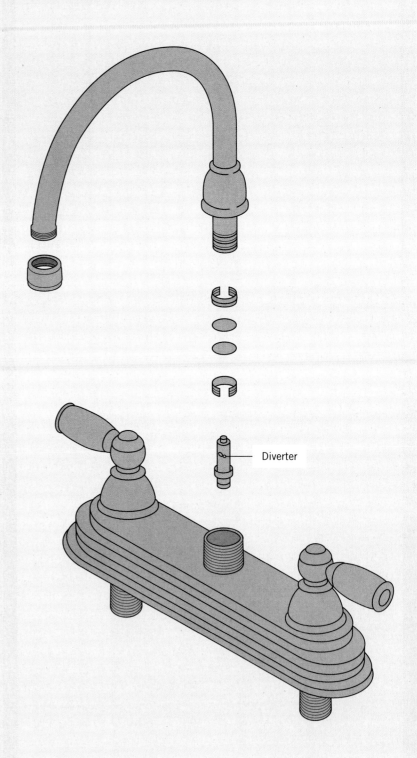

Diverter

How to Replace a Sprayer Head

1

Replace a leaking sprayer head rather than the whole assembly to save money, time, and effort. Start by unscrewing the ridged base nut on the existing spray head. The spray head should come right off once the nut is entirely unscrewed.

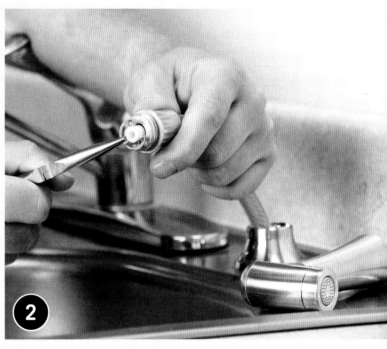

2

The spray head base is held in place by a small metal C-clip. Remove the rubber washer to expose the C-clip. Use needle-nose pliers to grab the clip and spread it until it pops out of its ridge and releases from the base. Remove the C-clip and base.

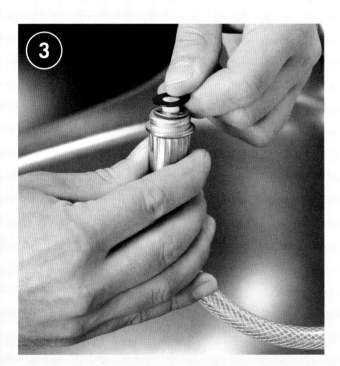

3

Secure the hose from slipping down the hole, if necessary. Buy a head to match the one you're replacing. Disassemble the new head, and slide the new base onto the existing hose. Secure the base in place with a C-clip, cover with the rubber washer, and secure the sprayer on the base by hand-tightening the mounting nut.

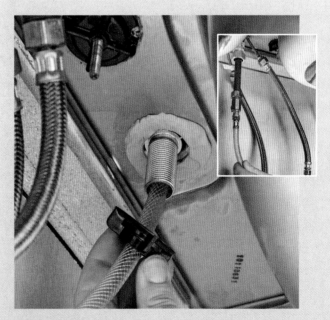

ALTERNATIVE: To remove the entire spray assembly, simply unscrew the mounting nut for the sprayer on the underside of the deck, then use a crescent wrench or basin wrench to unscrew the nut on the connection between the end of the spray hose and the faucet nipple (inset). Reverse the process to install the new sprayer.

Fixing Leaky Tub + Shower Faucets

Tub and shower faucets have the same basic designs as sink faucets, and the techniques for repairing leaks are the same as described in the faucet repair. To identify your faucet design, you may have to take off the handle and disassemble the faucet.

When a tub and shower are combined, the showerhead and the tub spout share the same hot and cold water supply lines and handles. Combination faucets are available as three-handle, two-handle, or single-handle types. The number of handles gives clues as to the design of the faucets and the kinds of repairs that may be necessary.

With combination faucets, a diverter valve or gate diverter is used to direct water flow to the tub spout or the showerhead. On three-handle faucet types, the middle handle controls a diverter valve. If water does not shift easily from tub to showerhead, or if water continues to run out the spout when the shower is on, the diverter valve probably needs to be cleaned and repaired.

Two-handle and single-handle types use a gate diverter that is operated by a pull lever or knob on the tub spout. Although gate diverters rarely need repair, the lever occasionally may break, come loose, or refuse to stay in the up position. To repair a gate diverter set in a tub spout, replace the entire spout.

Tub and shower faucets and diverter valves may be set inside wall cavities. Removing them may require a deep-set ratchet wrench.

If spray from the showerhead is uneven, clean the spray holes. If the showerhead does not stay in an upright position, remove the head and replace the O-ring.

To add a shower to an existing tub, install a flexible shower adapter. Several manufacturers make complete conversion kits that allow a shower to be installed in less than one hour.

Tub/shower plumbing is notorious for developing drips from the tub spout and the showerhead. In most cases, the leak can be traced to the valves controlled by the faucet handles.

Tub + Shower Combination Faucets

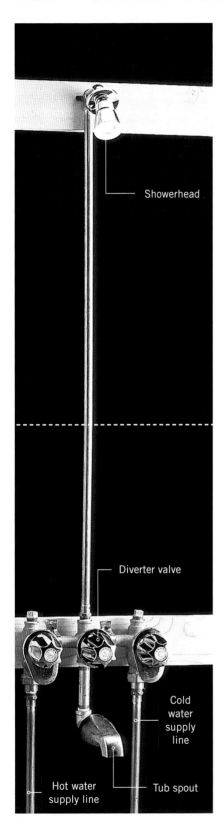

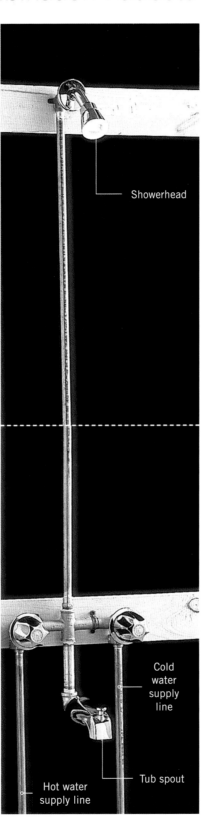

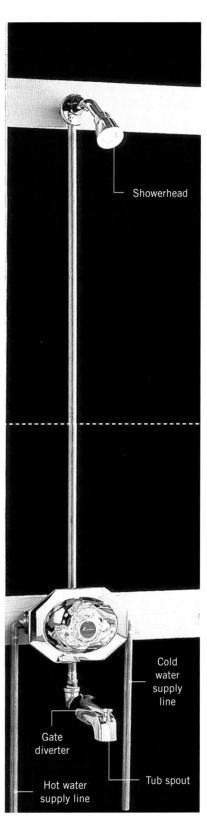

Three-handle faucets have valves that are either compression or cartridge design.

Two-handle faucets have valves that are either compression or cartridge design.

Single-handle faucets have valves that are cartridge, ball-type, or disc design.

Fixing Three-Handle Tub + Shower Faucets

A three-handle faucet type has two handles to control hot and cold water, and a third handle to control the diverter valve and direct water to either a tub spout or a showerhead. The separate hot and cold handles indicate cartridge or compression faucet designs.

If a diverter valve sticks, if water flow is weak, or if water runs out of the tub spout when the flow is directed to the showerhead, the diverter needs to be repaired or replaced. Most diverter valves are similar to either compression or cartridge faucet valves. Compression-type diverters can be repaired, but cartridge types should be replaced. Remember to turn off the water supply before beginning work.

TOOLS + MATERIALS

Screwdriver

Adjustable wrench or channel pliers

Ratchet wrench set

Small wire brush

Replacement diverter cartridge or universal washer kit

Faucet grease

Vinegar

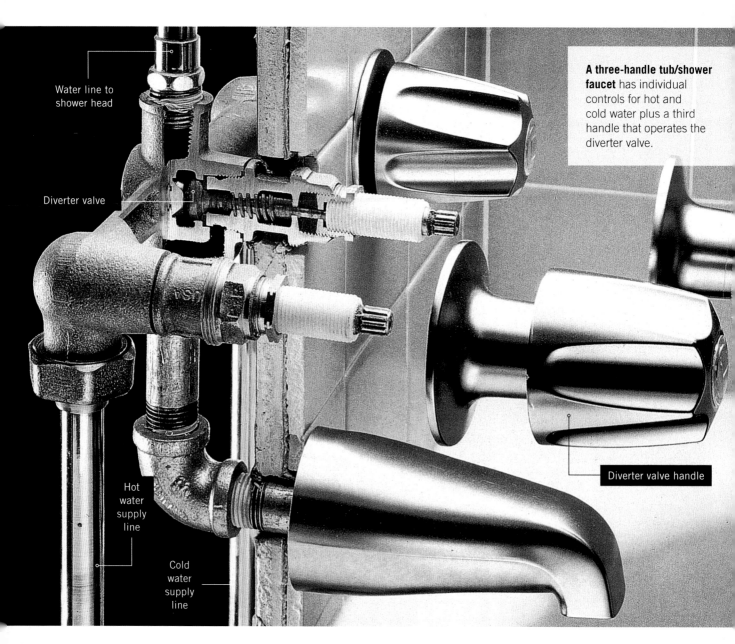

Water line to shower head

Diverter valve

Hot water supply line

Cold water supply line

A three-handle tub/shower faucet has individual controls for hot and cold water plus a third handle that operates the diverter valve.

Diverter valve handle

How to Repair a Compression Diverter Valve

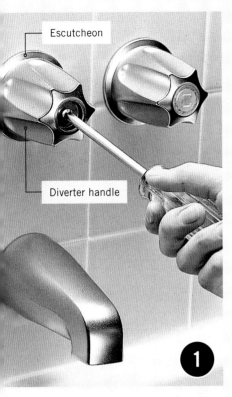

Escutcheon

Diverter handle

Bonnet nut

3

Unscrew the stem assembly using a ratchet wrench with an extension or deep socket. If necessary, chip away any mortar surrounding the bonnet nut.

1

Remove the diverter valve handle with a screwdriver. Unscrew or pry off the escutcheon.

2

Remove the bonnet nut with an adjustable wrench or channel pliers.

4

Stem washer

Stem screw

Remove the brass stem screw. Replace the stem washer with an exact duplicate. If the stem screw is worn, replace it.

5

Retaining nut

Threaded spindle

Unscrew the threaded spindle from the retaining nut.

6

Clean sediment and lime buildup from the nut using a small wire brush dipped in vinegar. Coat all parts with faucet grease, and reassemble the diverter valve.

Fixing Two-Handle Tub + Shower Faucets

Two-handle tub-and-shower faucets are either cartridge or compression design. Because the valves of two-handle tub-and-shower faucets may be set inside the wall cavity, a deep-set socket wrench may be required to remove the valve stem.

Two-handle tub-and-shower designs have a gate diverter, which is a simple mechanism located in the tub spout. A gate diverter closes the supply of water to the tub spout and redirects the flow to the shower head. They seldom need repair. Occasionally, the lever may break, come loose, or refuse to stay in the up position.

If the gate diverter fails to work properly, replace the tub spout. Tub spouts are inexpensive and easy to replace.

Remember to turn off the water supply before beginning any work.

TOOLS + MATERIALS

Screwdriver
Allen wrench
Pipe wrench
Channel pliers
Small cold chisel
Ball-peen hammer
Ratchet set
Masking tape or cloth
Pipe joint compound
Replacement faucet parts, as needed

Water line to shower head

Bonnet nut

Valve stem

Cold water supply line

Hot water supply line

Diverter lever

Gate diverter

A two-handle tub/shower faucet can operate with compression valves, but more often these days they contain cartridges that can be replaced. Unlike a three-handle model, the diverter is a simple gate valve that is operated by a lever.

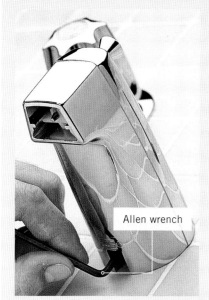

Check underneath the tub spout for a small access slot. The slot indicates the spout is held in place with a set screw. Remove the screw using an Allen wrench. The spout will slide off.

Allen wrench

Unscrew the faucet spout. Use a pipe wrench or insert a large screwdriver or hammer handle into the spout opening, and turn spout counterclockwise.

Spout nipple

Spread pipe joint compound on the threads of the spout nipple before replacing the spout. If you have a copper pipe or a short pipe, buy a spout retrofit kit, which can attach a spout to most any pipe.

 How to Remove a Deep-Set Faucet Valve

1 Escutcheon
Masking tape
Stem nipple

2
Bonnet nut

3

Remove the handle and unscrew the escutcheon with channel pliers. Pad the jaws of the pliers with masking tape to prevent scratching the escutcheon.

Chip away any mortar surrounding the bonnet nut using a ball-peen hammer and a small cold chisel.

Unscrew the bonnet nut with a deep-set socket. Remove the bonnet nut and stem from the faucet body.

Fixing Single-Handle Tub + Shower Faucets

A single-handle tub and shower faucet has one valve that controls both water flow and temperature. Single-handle faucets may be ball, cartridge, or disc designs.

If a single-handle control valve leaks or does not function properly, disassemble the faucet, clean the valve, and replace any worn parts. Repairing a single-handle cartridge faucet is shown on the opposite page.

Direction of the water flow to either the tub spout or the showerhead is controlled by a gate diverter. Gate diverters seldom need repair. Occasionally, the lever may break, come loose, or refuse to stay in the up position.

Remember to turn off the water before beginning any work; the shower faucet shown here has built-in shutoff valves, but many other valves do not. Open an access panel in an adjoining room or closet, behind the valve, and look for two shutoffs. If you can't find them there, you may have to shut off intermediate valves or the main shutoff valve.

TOOLS + MATERIALS

Screwdriver	Adjustable wrench	Channel pliers	Replacement faucet parts, as needed

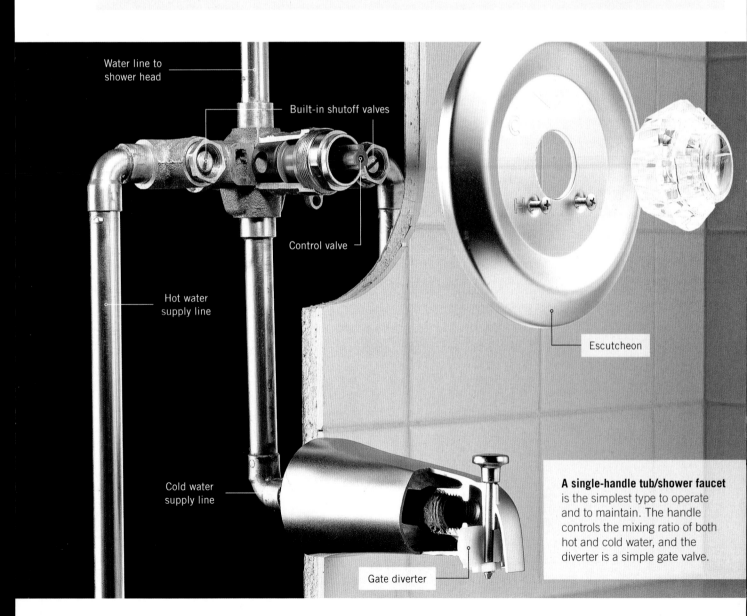

Water line to shower head

Built-in shutoff valves

Control valve

Hot water supply line

Escutcheon

Cold water supply line

Gate diverter

A single-handle tub/shower faucet is the simplest type to operate and to maintain. The handle controls the mixing ratio of both hot and cold water, and the diverter is a simple gate valve.

How to Repair a Single-Handle Cartridge Tub + Shower Faucet

Handle

Escutcheon

1

Use a screwdriver to remove the handle and escutcheon.

Built-in shutoff valves

2

Turn off the water supply at the built-in shutoff valves or the main shutoff valve.

Bonnet nut

3

Unscrew and remove the retaining ring or bonnet nut using adjustable wrench.

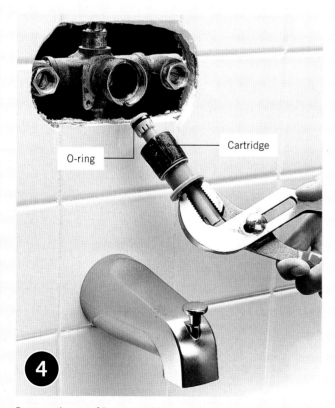

O-ring

Cartridge

4

Remove the cartridge assembly by grasping the end of the valve with channel pliers and pulling gently.

5

Flush the valve body with clean water to remove sediment. Replace any worn O-rings. Reinstall the cartridge, and test the valve. If the faucet fails to work properly, replace the cartridge.

Single-Handle Tub + Shower Faucet with Scald Control

In many plumbing systems, if someone flushes a nearby toilet or turns on the cold water of a nearby faucet while someone else is taking a shower, the shower water temperature can suddenly rise precipitously. This is not only uncomfortable; it can actually scald you. For that reason, many one-handle shower valves have a device, called a "balancing valve" or an "anti-scald valve," that keeps the water from getting too hot.

The temperature of your shower may drastically rise to dangerous, scalding levels if a nearby toilet is flushed. A shower fixture equipped with an anti-scald valve prevents this sometimes dangerous situation.

How to Adjust the Shower's Temperature

To reduce or raise the maximum temperature, remove the handle and escutcheon. Some models have an adjustment screw, others have a handle that can be turned by hand.

To remove a balancing valve, you may need to buy a removal tool made for your faucet. Before replacing, slowly turn on water to flush out any debris; use a towel or bucket to keep water from entering the inside of the wall.

Fixing + Replacing Showerheads

If spray from the showerhead is uneven, clean the spray holes. The outlet or inlet holes of the showerhead may get clogged with mineral deposits. Showerheads pivot into different positions. If a showerhead does not stay in position, or if it leaks, replace the O-ring that seals against the swivel ball.

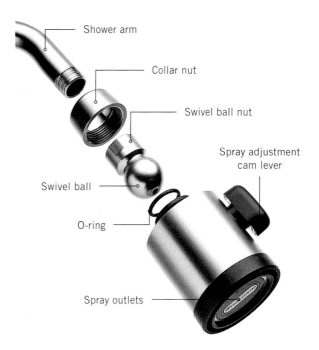

A **typical showerhead** can be disassembled easily for cleaning and repair. Some showerheads include a spray adjustment cam lever that is used to change the force of the spray.

TOOLS + MATERIALS

Adjustable wrench or channel pliers

Pipe wrench

Drill + bits

Glass + tile bit

Mallet

Screwdriver

Masking tape

Teflon tape

White vinegar (optional)

Thin wire (paper clip)

Faucet grease

Rag

Replacement O-rings

Masonry anchors

Flexible shower adapter kit (optional)

Work gloves

Safety glasses

How to Clean + Repair a Showerhead

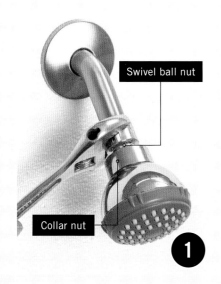

1 Unscrew the swivel ball nut using an adjustable wrench or channel pliers. Wrap the jaws of the tool with masking tape to prevent marring the finish. Unscrew the collar nut from the showerhead.

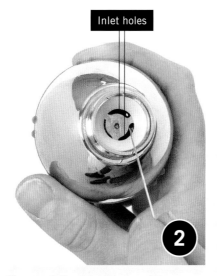

2 Clean outlet and inlet holes of the showerhead with a thin wire. Flush the head with clean water. You can also soak the entire head in a 50-50 solution of white vinegar and hot water.

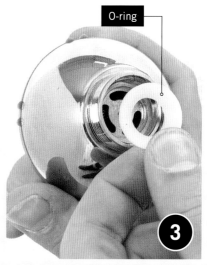

3 Replace the O-ring, if necessary. Lubricate the O-ring with faucet grease before installing.

How to Replace a Showerhead with a Handheld Spray Head

1

Make sure when shopping for a new handheld showerhead that the head mounting bracket is compatible with your existing shower arm. Ask an associate for help if you're not sure. Remove the existing fixed head by unscrewing the mounting nut with an adjustable wrench.

2

Attach the new showerhead mounting bracket by screwing the mounting nut end onto the end of the shower arm (you don't need Teflon tape for this because the bracket has an internal rubber washer). Hand-tighten the bracket until it is snug and the large side of the mounting slot on the end is pointing up and the hose connection is pointing down.

3

Attach the mounting nut end of the showerhead hose to the hose connection on the bracket. Hand-tighten the hose mounting nut. Do not use pliers for this.

4

Screw the showerhead base onto the conical end of the showerhead hose, and slip the cone base into the mounting bracket. Turn on the water, and check that there are no leaks. If you find any, turn the water off and hand-tighten the connection further until it does not leak.

NOTE: The hose may curl up awkwardly; time and exposure to hot water will soon slacken the hose to hang normally.

Variation: Shower Conversion Kit

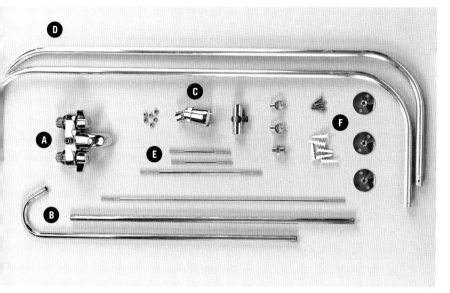

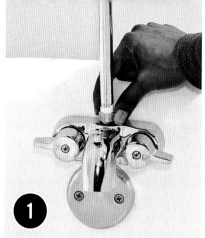

A packaged kit for adding a shower to your tub features a faucet with diverter (A), shower riser plumbing (B), showerhead (C), a frame for the shower curtain (D) that mounts on the wall and ceiling with threaded rods (E), and fasteners and fittings (F).

1

Remove the old tub faucet and replace it with the new diverter-type faucet from the kit. Fit the assembled shower riser into the top of the faucet and hand-tighten. Apply Teflon tape to the threads before making the connection. This assembly includes one straight and one curved section, joined by a coupling. The top, curved pipe includes a connector to a wall brace. Shorten the straight section using a tubing cutter to lower the showerhead height, if desired. Slip the compression nut and washer onto the bottom end of the shower riser, and attach the riser to the top of the faucet, hand-tightening for the time being.

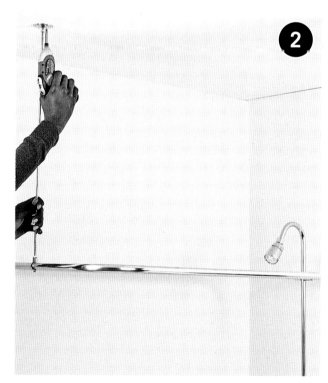

2

With a helper, assemble the curtain frame, securing with setscrews. Hold the frame level, and measure to the ceiling to determine the ceiling brace pipe length. Cut the pipe, and complete the ceiling brace assembly. Set the shower riser to the desired height, and connect the brace to the wall (ensure strong connections by driving the mounting screws into a wall stud and ceiling joist, if possible).

3

After the curtain frame is completely assembled and secured, tighten the faucet connection with a wrench. Full-size shower kits require one shower curtain on each side of the curtain frame. The hooks seen here feature roller bearings on the tops so they can be operated very smoothly with minimal resistance.

Slide-Bar Dual Showerheads

You may not have the space or inclination to install a super-luxe walk-in shower with multiple heads and Bluetooth stereo, but you can have luxury in even the most basic bath-shower combo. That's the good news. The even better news? It won't break the bank and it's a simple installation that you can complete in a weekend afternoon.

The secret is a dual-head slide bar assembly. These wonderful shower conversions replace a single droopy showerhead with a new, upscale fixed head and a hand-held showerhead that can be adjusted for a custom blast even when it's not in your hand. These wonderful bathroom upgrades come in just about every style imaginable, and boost your shower experience every bit as much as it dials up your bathroom's look.

TOOLS + MATERIALS

Slide-bar showerhead assembly	Grease pencil
4' level	Drill + bits
Teflon tape	Adjustable wrench
Tape measure	Gloves
	Safety glasses

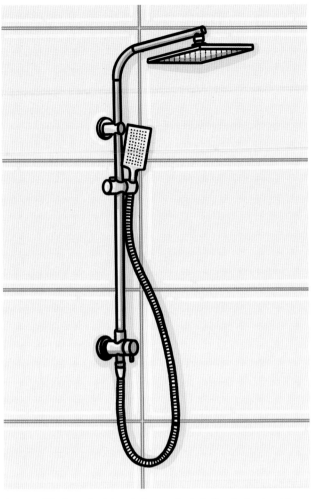

A new slide-bar, dual-head shower installation is the best type of home improvement project. It offers a style upgrade and a more enjoyable shower experience with a minimum of time, effort, or expense.

How to Install a Slide-Bar Dual Showerhead

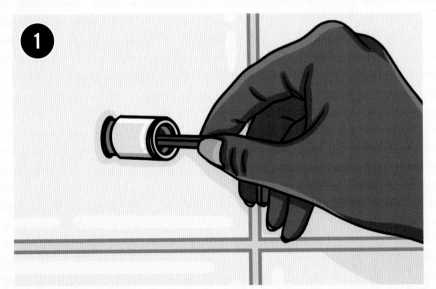

1

Turn off the water to the shower. Remove the existing shower head and shower head arm. Wrap the new nipple threads (both sides) with Teflon tape and screw into the water supply in the wall, where the showerhead arm was connected. Screw the connector to the nipple.

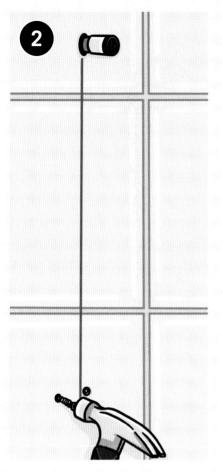

Use a level
to determine a plumb line from the nipple. Mark 24½" (the distance in this case; use the measurement indicated by the manufacturer) down from the bottom of the nipple. Disassemble the bottom support. Center the support base on the plumb mark, and mark through the holes on either side for the screw anchors. Drill holes and tap in anchors for the screws.

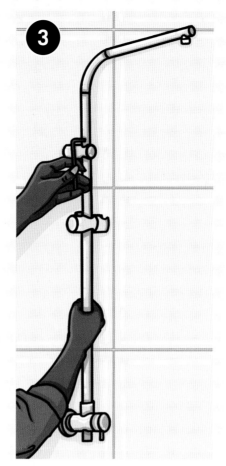

Screw the base
to the wall. Fasten the top showerhead arm onto the slide bar, using the set screw and hex key provided (the arm should be oriented directly opposite the water supply connection). Slip the mounting flange over the slide-bar water supply.

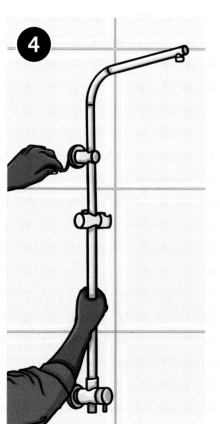

Slide the assembly water inlet onto the coupling as you align the bottom support body with the base that you screwed to the wall. Screw the bottom support body's mounting collar to the base. Ensure that the inlet is all the way onto the water supply coupling, and tighten it in place with the set screw on the line body.

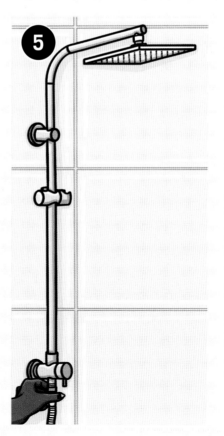

Slide the rubber washer onto the top showerhead connector and fasten the showerhead to the connector. Be careful not to overtighten the head. Follow the same process for installing the end of the handheld showerhead hose onto the bottom of the slide bar, and the opposite end to the handheld showerhead. Turn the water on and check for leaks at any of the connections. Adjust as necessary.

Tubs + Shower Drains

Tub or shower not draining? First, make sure it's only the tub or shower. If your sink is plugged too, it may be that a common branch line is plugged. A sure sign of this is when water drains from the sink into the tub. This could require the help of a drain cleaning service.

If the toilet also can't flush (or worse, water comes into the tub when you flush the toilet), then the common drain to all your bathroom fixtures is plugged. Call a drain cleaning service. If you suspect the problem is only with your tub or shower, then read on. We'll show you how to clear drain lines and clean and adjust two types of tub stopper mechanisms. Adjusting the mechanism can also help with the opposite problem: a tub that drains when you're trying to take a bath.

As with bathroom sinks, tub and shower drain pipes may become clogged with soap and hair. The drain stopping mechanisms can also require cleaning and adjustment.

TOOLS + MATERIALS

Phillips screwdriver
Plunger
Scrub brush
White vinegar
Old toothbrush

Needlenose pliers
Dishwashing brush
Faucet grease
Augers

MAINTENANCE TIP

Like bathroom sinks, tubs and showers face an ongoing onslaught from soap and hair. When paired, this pesky combination is a sure-fire source of clogs. The soap scum coagulates as it is washed down the drain and binds the hair together in a mass that grows larger with every shower or bath. To nip these clogs in the bud, simply pour boiling hot clean water down the drain from time to time to melt the soapy mass and wash the binder away.

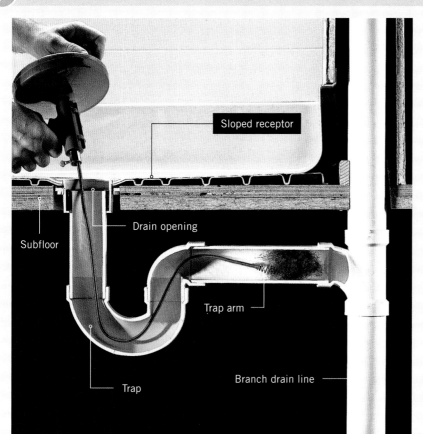

Sloped receptor

Drain opening

Subfloor

Trap arm

Trap

Branch drain line

On shower drains, feed the head of a hand-crank or drill-powered auger in through the drain opening after removing the strainer. Crank the handle of the auger to extend the cable and the auger head down into the trap and, if the clog is farther downline, toward the branch drain. When clearing any drain, it is always better to retrieve the clog than to push it farther downline.

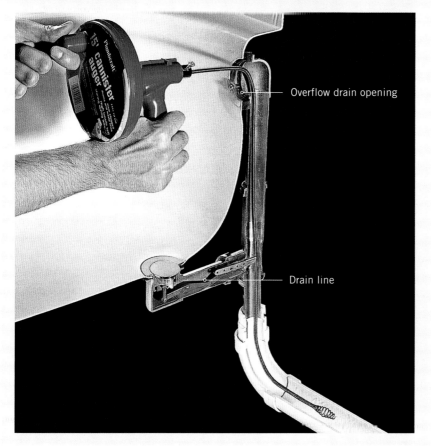

Overflow drain opening

Drain line

On combination tub/showers, it's generally easiest to insert the auger through the overflow opening after removing the coverplate and lifting out the drain linkage. Crank the handle of the auger to extend the cable and the auger head down into the trap and, if the clog is farther downline, toward the branch drain. When clearing any drain, it is always better to retrieve the clog than to push it farther downline.

How to Fix a Plunger-Type Drain

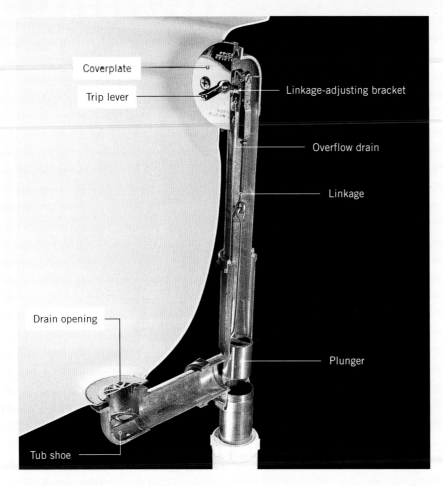

Coverplate

Trip lever

Linkage-adjusting bracket

Overflow drain

Linkage

Drain opening

Plunger

Tub shoe

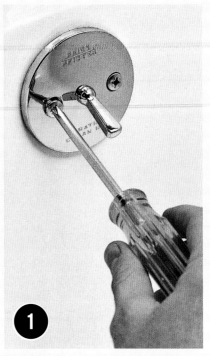

1

A plunger-type tub drain has a simple grate over the drain opening and a behind-the-scenes plunger stopper. Remove the screws on the overflow coverplate with a Phillips screwdriver. Pull the coverplate, linkage, and plunger from the overflow opening.

Clean hair and soap off the plunger with a scrub brush. Mineral buildup is best tackled with white vinegar and a toothbrush or a small wire brush.

2

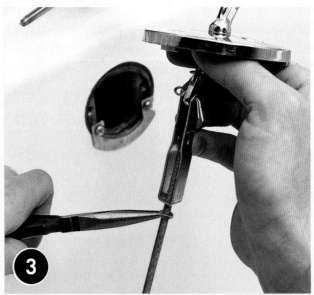

3

Adjust the plunger. If your tub isn't holding water with the plunger down, it's possible the plunger is hanging too high to fully block water from the tub shoe. Loosen the locknut with needlenose pliers, then screw the rod down about ⅛". Tighten the locknut down. If your tub drains poorly, the plunger may be set too low. Loosen the locknut, and screw the rod in ⅛" before retightening the locknut.

How to Fix a Pop-Up Drain

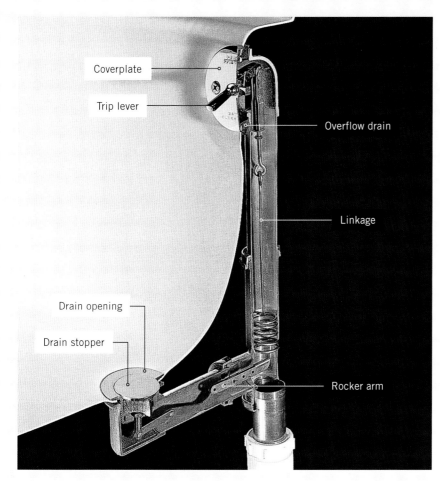

- Coverplate
- Trip lever
- Overflow drain
- Linkage
- Drain opening
- Drain stopper
- Rocker arm

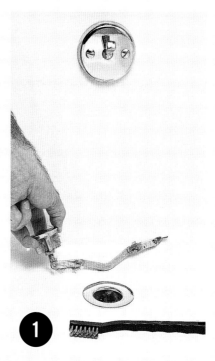

1

Raise the trip lever to the open position. Pull the stopper and rocker arm assembly from the drain. Clean off soap and hair with a dishwashing brush in a basin of hot water. Clean off mineral deposits with a toothbrush or small wire brush and white vinegar.

Remove the screws from the coverplate. Pull the trip lever and the linkage from the overflow opening. Clean off soap and hair with a brush in a basin of hot water. Remove mineral buildup with white vinegar and a wire brush. Lubricate moving parts of the linkage and rocker arm mechanism with faucet grease.

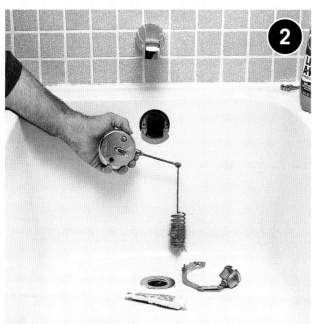

2

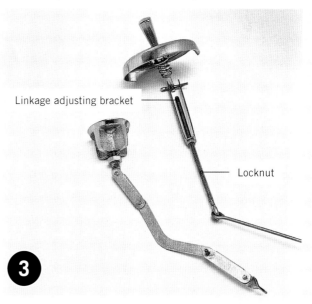

- Linkage adjusting bracket
- Locknut

3

Adjust the pop-up stopper mechanism by first loosening the locknut on the lift rod. If the stopper doesn't close all the way, shorten the linkage by screwing the rod ⅛" farther into the linkage-adjusting bracket. If the stopper doesn't open wide enough, extend the linkage by unscrewing the rod ⅛". Tighten the locknut before replacing the mechanism and testing your adjustment.

Sink Drains

Every sink has a drain trap and a fixture drain line. Sink clogs usually are caused by a buildup of soap and hair in the trap or fixture drain line. Remove clogs by using a plunger, disconnecting and cleaning the trap (this page), or using a hand auger (see page 275).

Many sinks hold water with a mechanical plug called a pop-up stopper. If the sink will not hold standing water, or if water in the sink drains too slowly, the pop-up stopper must be cleaned and adjusted.

Clogged lavatory sinks can be cleared with a plunger (not to be confused with a flanged force-cup). Remove the pop-up drain plug and strainer first, and plug the overflow hole by stuffing a wet rag into it, allowing you to create air pressure with the plunger.

TOOLS + MATERIALS

Plunger	Bucket
Channel pliers	Replacement gaskets
Small wire brush	Teflon tape
Screwdriver	Work gloves
Flashlight	Safety glasses
Rag	

How to Clear a Sink Trap

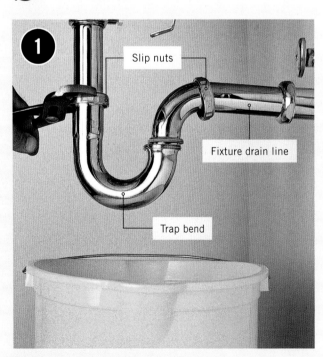

①

Slip nuts

Fixture drain line

Trap bend

Place a bucket under the trap, and loosen the slip nuts on the trap bend with channel pliers. Unscrew the nuts by hand and slip them away from the connections. Pull off the trap.

②

Remove any debris. Clean the trap bend with a small wire brush. Inspect the slip nut washers and replace if necessary. Reinstall the trap bend, and tighten the slip nuts.

How to Clear a Kitchen Sink

Plunging a kitchen sink is not difficult, but you need to create an uninterrupted pressure lock between the plunger and the clog. If you have a dishwasher, the drain tube needs to be clamped shut and sealed off at the disposal or drainline. The pads on the clamp should be large enough to flatten the tube across its full diameter (or you can clamp the tube ends between small boards).

If there is a second basin, have a helper hold a basket strainer plug in its drain or put a large pot or bucket full of water on top of it. Unfold the skirt within the plunger and place this in the drain of the sink you are plunging. There should be enough water in the sink to cover the plunger head. Plunge rhythmically for six repetitions with increasing vigor, pulling up hard on the last repitition. Repeat this sequence until the clog is removed. Flush out a cleared pipe with plenty of hot water.

 # How to Use a Hand Auger at the Trap Arm

If you suspect the clog is downstream of the trap, remove the trap arm from the fitting at the wall. Look in the fixture drain with a flashlight. If you see water, that means the fixture drain is plugged. Clear it with a hand-crank or drill-powered auger.

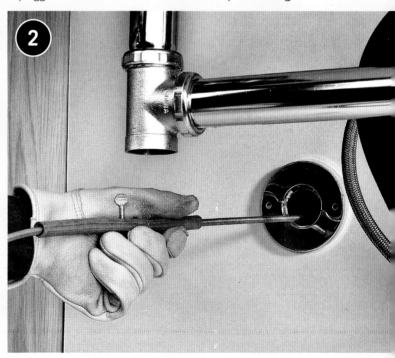

If plunging doesn't work, remove the trap and clean it out. With the trap off, see if water flows freely from both sinks (if you have two). Sometimes clogs will lodge in the tee fitting or one of the waste pipes feeding it. These may be pulled out manually or cleared with a bottlebrush or wire. When reassembling the trap, apply Teflon tape clockwise to the male threads of metal waste pieces. Tighten with your channel pliers. Plastic pieces need no tape and should be hand tightened only.

Branch + Main Drains

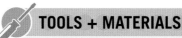
Adjustable wrench or pipe wrench	Penetrating oil
	Cleanout plug (if needed)
Hand auger	Pipe joint compound
Cold chisel	Electrical drum auger
Ball-peen hammer	Gloves
Bucket	Teflon Tape
Ladder	Eye protection
Phillips screwdriver	N95 mask
Rags	

If using a plunger or a hand auger does not clear a clog in a fixture drain line, it means that the blockage may be in a branch line, the main waste-vent stack, or the sewer service line.

First, use a hand-crank or drill-powered auger to clear the branch drain line closest to any clogged fixtures. Branch drain lines may be serviced through the cleanout fittings located at the end of the branch. Because waste water may be backed up in the drain lines, always open a cleanout with caution. Place a bucket and rags under the opening to catch waste water. Never position yourself directly under a cleanout opening while unscrewing the plug or cover.

If using an auger on the branch line does not solve the problem, then the clog may be located in a main drainage stack. To clear the stack, run an auger cable down through the roof vent. Make sure that the cable of your auger is long enough to reach down the entire length of the stack. If it is not, you may want to rent or borrow another auger. Always use extreme caution when working on a ladder or on a roof.

If no clog is present in the main stack, the problem may be located in the sewer service line. Locate the main cleanout, usually a wye-shaped fitting at the bottom of the main drainage stack. Remove the plug and push the cable of a hand auger into the opening.

Some sewer service lines in older homes have a house trap. The house trap is a U-shaped fitting located at the point where the sewer line exits the house. Most of the fitting will be beneath the floor surface, but it can be identified by its two openings. Use a hand auger to clean a house trap.

If the auger meets solid resistance in the sewer line, retrieve the cable and inspect the bit. Fine, hair-like roots on the bit indicate the line is clogged with tree roots. Dirt on the bit indicates a collapsed line.

Use a power auger to clear sewer service lines that are clogged with tree roots. Power augers are available at rental centers. However, a power auger is a large, heavy piece of equipment. Before renting, consider the cost of rental and the level of your do-it-yourself skills versus the price of a professional sewer cleaning service. If you rent a power auger, ask the rental dealer for complete instructions on how to operate the equipment.

Always consult a professional sewer cleaning service if you suspect a collapsed line.

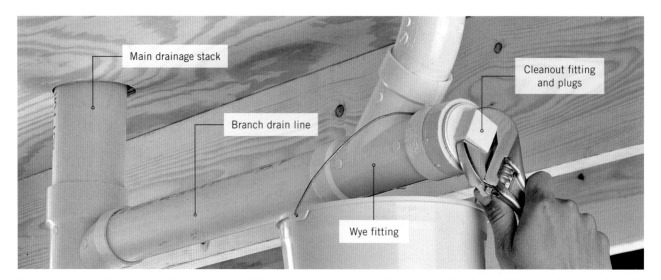

Clear a branch drain line by locating the cleanout fitting at the end of the line. Place a bucket underneath the opening to catch waste water, then slowly unscrew the cleanout plug with an adjustable wrench. Clear clogs in the branch drain line with a hand auger.

How to Clear a Branch Drain Line

Clear the house trap in a sewer service line using a hand auger. Slowly remove only the plug on the "street side" of the trap. If water seeps out the opening as the plug is removed, the clog is in the sewer line beyond the trap. If no water seeps out, auger the trap. If no clog is present in the trap, replace the street-side plug and remove the house-side plug. Use the auger to clear clogs located between the house trap and main stack.

If all else fails, you can try to clear the main drainage stack by running the cable of a hand-crank or drill-powered auger down through the roof vent. Always use extreme caution while working on a ladder or roof.

 # How to Replace a Main Drain Cleanout Plug

Remove the cleanout plug using a large wrench. If the plug does not turn out, apply penetrating oil around the edge of the plug, wait 10 minutes, and try again. Place rags and a bucket under fitting opening to catch any water that may be backed up in the line.

Remove stubborn plugs by placing the cutting edge of a cold chisel on the edge of the plug. Strike the chisel with a ball-peen hammer to move the plug counterclockwise. If the plug does not turn out, break it into pieces with the chisel and hammer. Remove all broken pieces.

Replace the old plug with a new plug. Apply pipe joint compound to the threads of the replacement plug, and screw it into the cleanout fitting.

ALTERNATIVE: Replace the old plug with an expandable rubber plug. A wing nut squeezes the rubber core between two metal plates. The rubber bulges slightly to create a watertight seal.

Noisy Pipes

Air pockets in flowing water that move when appliances or fixtures cycle on or off can cause pipes to bang against framing. Noise comes from the air pockets lurching in the pipes and the pipes hitting structural elements. The effect is called water hammer.

Water hammer can be more than an annoyance. The shockwave can cause damage and eventually failure in pipes and fittings. If a pressure-relief valve on your water heater leaks, it may not be a faulty valve but a pressure surge in the supply system.

You can eliminate water hammer by installing a simple device called a water hammer arrester in the supply line. Inexpensive point-of-use arresters are small enough to be installed easily near the noisy valve or appliance (the closer the better). They can be positioned horizontally or vertically or at an angle without any change in effectiveness. Unlike with old-style air chambers, water cannot fill a water hammer arrester, so they should be effective for the life of the system.

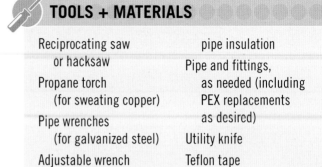
Pipes that bang against studs or joists can be quieted by cushioning them with pieces of pipe insulation. Make sure pipe hangers are snug and that pipes are well supported.

Of course, a more involved but still easy solution is to replace noisy copper pipes with PEX pipes and fittings. Noise is rarely problem with PEX.

Loose pipes may bang or rub against joist hangers, creating noise. Use pieces of foam rubber pipe insulation to cushion pipes.

A tube strap holds pipe away from a framing member. Just snap the strap on and drive in a nail.

How to Install a Water Hammer Arrester

Install a tee fitting as close to the valve as possible.

②

①

Shut off the water supply, and drain the pipes. Use a tubing cutter or reciprocating saw to cut out a section of horizontal pipe long enough for a tee fitting.

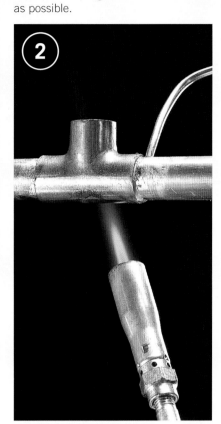

Short pipe

Branch arm

T-fitting

③

Install a short piece of pipe in the branch arm of the tee fitting. This short pipe will be used to attach a threaded fitting.

④

Install a threaded fitting. Use a fitting recommended by the manufacturer of your arrester.

⑤

Wrap the threads of the arrester in Teflon tape. Thread the arrester onto the fitting by hand. Tighten by holding the fitting with one adjustable wrench and turning the arrester with the other. Do not overtighten. Turn the water on, and check for leaks.

Measurement Conversions

LUMBER DIMENSIONS

NOMINAL - U.S.	ACTUAL - U.S. (IN INCHES)	METRIC	NOMINAL - U.S.	ACTUAL - U.S. (IN INCHES)	METRIC
1 × 2	¾ × 1½	19 × 38 mm	1½ × 4	1¼ × 3½	32 × 89 mm
1 × 3	¾ × 2½	19 × 64 mm	1½ × 6	1¼ × 5½	32 × 140 mm
1 × 4	¾ × 3½	19 × 89 mm	1½ × 8	1¼ × 7¼	32 × 184 mm
1 × 5	¾ × 4½	19 × 114 mm	1½ × 10	1¼ × 9¼	32 × 235 mm
1 × 6	¾ × 5½	19 × 140 mm	1½ × 12	1¼ × 11¼	32 × 286 mm
1 × 7	¾ × 6¼	19 × 159 mm	2 × 4	1½ × 3½	38 × 89 mm
1 × 8	¾ × 7¼	19 × 184 mm	2 × 6	1½ × 5½	38 × 140 mm
1 × 10	¾ × 9¼	19 × 235 mm	2 × 8	1½ × 7¼	38 × 184 mm
1 × 12	¾ × 11¼	19 × 286 mm	2 × 10	1½ × 9¼	38 × 235 mm
1¼ × 4	1 × 3½	25 × 89 mm	2 × 12	1½ × 11¼	38 × 286 mm
1¼ × 6	1 × 5½	25 × 140 mm	3 × 6	2½ × 5½	64 × 140 mm
1¼ × 8	1 × 7¼	25 × 184 mm	4 × 4	3½ × 3½	89 × 89 mm
1¼ × 10	1 × 9¼	25 × 235 mm	4 × 6	3½ × 5½	89 × 140 mm
1¼ × 12	1 × 11¼	25 × 286 mm			

METRIC CONVERSIONS

TO CONVERT:	TO:	MULTIPLY BY:	TO CONVERT:	TO:	MULTIPLY BY:
Inches	Millimeters	25.4	Millimeters	Inches	0.039
Inches	Centimeters	2.54	Centimeters	Inches	0.394
Feet	Meters	0.305	Meters	Feet	3.28
Yards	Meters	0.914	Meters	Yards	1.09
Square inches	Square centimeters	6.45	Square centimeters	Square inches	0.155
Square feet	Square meters	0.093	Square meters	Square feet	10.8
Square yards	Square meters	0.836	Square meters	Square yards	1.2
Ounces	Milliliters	30.0	Milliliters	Ounces	.033
Pints (U.S.)	Liters	0.473 (Imp. 0.568)	Liters	Pints (U.S.)	2.114 (Imp. 1.76)
Quarts (U.S.)	Liters	0.946 (Imp. 1.136)	Liters	Quarts (U.S.)	1.057 (Imp. 0.88)
Gallons (U.S.)	Liters	3.785 (Imp. 4.546)	Liters	Gallons (U.S.)	0.264 (Imp. 0.22)
Ounces	Grams	28.4	Grams	Ounces	0.035
Pounds	Kilograms	0.454	Kilograms	Pounds	2.2

COUNTERBORE, SHANK + PILOT HOLE DIAMETERS

SCREW SIZE	COUNTERBORE DIAMETER FOR SCREW HEAD (IN INCHES)	CLEARANCE HOLE FOR SCREW SHANK (IN INCHES)	PILOT HOLE DIAMETER	
			HARD WOOD (IN INCHES)	SOFT WOOD (IN INCHES)
#1	9/64	5/64	3/64	1/32
#2	¼	3/32	3/64	1/32
#3	¼	7/64	1/16	3/64
#4	¼	⅛	1/16	3/64
#5	¼	⅛	5/64	1/16
#6	5/16	9/64	3/32	5/64
#7	5/16	5/32	3/32	5/64
#8	⅜	11/64	⅛	3/32
#9	⅜	11/64	⅛	3/32
#10	⅜	3/16	⅛	7/64
#11	½	3/16	5/32	9/64
#12	½	7/32	9/64	⅛

Resources

Accessibility Resource Center (ARC)
Shower and wet room kits, aging in place
   and accessibility accessories
877-319-6521
www.arcfirst.net

American Standard
800-442-1902
www.americanstandard-us.com

Black + Decker
Power tools and accessories
800-544-6986
www.blackanddecker.com

International Code Council
888-422-7233
www.iccsafe.org

John Guest Co.
Speedfit push-in fittings
www.johnguest.com

Kohler
800-456-4537
www.kohler.com

Laticrete
Floor-warming mats and supplies
800-243-4788
www.laticrete.com

Moen
Bathroom faucets, shower fixtures, safety
   and accessibility accessories
800-289-6636
www.moen.com

MTI
Tubs, shower bases and enclosures,
   sinks, accessories
800-783-8827
www.mtibaths.com

**National Kitchen + Bathroom Association
   (NKBA)**
800-843-6522
www.nkba.com

Plumbing and Drainage Institute
978-557-0720
www.pdionline.org

**Plumbing, Heating, Cooling Contractors
   Association (PHCC)**
Producers of the National Standard
   Plumbing Code
800-533-7694
www.phccweb.org

Price Pfister
800-732-8238
www.pfisterfaucets.com

Swanstone
800-325-7008
www.swanstone.com

Toto
888-295-8134
www.totousa.com

Water Sense
www.epa.gov/watersense

Photo Credits

Photo courtesy of American Standard,
   americanstandard-us.com: 132

Photo courtesy of D-Link, us.dlink.com, (844)
   883-5465: p. 13 (lower)

Rich Fleischman: 25 (middle left), 26
   (middle), 56 (all), 57 (top inset, middle
   left and right, bottom), 35 (top), 37–39
   (all), 79 (top right), 244–245 (all), 259
   (all), 269 (bottom, all), 270 (all)

Photo courtesy of Kohler, www.us.kohler.com:
   98, 200 (both), 256

Photo courtesy of Pfister, www.pfisterfaucets.com:
   99 (all)

Shutterstock, Shutterstock.com: pp. 6, 14,
   15, 46, 68, 84 (top), 92, 133, 158, 165,
   178, 189, 225 (top), 234

Photo courtesy of Sioux Chief Manufacturing,
   www.siouxchief.com, 800-821-3944:
   pp. 86 (middle right), 86 (lower right)

Photo courtesy of TOTOUSA, www.totousa.com,
   (888) 295-8134: p. 93 (top)

Index

ABS (acrylonitrile butadiene styrene) pipes, 22–23, 42–43

access panels, 70, 73

accessibility
    and shower design, 169
    and sinks, 202

air admittance valve, 72, 212

alcove bathtubs, 178–183

appliances. *see* individual appliances

arresters and water hammers, 282–283

augers
    for kitchen sinks, 279
    plumbing lines and, 280–281
    for shower clogs, 275
    for toilet clogs, 21, 241
    types of, 21

ball faucets, 254. *see also* faucets

ball valves, 53, 57, 60, 61. *see also* valves

banded couplings, 47

basement bath, installing pipes, 83

bathrooms
    bathtubs. *see* bathtubs
    bidets, 95–97
    drains, 140–143, 274–278
    faucets, 132–139, 260–268
    shower conversion kits, 271
    showerheads, 269–270, 272–273
    showers, 144–177, 274–275
    sinks, 200–201, 202–205, 208–209
    toilets. *see* toilets
    see also wet walls

bathtubs
    alcove, 178–183
    clogged drains, 274–277
    faucet repairs, 260–268
    freestanding (clawfoot), 214–217
    jetted, 188–195
    shower conversion kits, 271
    sliding doors, 184–187

bathtub-shower combination
    faucet repairs, 260–268
    sliding doors, 184–187

bidets, 95–97

black (iron) pipes, 22–23

black water, 15

blocking, 88

braided metal pipes, 22–23

branch drain lines
    clogs or blockages, 280–281
    gas, 82
    pipe sizing, 85
    sample layouts, 9, 33
    water supply, 8

building drain. *see* drain-waste-vent system (DWV)

cartridge faucets, 252–253, 255.
    see also faucets

cast iron pipes
    about, 22–23
    cutting, 47
    joining, 48–49
    working with, 46

cementing PVC pipe, 44–45

cements (solvent), 42

chases, 72

chromed brass pipes, 22–23

chromed copper supply tubes, 22–23

clamp connections, 37

clawfoot (freestanding) tubs, 214–217

cleanouts, 81, 281

closet augers, 241. *see also* augers

closet flanges, 243

CO2 injection plunger, 239

cold water line, 8, 10

compression faucets, 249–250.
    see also faucets

compression fittings, 62–63. *see also* fittings and connectors

compression stop valves, 89

connectors, PEX, 35. *see also* fittings and connectors

control valves, 69, 73, 266. *see also* valves

copper pipes and tubes
    compression fittings, 62–63

cutting and soldering copper, 26–30
    flared fittings, 64–65
    types of, 22–23
    working with, 24–25

CPVC (chlorinated polyvinyl chloride) pipes, 22–23, 42–43

crawl spaces and fittings, 62

crimp connections, 36

curbless showers, 168–177

cutting
    cast-iron pipe, 47
    copper pipes, 26–27
    outdoor flexible plastic pipes, 51
    rigid plastic pipes, 43

disc faucets. *see* faucets

dishwashers, 108–111

diverter gates, 266

diverter valves, 14, 247, 252, 256–258, 260–263. *see also* valves

drains
    bathtubs, 69, 274–277
    choosing, 105
    fittings, 52
    kits, 105
    plunger-type, 276
    pop-up, 140–143, 277
    sinks, 104–107, 140–143, 278–279
    standpipe, 212–213
    toilets, 69, 81

drain-waste-overflow (DWO) and bathtubs, 179, 181–183

drain-waste-vent system (DWV)
    basic information, 8–9, 11
    bathtubs, 179
    fittings, 52–55
    layouts, 9, 11, 76–77
    new installations, 80–81, 83
    see also branch drain lines

dual-flush valves, 234–237

expansion connections, 38